HISTORY (

FROM A SCIENTIST'S POINT OF VIEW

Michael Disney

For my grandson Rudi (b 2005) and his generation who will need to understand all this much better than we did.

COPYRIGHT PAGE

mjd@astro.cf.ac.uk

Published by Kindle Direct Publishing.

ISBN – 9 781086157499

A HISTORY OF THE BRITS
TABLE OF CONTENTS

A HISTORY OF THE BRITS

FROM A SCIENTIST'S POINT OF VIEW

PREFACE: ANOTHER HISTORY; WHAT ON EARTH FOR?

"The most effective way to destroy people is to deny and obliterate their own understanding of their own history." George Orwell

What we aim for, and what we can achieve, are largely determined by who we think we are, by our self-confidence. And that is as true for nations as it is for individuals. Where we British go in future will be decided by what we think about our past. So this is a history of the Brits with its eye on the future. It is different partly because it is written by a scientist who believes that technology, mathematics and science have been so crucial to history that historians without a scientific background are virtually condemned to miss the point. Have you ever wondered how a bunch of bestial gangsters based in Rome were able to enslave most of the West for over a thousand years? It was, according to the engineer F. W. Lanchester, because of a trick which relied on simple mathematics for its success. If only we'd been able to work it out at the time we might have advanced progress by a millennium, to say nothing of saving millions of poor devils from that Roman speciality, crucifixion.

Think of the following: vaccination, Darwinism, universal sewage and clean water, calculus, broadcasting, the industrial revolution, representative democracy, the telescope, organised sport, tourism, railways, megacities, the middle class, the jet engine, anti-sepsis, artificial fertilizers, computing, expert committees, the abolition of slavery, bicycles, electronics, nursing, the electric motor, mass-produced steel, the steam-ship, economics, astro-navigation, chemistry, the concept of Energy, anti-scorbutics, atomic theory, artificial dyes, photography, radar, sea-bathing, television, tanks, mountaineering, refrigeration, limited liability, ATMs, the atomic nucleus, the spinning jenny, national newspapers, antibiotics, statistics, IVF, float-glass …… one could go on an on. They were all British developments or insights which have revolutionised mankind's life worldwide. No other society has left such a legacy – or anything approaching it. Surely it is vital to try and understand how it came about – if only to prevent the magic spring from drying up, and that is what this book is mainly about. I don't believe it has to do with native genius – as I shall argue at some length – so it must surely be something to do with our location, our institutions or our culture. But what?

Tyrants, conquerors, media magnates, priests and politicians all want to control what is taught as history – because it is a damned effective way of controlling the present and determining the future. Thus ordinary citizens have a hell of a struggle to find out what really happened in the past. Apart from a long-standing fascination with the subject, going back to a childhood in the Second World War, my main qualification to attempt a history is a lifetime spent as a scientist (astronomer) trying to sift through and make sense of conflicting evidence. A sceptical, outsider's point of view is essential for that, as well as a willingness to change one's mind – which is never easy. It helps that I have lived and worked in many countries including America (thrice), Australia, Holland, Germany, the Soviet Union, India, South Africa, Switzerland … experiences which I hope help me to see Britain in a more impersonal light. Even so every essay in history is a personal journey ending in a personal point of view. That makes this an unbalanced, idiosyncratic and self-indulgent exercise, but I hope my journey at least entertains, stimulates and even provokes, as it tries to shed light in some dark corners. Anyway, despite protestations to the contrary, any history is bound to be a personal affair. It is a portrait, even a caricature, and can never become a dispassionate science. I'm hoping that my portrait of Britain will show her from a new angle, and so by a rather different light.

Let me be clear though : a scientist's portrait of British history is deserving of no more respect than anybody else's. It will just be different, as it happens very different, simply because most conventional historians have been both innumerate and scientifically illiterate. Any scientist who claims a special channel into wisdom is no better than any other priest, and priests have been , and still are in my opinion, the bane of humankind. According to Einstein there is only one fruitful way to think – and that is to use Common Sense. Priests, including scientific priests who claim otherwise, are either frauds or fools. So this will be a different portrait, not necessarily a better one. Only the reader can judge that.

The Brexit referendum, and its aftermath, make this an apposite moment to ponder Britain's past. There are those who think that Britain will shrink and fade outside the European Union, and there are those, like me, who disagree. I suspect that both our points of view are, to a great extent, the outcome of our respective historical inheritances, however capricious they may be. Having made my preference plain, as any historian should, I hasten to add that nearly all my views were formed long before Brexit ever appeared on the horizon. Thus this is studiously not a political tract. What I do believe is that Britain has so far left behind an unexampled historical legacy. But how and why? We humans, British or not, need to find out before she fades unheeded into the past. If Ancient Greece was interesting; Modern Britain is vastly more.

The history of ideas teaches us that it is much easier to spot what is wrong with an argument than to spot what has been left out. This is a series of essays about some of the vital factors that have been largely or entirely left out of British history so far. Consider for instance:

- Much of human activity is dominated by underlying mathematical principles, but conventional historians don't 'do' mathematics. Thus, for example, they don't understand why nations, including the British, have been forced into continually fighting with one another. Wars have been inevitable, their proximate causes being irrelevant. But in the atomic age such wars clearly cannot continue. But if we don't identify the underlying mathematical compulsion for war how are we to give up the destructive habit? [Ch.4]

- Civilization grows out of great cities, but sustainable cities require vast amounts of cheap power just to feed and fuel themselves. Why did London and Glasgow succeed where Rome and Athens failed. It was Moon-power. [Ch.2]

- Why do people go to hot countries to relax, but risk their lives to come and live in cool ones where they are generally not welcome any more because they are already far too crowded? It has all got to do with The Second Law of Thermodynamics – which dominates all of human existence. But what is it and how is it so affecting our lives? [Ch.1]

- Phillip of Spain's Armada and Adolf Hitler's Luftwaffe were both repulsed by expert committees. The former by the Navy Board, the latter by the Tizard Committee. But how on earth.... And why are expert committees probably Britain's greatest legacy to civilization? [Ch.6]

- All successful organisms, be they harvest mice or nation states, have to be able to change their minds. But why and how? It's all about the provisionality of Inductive Thought. But what is that and why didn't they teach us about it at school..... or university? [Ch.5]

- Healthy societies progress. But what exactly is progress? If we could pin it down we might all get on much faster. [Ch.5]

The conclusions one draws from history must surely depend on the methods one employs to reach them. Thus some chapters are addressed specifically to our methods, which are by no means orthodox [e.g. chapters 4,5&8]. If you can't stomach my methods my conclusions are likely to disagree with you too. At least they are transparent .

So this is, to repeat, a series of loosely connected essays about the things that other historians, because of their background, or rather their lack of scientific background, have left out. I have tried to crop it as short as possible by:

- Ignoring all topics where I have nothing original to say.
- Avoiding issues where a great deal of evidence would have to be compiled and analysed before a considered conclusion could be reached. In other words if it is not clear-cut it is not in.
- By starting as late as 1588 with the repulse of the Armada. Before that Britain was hardly a secure and distinctive state, just another European province dominated by the Roman Church and its various puppets , unable to evolve in its own way.

NB The author is starting a website associated with this book. It will build up gradually. It will be called : **thinkingforourselves.org**

A HISTORY OF THE BRITS

CHAPTER 1

: BRITAIN'S UNIQUE GEOGRAPHY

"...this sceptred isle,...this other Eden, demi paradise. This fortress built by Nature for herself Against infection and the hand of war...."
Shakespeare, Richard II

The history of a region is often dominated by its geography. If I list the features which, in my opinion, render a region desirable as a home for long term human occupation they are, in order of importance:

(i) Secure from invasion – therefore probably a large island.
(ii) Free from the affects of volcanoes and earthquakes.
(iii) Fertile enough to sustain a healthy population.
(iv) Not too isolated from trade, and the exchange of ideas.
(v) Richly supplied with useful minerals.
(vi) In the 'right' climatic region.

This last demands discussion. Humans have evolved a unique, and on the face of it, a foolhardy strategy – they are warm-blooded but naked. And yet they are, by almost any measure, the most dominant large species on Earth. Could strategy and dominance be linked? This leads us to the critical topic of Human Thermodynamics, which seems to have been missed by every predecessor historian.

All animals are 'heat-engines', that is to say they ingest fuel, burn (metabolize) it, and transform the output into some combination of energy, fat-storage and waste-heat. What proportion of it can be transformed into the useful forms (energy and fat) is entirely determined by the "Second Law of Thermodynamics" (SLOT). SLOT proclaims, on unarguable grounds, that the Thermodynamic Efficiency of any heat-engine, i.e. :

$$\frac{\text{Useful Energy Generated}}{\text{Fuel ingested}} < 1-\left(\frac{T_s}{T_E}\right) \qquad (1)$$

where T_E is the (Absolute) Temperature of the engine in question, T_s of its surroundings, and < means "less than"[Absolute Temperature = Centigrade Temperature + 273 degrees],.

Now our body temperature is 37 deg. C (310 deg. Absolute) so that in comfortably warm surroundings, 27 deg. C say, (300 deg. Abs.):

$$\text{Thermodynamic Efficiency} < 1-\left(\frac{300}{310}\right) = .03 \text{ or 3 per cent.}$$

Surely that can't be right? Surely. I mean think of the implications. If we eat a typical diet of 2000 Calories a day, that is equivalent to about 8 million Joules of energy which, if we turn it into useful output at only 3% efficiency, yields an average useful power, spread over 24 hours, of only 3 Watts ! That's ridiculously small – even a normal light bulb has a power of about 100 Watts. It can't be right. There's something wrong. Surely?

Alas there isn't. The Second Law of Thermodynamics has a far more vital bearing on History than The Divine Right of Kings, Catholic Emancipation, Capitalist Economics – or any of the other pre-occupations of conventional historians. That renders them thoroughly unreliable sources of understanding. The novelist C.P. Snow famously remarked that ignorance of the Second Law of Thermodynamics marks anyone as uneducated – and you can see why.

All the same; 3 Watts! We have to walk, work, think, rear children…and keep ourselves warm with less power than a feeble torch. Whether we know it or not, most of our lives , indeed most of human history going back to our hairy forbears, has been dominated by the need to generate more useful power, and conserve what energy we've got.

But what can we do about the situation? According to Equation (1) our only option is to live somewhere colder. If I move to a region where the surrounding temperature is only 17 deg. instead of 27 I immediately double my useful power output to 6 Watts ! That could revolutionize my life – transform it completely [Whereas if I moved to the Tropics where T_s is about 35 deg. I would have to survive on no more than a single Watt!]

To return to geography more generally, it is obviously advantageous to live in a cool climate – but not one so cold that all ones' useful energy has to be spent in keeping warm – and anyway if it's too cold one cannot grow crops. It turns out that cool-temperate is just about optimum. [For the whole fascinating and fateful subject of Human Thermodynamics, which seems to have been neglected by almost everybody, see Note 1 below]

So a cool-temperate, large island just off the shore of a relatively civilized continent looks like the ideal place on which to live.

But why large? It is a simple scientific argument once again. The population of a country can rise roughly with its area—that is to say with the square of its diameter, but the length of its borders will only rise proportionately with its diameter (i.e. 'linearly'). Other things being equal larger countries will therefore be more secure because they can deploy larger numbers of troops per mile to defend their borders. Indeed that is one of the single most important factors in History [See Ch.7 for a more detailed explanation]. The Square-Linear law (SLL) has forced groups into tribes, tribes into clans, clans into confederations, confederations into nations, nations into empires. There was really no choice – either you expanded, or you were over-run. Basically that's why men have to fight, whether they desire to or not. People tend to forget this very hard fact – particularly when they are clamouring for their independence. For instance Scotland has a 6000 mile long coast-line making it particularly vulnerable to sea-born invasion. Who else but the rest of the British islanders could get there in time to defend them? The Square-Linear Law and the Second Law of Thermodynamics are the two of the three dominating forces in History. In the modern context an island needs to sustain a population of something like ten million to be reasonably secure from invasion [Thus the Crimea (pop. 2 million) fell to Russia in 2015, Corsica (120,000) to France in 1769].

To return to our ideal human habitation – a fertile island at least 100 miles across, in a cool-temperate region, just off the coast of a reasonably civilized continent; when you look at the atlas there is not much choice:

TABLE (2:1) POTENTIAL PARADISES ON EARTH

Japan
Taiwan
Vancouver Island
Newfoundland
Britain
Ireland
Tasmania

The first three are tectonically far too unstable, particularly Vancouver Island. Newfoundland is, from the point of view of the Coriolis Forces which dictate currents, winds and climate, on the wrong side of an ocean. Until very recently Tasmania was too remote – leaving only Britain and Ireland. Ireland is probably an island too far – it will always be dominated by its larger inshore neighbour – and anyway it is almost entirely lacking in valuable minerals such as iron and coal.

That leaves Britain as the pretty well unique best location on the planet for human beings to thrive. It is large enough, fertile, thermodynamically ideal, well watered, exactly the right distance off the coast of Europe, seismically quiescent and, guess what, richer geologically than any area of equivalent size on Earth: tin, copper, flint, iron, coal, salt, oil, gas, china-clay, phosphates…….If the Almighty were to carry out an experiment to see if humans could civilize themselves he would almost certainly choose Britain to start. We are lucky, incredibly lucky. And we have another unique but unremarked advantage – as we shall next see.

NOTES CHAPTER 1

1 The fascinating but wholly neglected subject of HUMAN THERMODYNAMICS can be followed up at

https://tinyurl.com/y448gw3z

A HISTORY OF THE BRITS

CHAPTER 2

CIVILIZATION AND MOON-POWER

Before all, dwelling in cities – which is what civilization literally means – requires massive amounts of cheap and reliable transport. A household requires roughly ten kilos of raw food, and ten kilos of fuel a day. If it is to come from twenty kilometres or more away, as most of it must, we are talking very roughly of one Unit of Transport required per household, where one Unit corresponds to one 'ton-kilometre-per-day'. This is a sensible unit because an extremely fit man could carry on his back forty kilograms for 25 kilometres if he marched all day. In other words every city-household would turn its menfolk (or womenfolk in Africa where most men don't deign to carry things) into beasts of burden, leaving nobody left to create the very culture the city was supposed to promote. Horses and carts could help, but not by much when you take into account the effort needed to build roads and supply fodder. Athens and Rome got by only because they were brutal slave states dependent on constant conquest to resupply the poor devils whose backs and spirits they then broke. They deservedly passed into oblivion because they never remotely solved the Transport Problem and so instead imposed endless cruelty on their fellow men and women. Almost the first act of the Romans after they landed in Britain was to crucify some locals.

So how did mankind first solve 'The Transport Problem'? The short answer is by harnessing Moon-power. My grandmother lived at Leigh-on-Sea on the Thames estuary, where it is about ten miles across. In the nineteen forties and fifties one could usually see from there a dozen Thames Barges with their tan spritsails working the wind and tide or waiting patiently, sails furled, anchors down, crew asleep, for the next favourable stream. In 24 hours there are two tides running in the same direction for 6 hours each at an average speed of around 2 knots. So that's 24 miles a day in your desired direction. And given they had a crew of only two men (and a boy) and could carry a hundred tons, each Thames sailing barge could transport more than a thousand fit men. No wonder London became the greatest commercial city on Earth. The tides running down and up the estuary as far as Tower Bridge were the great pulsing heart of modern civilization.

With that insight a vital chapter of history becomes explicable for the first time. Big tides are uncommon – none to speak of in most oceans, the Mediterranean or the Baltic. But in North Western France, the Low Countries, and Britain in particular, they are immensely powerful, reaching a height of fifty feet at the headwaters of the Bristol Channel. And that is most likely why civilization, stable enduring civilization, first developed there. London, Antwerp, Amsterdam, Liverpool, Rouen, Glasgow, Rotterdam, Bruges, Bristol….and their hinterlands, didn't need slaves. They flourished on Moon-power. Food and fuel, building stone and timber, sand and salt, leather, iron-work and bricks, slate, night-soil, fodder and road-stone, flax, wool and beer…..all the necessities and luxuries of a civilized life could glide long distances on tide and wind….thanks to the tidal sailing barge.

The problem with tidal waters is that they don't generally get very far inland – or stay there for long if they do. But it didn't take much for someone to think of closing a gate or barrage to hold the tide up and allow vessels to take their cargoes to the utter extremities of tidal reaches. Then of course someone had to build locks in the barrages to allow the captive barges out and back down to the sea without letting too much of the precious water out. But once you have such a lock for letting vessels down why not reverse its action and lift vessels up? Thus in 1300 near Bruges was born what is perhaps the most ingenious contrivance of the human mind: the lock. Ships could now travel up hill by the aid of rainwater – and a little horse-power. Thus the prosperous, and sustainable modern world was born – without the need for a single slave. Tides led to barrages, to canals, to locks and so to industrial cities like Birmingham, far, far inland.

All would have been well if prosperous Tidal Man could have restrained himself . But he didn't. Temporarily provided for by waterborn wealth he bred like the proverbial rabbit. In a couple of centuries the tidelanders, and in particular the Brits, had cut down most of their trees, precipitating a catastrophic firewood crisis. There was nothing for it but to turn themselves back into slaves and dig coal from underground like blind worms. But if it hadn't been for the canals and barges, that life-giving coal would never have made it to the shivering cities. The entire South Wales Coal and Steel Industry, which once (1880) ruled the world, was entirely enabled by a pair of lock gates 60 feet high built in Cardiff to hold in the tide. They're still there.

Coal mines and rain water obviously don't mix. Steam power had to be invented to pump out the mines and with steam, eventually came the steam train with a transport capability greater than either the tidal or the canal barge. Their gentle days were numbered.

The tidal sailing barge and the canal lock were the miraculous developments which gave rise to true civilization. And if we hadn't bred so improvidently we might still be living off their backs today. Even by the standards of modern mechanized transport they were pretty efficient as the following table illustrates, where the Units are equivalent to what one very fit man can carry in a day i.e. roughly 1 Ton-kilometre. Attempts have been made to factor in the costs of crews, of forage, of fuel and of the building and maintenance along the ways on which they ran. But that is not easy to do given that governments often tax or subsidize the different factors in haphazard ways.

Usage then becomes a vital factor in the relative costs of alternative modes of transport. For instance the British canal system collapsed so rapidly because as railways stole freight away their fixed maintenance costs had to be charged upon fewer and fewer barges (Also railway companies bought up canals and vandalized them deliberately).

TABLE (2:1) RELATIVE TRANSPORT CAPABILITIES

In units of 1 Ton-kilometres per day per man required.

PORTER	1
BARROW-BOY (Wheels; common in India still)	4
CYCLE (No track costs included)	10
HORSE WAGON (forage costed but not roads)	8
TIDAL SAILING BARGE (Britain; 2.5 crew)	1200
CANAL BARGE (30 Tons; including canal costs)	90
CLIPPER SHIP (limited to trade wind routes)	3000
RAILWAY* (incl track and fuel costs)	2400
TRAMP STEAMER (incl 30 crew and 50 miners)	4000
MODERN TRUCK (2 crew, fuel and road costs)	3000
CONTAINER SHIP	8000
JET CARGO-PLANE	600

* I have everywhere converted fuel costs into manpower units by assuming a man can mine about half a ton of coal a day and that oil will be taxed until it is more expensive than coal per unit of energy stored.

In short we can see that it was the tidal sailing barge which first made true civilization possible. The North Western Europeans were blessed with this rare magic, and of course the Brits, as usual, with far more than anyone else.

15

With all this geography, geology and geophysics on our side its hardly surprising we've done better than most. Indeed we may have to contemplate the opposite question at times: 'Why did the Brits make such a hash of it?'

NB: This has been an entirely quantitative argument (see table). Some arguments are bound to be of this nature. This is why mathematics has to play a significant, sometimes over-riding role in History [Ch.4].

HISTORY OF THE BRITS

CHAPTER 3

THE ROYAL NAVY

"The royal Navy of England hath ever been its greatest defence and ornament; it is its ancient and natural strength; the floating bulwark of our island."
William Blackstone, 1765, 'Commentaries on the Laws of England'.

A nation only truly becomes so once it secures its borders, which Britain did not manage until the late 16th century, which is why my History only commences then. Even then it wasn't safe to live near the coast: as late as 1800 Barbary Pirates were snatching citizens from our coasts for sale in the slave-markets of North Africa.

Without it's own strong and permanent fighting navy any island is a dangerous abode. But a standing navy is damned expensive. Ships take years to build but quickly become obsolete or rot; naval gunnery is tricky while men capable of fighting a ship effectively need to be highly trained and kept at the ready. In other words an effective fighting navy is an endlessly expensive weapon – but indispensable to any would-be island nation.

Henry the VIIIth (reigned 1509 to 47) tried to build such a navy using money acquired through dissolution of the monasteries. He built shipyards and ships but most importantly in 1545 established a standing committee of skilled professionals, the Navy Board, to oversee shipbuilding, ordnance, stores, finance, rigging, sails etc. In the long run that was to prove crucial because none of Britain's European rivals did likewise. Its deliberations led eventually to superior ship designs (the galleon), cheap and deadly cast-iron cannon ('seed-guns' they were called, cast out of Kent & Sussex iron using flux from their white cliffs which bestowed such strength that they could be fired far and often without bursting), astro-navigation, anti-scorbutics, copper sheathing against dragging weed and devouring worm, and a highly professional officer class controlled by the government through The Articles of War.

The committee though could not solve the overwhelming problem – how to fund the navy. King Charles the First tried and failed with the Ship-Money Tax, against which Parliament rebelled – which led to the Civil War in which Charles lost his head. Parliament prevailed in part because the Navy took its side. Parliament then solved the problem by raising Customs and Excise Duty specifically to fund the fleet – after which it would be a match for anyone. It had already seen off The Armada in 1588 – thanks in large measure to its superior complement of naval cannon, and in 1653 it pulverized the Dutch, our other main rival, in the North Sea at the Gabbard Shoals. Then Admiral Blake sailed South to try and put an end to the menace of Barbary Pirates. Parliament also wisely passed the Navigation Acts (1660s) mandating that British overseas trade should travel in 'British bottoms' manned largely by British seamen. Britain was now, and would remain for three hundred years, mistress of the seven seas. She had become so partly because of her very favourable location, partly because of her standing committee, mainly because she depended on her navy more than any of her continental rivals. For them an army had to come first while a navy was a luxury; for her it was a matter of survival.

What was to happen afterwards had already been foreseen by thoughtful members of Elizabeth's largely Welsh court:

A permanent navy was "the Master Key wherewith to open all locks that keep out or hinder this incomparable British Empire." (John Dee, the court mapmaker and mathematician, and first prophet of empire).

"Whosoever commands the sea, commands the trade; whosoever commands the trade of the world commands the riches of the world and consequently the world itself." (Walter Raleigh, languishing in the Tower before his execution by James the 1st. Elizabeth's successor).

What brought the dominance of the Royal Navy to an end was the development of the aeroplane, particularly in the 1930's. A flimsy dive-bomber costing thousands of pounds with a crew of one or two could all too easily sink a battleship costing tens of millions with a crew of thousands. Simple calculation reveals that no conceivable armour could resist the plunging momentum of an aerial bomb. The sinkings of the Bismarck and the Tirpitz, the Repulse and the Prince of Wales, Pearl Harbour and the humiliation of the Yamamoto, the worlds' largest ever battleship, brought an era which began in 1588 to a hasty and irrevocable end. The US Navy likes to the maintain the fiction of naval power with its colossal nuclear-powered aircraft-carriers. But none of them would survive the first minutes of a serious nuclear war.

NOTES.

One can read about the history of the RN in:

1 *To Rule the Waves* by Arthur Herman (US). Hodder 2005. The best short account of a huge subject that I know of.

2 CS Forester's Hornblower novels are an exciting and authentic evocation of the Navy in Nelson's time.

3 *The Command of the Ocean* Nicholas Rodger, 2004, Allen Lane. Naval history 1649-1815.

4 *Business in Great Waters*, John Terraine, 1989 Cooper, re-issued by Wordsworth Editions 1999. A truly magnificent account of the battles for the Atlantic in the First and Second World wars.

5 *The War at Sea*, by Capt. S W Roskill is the 3-volume official account of the RN in WW II. Don't be put off by 'Official'; what an achievement! Can be found in paperback and on Kindle (Amazon).

6 Samuel Pepys was secretary of the Navy Board in the late 18th century. His *Diaries* make good reading at many levels.

7 *The Cruel Sea* by Nicholas Montserrat, though a novel, was written by one who served out there on the deep and did it rare justice.

HISTORY OF THE BRITS
CHAPTER 4.
A MATHEMATICAL PORTRAIT OF HISTORY

"Facts are the mere dross of history. It is from abstract truth which inter-penetrates, and lies latent among them like gold in the ore, that the mass derives its value."
Lord Macauley, *Critical and Historical Essays*

(4:1) INTRODUCTION The sky is dark at night, stars shine, we've got long intestines, big spiders are hairy, there are no giants, uranium atoms decay – all for mathematical reasons. Just as stars and atoms must obey the profound laws of proportion so must nations. Histories written without appreciating the mathematical dimension risk being dummies without a skeleton. Let's look at some examples.

My interest in this unlikely proposition was aroused by two brilliant essays in the same anthology.[1] F.W. Lanchester, the engineer who invented the hydraulic gearbox, proved that the fighting strength of a military force was in proportion to the square of its numerical size. I was shocked; it sounded counter-intuitive. But Lanchester argued that the soldiers on the numerically inferior side, being the target of more missiles, would survive less long, and therefore individually fire off less missiles of their own. Obvious really – when you think in mathematical terms. But that argument only applies if the weapons have sufficient range to strike every member of the opposing force. So Lanchester considered the alternative extreme, which applied in Roman times, when the killing short- sword extended not much further than a man's reach. In that context numbers become irrelevant because the only fighting would be at the interface of the two forces. In that case only individual prowess (and rigid discipline) would count. Thus a Roman Legion, uniquely made up of entirely professional soldiers, could cut its way through a "barbarian" army of unlimited size like a hot knife through butter. At a stroke Lanchester had explained the previously inexplicable – how a bunch of dim gangsters based on Rome had managed to subdue and brutalize much of the known world. [Incidentally the bloodthirsty Zulus used identical tactics to the same effect 2000 years later. Their leader Chaka's idea of an evening's entertainment was to have several thousand victims thrown off a precipice one by one while he looked on. The Romans would have approved. Their Consul Crassus had 5000 rebellious slaves crucified along the Appian Way on one day.]

Another great puzzle – the origin of the First World War – was tackled afterwards by Lewis Fry Richardson the Quaker meteorologist. He analysed the mathematics of the arms-race which preceded it and showed that if the contestants could arm faster than they could disarm, as was the case at the time, conflagration was inevitable. Of course one cannot prove that it was the actual spark which ignited that tragedy – but it does sound more plausible to me than the numerous competing theories. At any rate, following the Cuban Missile Crisis of 1962, the commanders on both sides, rightly frightened out of their wits, installed a hot line between the Kremlin and the White House in order to obey Richardson's criterion for peace.

Let us, as an example, consider the Second World War to see what Mathematics can tell us about code-breaking, the Eastern Front and the Battle of the Atlantic.

(4:2) CIPHER BREAKING

We all know that code-breaking, as it is more usually called, played a significant role in shortening that war, though the story is often personalized (Alan Turing) and told from an exclusively Allied point of view. We don't like to admit that we lost thousands of ships and tens of thousands of lives to U-boats because Berlin had broken the naïve Admiralty Convoy Code. The idea that a few brilliant dons, from Oxbridge of course, won the war at Bletchley Park in between solving crossword puzzles, is now the popular myth. As I see it the truth 'was rather more nuanced'. In war every side breaks codes, and has their own broken in turn. The secret is to break them fast enough and often enough for the information to be of use – and by the Second World War that required machines – electro-mechanical business machines that could try out many different guesses at high speed. For instance the German Enigma enciphering machine had 3 rotors, each with 26 possible settings, which changed from letter to letter, and a plug-board which changed once a day. It could generate 159,000,000,000,000,000,000 (= 'Godzilla') different cipher combinations. Each letter you could correctly guess (a 'Crib') reduced the number of settings to be tried by a multiple of 26, so that if you could guess 15 you had enough information in principle to break into the wheel-setting for that message (because 26^{15} is larger than Godzilla). Principle is one thing, practice another. So complex electro-mechanical machines (christened 'bombes' by the Poles who originally devised them) were built at Bletchley Park to shuffle through the possible settings until a message in plaintext German emerged. But that could take hours, days or even weeks.

The crucial 'Cipher Breakers' Equation' (CBE) is:

$$\frac{T}{\tau} > P \times (26)^{W-N} \qquad (4:1)$$

Where > means 'more than' and:

T is the time needed to break a cipher.

τ is the cycle-time of the cracking-machine (i.e. time to test a single possibility)

W = number of rotor wheels in enciphering machine (Enigma had 3 or 4, *Geheimschreiber* had 12)

N = number of correctly guessed letters in Crib

P = number of plug-board settings of day (10^{16})

The original Bletchley bombes were OK for the Enigma 3-wheel cipher, too slow for the 4-wheel, almost hopeless for the 12-rotor Geheimschreiber which Hitler used to keep in touch with his top commanders. Bletchley Park would have failed but then someone had the bright idea of contacting Tommy Flowers a GPO engineer who was familiar with the much faster valve-based electronic circuits employed in automatic telephone exchanges. At least 1500 valves would, he said, be needed to build a cipher-cracker – which dismayed the Bletchley boffins who knew valves were notoriously unreliable. 'Not so' claimed Flowers, 'As long as they aren't being continually turned on and off'. But they wouldn't believe him so over Xmas 1943 he built the first electronic Cracker himself, partly out of his own pocket. It worked immediately and effectively and was a million times faster than Bletchley's electro-mechanical bombes. Colossus, as it was called, was in effect the world's first electronic computer. Tommy Flowers ought to have a column next to Nelson, but as he was a vulgar working-class type who went to night-school, and not to Oxbridge, there is no chance.

The great value of the Code Breaking Equation was that it would have provided a clear estimate of the challenge, and what might be achieved if the effort was put in. With tens of thousands of encrypted radio messages being intercepted each day (by the Y-service), and with their sources being located by bi-directional fixes, it wasn't impossible to guess what phrases some of them very likely contained – weather reports, routine situation reports, numbers of casualties, fuel remaining and so forth, and such material provided the 'Cribs' needed to make the break-ins feasible.

Thanks to Colossus, from January 1944 the Allies had a pretty complete picture of what was happening ‘on the other side of the hill’. For instance the knowledge that his opposite number Rommel had gone to Germany on leave helped Eisenhower to set the 6th. of June as D-day. For instance that the Nazis were not succeeding with the atom bomb – so Britain could relax on that score and divert precious resources elsewhere.

For those who understood the simple maths of the CBE the necessity for a cipher breaking organization with 10,000 souls was absolutely clear, and so it came to pass at ‘Station-X’.

(4:3) THE EASTERN FRONT

When Hitler launched his titanic attack against Russia in 1941, Operation Barbarossa, the civilized world, or what was left of it, held its collective breath. Few expected Russia to hold out but a ding-dong struggle ensued marked by epic battles such as Stalingrad and Kursk. Against all the odds the heroic Russians held on until 1945 when they reached the centre of Berlin to find Hitler immolated in his bunker. At least that is how the epic is generally portrayed

But if you look at the matter from the mathematical point of view things look very different. Hitler never stood a chance, any more than Napoleon did in 1812. Men can fight for only so long before they must halt and rest. At each stage of the advance casualties are incurred which can only get worse as you push deeper into enemy territory. Lengthening supply lines and depots must be defended against guerrillas operating in one’s rear, requiring more and more fighting troops to be left behind. Eventually, after 4 or 5 stages of advance the fighting spearhead of the attack will shrink to nothing, when the advance must grind to a halt. That’s what happened, that is what must happen according to what I call Napoleon’s Equation:

$$\frac{N(s)}{N(0)} = 1 - s(c+d) \qquad (4:2)$$

Where N(0) = number of assault troops who started out.

s = stage number

N(s) = number of troops who start out from stage s

c.N(0) = number of casualties suffered on each stage

d.N(0) = extra number left behind to defend the extending supply line after each stage of the advance.

The precise details don't matter, because the outcome is almost inevitable. For instance if c and d were both 0.2 (20%) the army wouldn't even reach stage 3, and even with implausibly low values of 10% there could be no advance beyond stage 5. Soldiers having to fight their way can hardly advance much more than 20 miles a day so a total advance of 5 times 6 times 20 miles (= 600) looks like the limit of rational ambition. But Hitler's troops had 800 miles to go even to reach Moscow – and many thousands more beyond that to reach their objective of Caucasian oil. They were doomed from the start. The killer feature of Napoleon's Equation is that as an assaulting army shrinks the casualties per stage do not, and neither do the requirements to leave men behind to defend the extending supply line. One by one Napoleon's star generals found this out when they tried to drive Wellington out of the Iberian Peninsula (1809 – 13). Napoleon himself learned his lesson at Borodino outside Moscow (1812) while the commanders on both sides in the North African campaign were crippled by the same mathematical iron boot. For instance Rommel reached the gates of Cairo in October 1942 – but with only a dozen still functioning tanks. That campaign could only be won, and was won, by supply from the sea. Churchill understood that when he risked nearly all to reinforce Malta in

August 1942 (Operation Pedestal) – one of the real turning points of that war.

(4:4) THE BATTLE OF THE ATLANTIC.

was however the real crux of that war, a battle in which Britain and Germany tried to strangle each other by starving their opponent into submission. It has no comparisons anywhere in history, unless it be the corresponding struggle in the First World War, and was, in my opinion, the most fateful battle of all time – Marathon, Salamis, Lepanto, Trafalgar and Stalingrad not excepted. It lasted 6 years and no less than 5,000 ships and 100,000 lives were lost – usually in the cruellest circumstances. It demanded every ounce of endurance, guts and ingenuity from both sides, while the outcome of the entire war, and with it the survival of European civilization, hinged on defeat or victory. Nor was the prospective outcome obvious. The Allies, principally Britain and Canada, were on their knees by April 1943, the US Navy had given up and the Admiralty were in despair. Three weeks later it was all over with Dönitz withdrawing his U-boat packs from the ocean – to which they were never to return in any numbers. What so unexpectedly and dramatically reversed the tide of battle? Was it cipher breaking, short wave radar, very long range aircraft, refuelling at sea, Support Groups, Escort carriers, depth-charge mortars, larger convoys, Huff-Duff (ship-born radio-direction finding), mass produced Liberty Ships, air-born acoustic torpedoes,….. all have their proponents. But after studying the battle for a lifetime, having grown up 50 yards from a Welsh beach where the grisly detritus washed ashore on every tide[2], I believe it was none of those things but an equation, The Convoy Equation:

$$P = e^{-\frac{E}{U}} \qquad (4:3)$$

where P = probability of an individual U-boat piercing the convoy escort screen and launching a successful torpedo attack and :

e is Euler's Number 2.7182

E = number of Escort Vessels protecting the convoy

U = number of U-boats in the attacking pack.

The Convoy Equation has an exponential nature as we say, [Ch.16] which means it can change value dramatically with modest changes in the relative numbers of U-Boats (U) to escort vessels (E) in the vicinity of a convoy(See Table).

TABLE (4:1): SHIP LOSSES BY U-BOAT PACK SIZE Probability (%) of μ ship-losses L(μ) per convoy as a function of wolf-pack size U, when there are 6 Escort vessels protecting it. A Tragedy is μ = 3 or more, a Catastrophe 6 or more.

U	L(zero)	L(μ =1)	L(2)	Tragedy	Catastrophe
1	100	0			
2	95	5	1		
3	70	25	3		
4	40	40	15	3	
5	20	40	30	15	
6	10	30	30	30	
9		2	5	90	75

According to the Convoy Equation increasing the number of U-boats from 3 to 9 multiplied the prospect of an individual U-boat's success by e^3 or no less than 20! So 9 U-boats will wreak 3 times 20 or 60 times as much havoc as 3.

Here, spelled out in elementary mathematics is the vital importance of concentration in battle, a principle which goes back at least as far as Thucydides (450 BC)

We almost lost the war for failure to understand one tiny equation which enshrines the vital need for concentration in battle. That failure meant that the people at the very top never quite allocated the Battle of the Atlantic the resources its vital importance demanded. In particular a dozen more extremely long range aircraft could have closed the mid ocean air-gap where the wolf packs concentrated. Fortunately, at the very last gasp, thanks in part to a mutiny amongst his admirals, Churchill was persuaded. Making one of his bravest decisions, and in despite of the violent protests of both Stalin and Roosevelt, he halted the Murmansk convoys (supplying Russia) – which were extravagant in their demands on the Escort fleet, and diverted 15 of those escort vessels into the Atlantic where, thanks to the Convoy Equation, they turned the tide. In May 1943 more U-boats were sunk than merchant ships, and the game was up for the Nazis. But, as Wellington said of Waterloo: "….it was a damned near run thing."

Individually none of my three equations conclusively proves the case for a mathematically tinted portrait of History. But I hope that together they at least supply an excuse for attempting one.

NOTES

1 "*Mathematics and the Imagination*", Kasner and Newman, Vol 2 of 3.

2 *Business in Great Waters*, John Terraine ; a magnificent account of the battles for the Atlantic in both World Wars.

3. *The War at Sea 1939 to 1945* by Captain S W Roskill, despite being the Royal Navy's official account, is a masterful and gripping read in 3 volumes. First published in the 1950's The Naval & Military press brought out an excellent

paperback addition in 2004. You can also download on Amazon Kindle. Deserves to be read for centuries. The small group of British and Canadian seamen, largely amateur, who fought and won the Battle of the Atlantic over the course of 6 years, somehow surviving in tiny corvettes and unseaworthy destroyers, literally saved our bacon, and in doing so performed the greatest military feat in history. Puts Trafalgar, Waterloo, Borodino, Stalingrad, Salamis, Lepanto….in the shade. Guts, guts, guts………… Because it was far too rough for journalists, politicians and cameramen to get out there, and because both sides were necessarily secretive, it was an epic that has never received the attention it deserves.

4 I have just completed a book on the scientific side of the Battle of the Atlantic in novel form entitled *Strangle* (Amazon, later this year 2020).

HISTORY OF THE BRITS

CHAPTER 5

PROGRESS: WHY NICE CHAPS COME IN FIRST

"We inherited the Earth from our parents, but we have stolen it from our children." Jane Goodall.

One cannot discuss history without considering the concept of Progress. But what is it, and can one find any objective criteria for defining it ? I believe we can, but that requires a detour into serious philosophy, Common Sense in fact.

As far as I can see Common Sense Thinking (CST henceforth) works like this: we all get ideas, they constantly bubble unasked to the surface of the mind; the real challenge is to decide which ones are sound. To determine that we look for evidence (clues) bearing on our idea or hypothesis H and place each clue in one of only 5 categories:

TABLE (5:1) The Weights of Clues bearing on Idea H

Clue	Weight	Symbol
	Strongly in favour of H	s
	Weakly in favour of H	w
	Neutral towards H	n
	Weakly against H (underlined)	$\underline{w}$
	Strongly against H (underlined)	$\underline{s}$

We then combine (symbol ★) the Weights in obvious ways thus:

w★w = s

w★$\underline{w}$ = n

s★s = ss

s★$\underline{w}$ = w   and so on.

And we finally decide to act on H only when the combined evidence reaches either sss [decide for H] or $\underline{s}\ \underline{s}\ \underline{s}$ [decide against H]. This is a precautionary measure which saves us from making premature, possibly fatal decisions based on only two strong clues, one of which might be unsound.

EXAMPLE

A detective is having to decide whether to charge X with a crime [her hypothesis is 'X is guilty'. Her thinking, based on the available evidence, might look like this:

TABLE (5:2) DETECTIVE's THINKING

Clue	Her Weight	Accumulated Weight	Outcome
Motive	s	s	
Opportunity	w	ws	
Alibi	$\underline{w}$	s	
Witness A	w	ws	
Witness B	$\underline{s}$	w	
Witness C	w	s	
Witness D	s	ss	
Forensics	s	sss	Charges X

My scheme is nothing more than the systematic Association of Ideas [H with different clues], combined with a simple precautionary mechanism for avoiding overhasty decisions. I suspect such CST is our main survival mechanism with roots that go back a billion years. You won't find it in text-books on Inference or Logic; they appeal instead to notions such as Probability Theory, Bayes' Theorem and Parsimony. The problem is that their authors disagree violently among themselves[1] –

so something must be seriously wrong. That's why scientists ignore them and go on using CST to progress.

Notice three important features of this scheme:

(i) The more evidence the better. With a sufficiently long string of clues, even when they conflict, we can eventually reach a decision [sss or $\underline{s}\ \underline{s}\ \underline{s}$] about H, one way or the other, provided (a major proviso) a record has been kept of the incoming clues, together with their Weights. For instance I was eventually able to bring my own tangled research project to a triumphant conclusion but only after using writing to compound 25 separate clues, some in stark conflict with the rest. This means the scheme can be used, but only by the literate, to handle highly complex tasks such as voyaging to the Moon

(ii) The process is open-ended; there is always room to add new evidence to the tally whenever it is found. Thus it is Provisional in nature, and even after a decision to act has been taken there must be room for a change of mind – in other words to Adapt.[2]

(iii) Rather than remember these unfamiliar symbols it turns out to be much easier to use betting Odds and replace "combine" by the multiplication sign ×, 'n' by the number 1, s by 4, w by 2, underlined-w by ½, and underlined-s by ¼ . Then a decision in favour takes place when the Odds are 64 to 1 on, and against at Odds of 64 to 1 against. In future that is what we do.[Website Page on 'Categorical Thinking' explains this all]

These outcomes of CST have six very definite implications for organizations which need to survive in a world of bitter rivalry – in other words for History

(A) The more evidence the better. More clues will enable decisions to be reached in more complex situations where the evidence is sometimes conflicting or uncertain. More evidence calls for more CURIOSITY on the part of both individuals and of the societies to which they belong. Curiosity is an absolutely vital survival mechanism. Autocracies which strangle curiosity are writing their own death warrants.

(B) Whereas the unaided human memory can hold maybe 3 or 4 clues [with their Weights] it has no chance of relating the dozen or even more required to reach a sound decision in a complex situation. This is why the invention of writing transformed human possibilities 5000 years ago. Before writing we were little better than apes; afterwards we joined the angels. LITERACY is the fairy dust of progress.

(C) Although, on the basis of current evidence, somebody else might appear to be categorically wrong, new evidence might tomorrow prove them right and you wrong. Thus TOLERANCE has to be an essential ingredient of any progressive society. Those without it may doom themselves to get stuck in a dead end.

(D) Once we can handle a whole string of evidence, ever more coming in, we must be able to change our minds. ADAPTABILITY has to be the watchword of progress, as it is of biological Evolution.

(E) We all have blind-spots, gaps in our knowledge and warps in our judgements. Thus a group of independent individuals who can bring their combined knowledge and wisdom to the table is more likely to decide soundly and do so more quickly. Progressive societies have to practice DEMOCRACY at all levels from government downwards. Less democratic societies will eventually lose out, especially in fatal confrontations, for instance in wars.

(F) Likewise in any competitive situation dishonesty (or corruption) must not be tolerated because it will lead to wrong or at least much delayed decisions. In the long run HONESTY will pay. To appreciate this point the following table illustrates how dramatically the 'decisiveness' of compounded evidence (i.e. D_N the accumulated Odds after N clues)) drops when the reliability or Weight of the average clue i.e. ($\bar{W}$) is diluted only from 2 to 1.5 by dishonesty. The honest group can make a sound decision (Odds D_N more than 60 to 1 on H) after only 6 clues while the dishonest group will need 10 or 11. No contest.

TABLE(5: 3) :HOW DISHONESTY DELAYS PROGRESS

N	D_N ($\bar{W}$ =2)	D_N ($\bar{W}$ =1.5)
1	2	1.5
2	4	2.2
3	8	3.7
4	16	5.1
5	32	7.6
6	64	11
7	128	17
8	256	26
9	512	38
10	1024	58
11	2048	86
12	4096	130

THE SIX REQUIREMENTS FOR PROGRESS

Thus there is a minimum set of 6 requirements demanded of any Progressive society:

Curiosity,

Honesty.

Adaptability

Tolerance

Literacy

Democracy. (Pneumonic CHATL(i)D)

Note that these requirements are not based on morality, but on the need to succeed in any competitive situation. Take one historical example of each:

EXAMPLES OF PROGRESSIVENESS

(A) Curiosity. The modern world largely derives from the curiosities of half a dozen scientists: Oersted (Denmark), Faraday, Maxwell, Heaviside, Hughes , Hertz (Germany) and Marconi (Italy). Between them they established that electromagnetic signals could race through empty Space at the speed of light. Astonishing! Radio, television, radar, broadcasting, mobile phones, the Internet, Relativity, Space-travel are all the outcome of naked human curiosity. Only Marconi made much money out of their discoveries while Oliver Heaviside allegedly died of malnutrition in Teignmouth and David Hughes, who first discovered radio in 1870, had his discovery spurned by the august Royal Society[3]. Fortunately it was re-discovered by Heinrich Hertz in Germany 17 years later.

(B) Literacy. For 35 years I was part of the Hubble Space Telescope Project – one of the most complex ever of Man's undertakings. So many teams were involved in building different but unavoidably interdependent components, and so many individuals rotated through each team with the passage of years, that stringent documentation was required of all teams at all times. It was a hell of a pain – but indispensible. Where it broke down (over the issue of military secrecy) disaster followed (launch with a hopelessly faulty mirror. Thanks to adaptability however we managed to put things right.)[4]

(C) Toleration. After Rutherford died in 1937 the leadership of nuclear physics passed from Britain to Germany and it was Hahn and Strassmann who discovered Uranium fission in Berlin in 1938. But the Nazis could not tolerate Jewish scientists while the British could. Thus Otto Frisch and Rudolf Peierls came to Birmingham University and there calculated the critical mass of Uranium 235 needed to build the Atomic Bomb – the essential secret of that fateful enterprise.[5]

(D) Democracy. Either the Germans or the British could have got that bomb first. The Germans entrusted the project to Werner Heisenberg the outstanding atomic physicist of his time. The British by contrast formed a committee. Heisenberg got the critical mass hopelessly wrong while the Maude Committee successfully worked out all the steps necessary to build a bomb, including isotope separation by gaseous diffusion. But when cipher traffic made it clear that the Nazis would be defeated without a bomb they handed over all those secrets to the Americans (who beforehand were sceptical of the Bomb's feasibility).[5]

(E) Adaptability. The decisive battle of the Second World War was the Battle of the Atlantic, fought between Hitler's U-boats and the British and Canadian navies. Over 6 years 5000 ships, 750 U-boats and 100,000 lives were lost. Both sides had their vital radio-ciphers broken by their adversaries. The U-boats wreaked such havoc largely because B-Dienst in Berlin had broken the Admiralty's Convoy Cipher, enabling Admiral Donitz to direct his submarines into a convoy's path even before it left port. Likewise the cipher breakers at Bletchley Park broke the U-boat Enigma ciphering machine, allowing allies to divert convoys around gathering wolf-packs. But the senior commanders on both sides refused to believe that their ciphers were compromised. Eventually however the Admiralty bowed to the evidence and changed its cipher system in mid 1943 (i.e. Adapted) while Donitz, even in the face of overwhelming evidence, never did. After May 1943 his U-boats were never a threat.[6,7,8]

(F) Honesty – or lack of it. My example here is "Ludendorff's Lie" that led directly not only to the rise of Hitler but to the world conflagration which followed. General von Ludendorff commanded the Kaiser's army in 1918. That army was comprehensively defeated by British, Commonwealth and French forces in front of Amiens in August 1918. Thereafter it went in irreversible retreat back towards Berlin. Ludendorff informed his government that if an armistice wasn't signed at once Germany would be occupied. They hastily signed. But afterwards Ludendorff claimed that his undefeated army had been 'stabbed in the back' by the politicians. Amongst many others Adolf Hitler unfortunately believed that lie. So the whole ghastly war had to be fought all over again – with Germany the greatest loser.[9]

P.S. If I have chosen most of my examples from war it is because war is such a stark test of a nation's mettle. In peace- time we often stumble along with the worst governments we can afford.

Readers might object that Curiosity, Literacy, Tolerance, Adaptability, Democracy and Honesty cannot be the only measures of Progress. That well may be – what about humanity or fairness for example? But those six are the only ones for which I can find a robust philosophical justification (But see Ch 15).

WHICH NATIONS ARE MOST PROGRESSIVE?

Now that we have our 6 criteria it is interesting to weigh some existing nations on the scales of Progress, judged by their relative performances over the past century. Table 3 shows my attempt to do so. Each society is awarded a mark between 1 and 5 for each of the 6 criteria, their marks are multiplied together(which helps to separate them into distinct classes) and the resulting totals are used to assign them to ranks. Since a perfect score amounts to $5\times5\times5\times5\times5\times5$ = 15,625 one way to do so would be place those nations within a factor 5 of the perfect score within the first rank, those within 5×5 of it in the second, and so on. Table 4 is the result:

TABLE (5:4)

13 NATIONS RANKED BY THEIR PROGRESSIVENESS

Nation	Curio.	Lity.	Demo.	Tol	Hon.	Adapt	Total	Rank
China	1	3	1	2	1	1	6	5
Congo	1	2	1	1	1	2	4	6
Denmark	2	5	5	5	5	4	5000	1
France	4	5	3	3	2	3	1080	2
Germany	4	5	2	2	2	4	640	2
India	1	2	2	2	2	2	32	4
Italy	3	4	2	2	3	3	432	3
Japan	3	5	2	2	2	3	360	3
Russia	2	4	1	1	1	1	8	5
Spain	1	4	2	1	3	4	96	4
Switz.	3	3	5	3	3	3	1215	2
UK	5	5	4	5	4	5	10000	1
USA	3	5	2	3	2	4	720	2

It will be easy to mock this scheme but I don't see how we can analyse history without some measure of progress and decline. Valueless people [you know who I mean] simply disqualify themselves from taking part – I don't intend to even argue about that. Alternative value systems are certainly possible, but they clearly need to be stated – and justified on fundamental grounds. It is at least much better than the gross and ephemeral measures so regularly used based on the numbers of dollars or warheads or tanks.

The most arbitrary feature of my list is its century timescale. For instance Japan and Germany might have done much better if I had chosen 50 years instead. But both countries only became progressive as a result of resounding defeats. Then there's America – but that's got a chapter [13] of its own.

There is too the fundamental question of whether Progress in itself is good. It has been well argued[10] that the best societies must be those that have endured the longest – in which case the Kalahari Bushmen easily come out on top (200,000 years). But after contact an unchanging society is likely to be overwhelmed by the influence of more progressive societies from outside. Look at Imperial China – which made a conscious effort to remain aloof – or the Bushmen themselves. Whether it is good or bad I think that progress is something we cannot avoid.

Britain comes out on top of the Progressive scale, narrowly above Denmark. And surely that is as it should be. She has done more to change herself, relatively peacefully, and to change the world, than anyone else, irrespective of size. She would do even better if she was more democratic and more honest with herself.

For me however the exciting point of this analysis is how positive it is, how optimistic we can all be, whatever our nationalities. Personally I find all six criteria for societal survival, from Curiosity to Honesty, most welcome. We can be confident I think that 'Nice guys will come in last' is untrue. On the contrary, if history is any guide, 'Nice chaps will definitely come in first.'

I can't resist finishing with an anecdote. In 1986 I went deep behind the Iron Curtain on a scientific mission. There I met a Jewish scientist who had been raised on the extremely remote Kamchatka Peninsula, where his mother still lived.

"Can't you get her out?" I asked.

"She will never leave" he replied.

"Why not?"

"Because only good people live there."

When I asked him what he meant he said that his people, the Moscow Jews, had been exiled to Kamchatka in the 1940s by Stalin in one of his paranoid rages. Intellectuals and bureaucrats, they'd been thrown out into the snow with an axe, a box of matches and a sack of potatoes each:

"According to my mother the bad people died during the first winter, the selfish people during the second and the dishonest during the third. Only the very best are left." [11]

NOTES

1 Jaynes E.T, 2003, *Probability Theory the Logic of Science*, CUP 2003. See especially his References with commentaries.

2 Tim Harford, 2011, *Adapt,* Abacus. Stories of successes which grew out of failure. The way the world really works.

3 Daniel Boorstin, 1985, *The Discoverers*, Vintage books. The History of Science is a huge and controversial subject, but this is a good place to start, and most readable.

4 Zimmerman, Robert, 2008, *The Universe in a Mirror*, Princeton University Press. Story of the Hubble Space Telescope. I have just myself brought out 4 self-contained novels about the Hubble Adventure on Amazon: in chronological order *Against the fall of Night*, *The Whispering Sky*, *Crouching Giant* and finally *Beyond the Western Stars*; all Amazon paperbacks 2020

5 Rhodes, Richard, 1983, *The Making of the Atomic Bomb*, Touchstone Books. I couldn't put this down.

6 John Terraine, 1989, *Business in Great Waters*; reissued by Wordsworth Military Library 1999. A wonderful book about an undeservedly neglected epic. Journalists never went out there to witness the battle of the Atlantic because it was far too tough for ordinary unsalted mortals to endure.

7 Stephen Roskill. *The War at Sea 1939 to 1945.* The all encompassing and magnificent Royal Navy official history in 3 volumes. Reissued in paperback by the Naval & Military Press 2004. Also on Amazon Kindle,

8 *Strangle.* (In preparation) My attempt to condense the scientific side of the epic Atlantic battle down in novel form. (Amazon 2020)

9 John Terraine, *To Win a War*, Cassel 1978. The story of the war in 1918 by a magnificent historian.

10 James Suzman, 2017, *Affluence without Abundance,* Bloomsbury. You can't rely on Laurence van der Post's famous '*Bushmen of the Kalahari*'; he made it up.

11 *The Siberians* by Farley Mowat is *the* book on the subject and absolutely gripping. When I asked my Jewish friend what Siberia was really like he put a finger to his lips. Remember this was still the Soviet Union. But next day he presented me with *The Classical Theory of Fields* by Landau and Lifschitz and winked. When, back in my room I opened that mathematical monster I found he had hollowed it out and concealed Mowat's book inside.

HISTORY OF THE BRITS

CHAPTER 6: COMMITTEES

" It seems important to me that men of good will should make an effort to understand how the world ticks; it is the only way to make it tick better." C.P. Snow, *'Science and Government' p 60.*

Twice since 1066 Britain has been on the verge of invasion and defeat – in 1588 and 1940 – and twice she was saved by a very British institution – the expert committee.

Henry the VIII th. (reigned 1509 - 47) made the first systematic attempt to build a navy that could defend these islands from sea-born marauders. Before his time it was unsafe to even live near the coast for fear of Barbary pirates. He built dockyards around the East and South coasts from Deptford near London to Portsmouth in lee of the Isle of Wight. There he began to build a formidable new fleet but unfortunately, or fortunately as it turned out, his superman in charge of the project William Gonson, Keeper of the King's Ordnance, died in 1545 before things were fairly underway. No one sufficiently versatile being found to succeed him Gonson was replaced by a standing committee of 7 fully professional experts called the Navy Board. There were different members in charge of ship design, of armaments, of sails and rigging, of finance, of Stores and so on. No other such corporate body controlled any other European navy and none ever would. The Navy Board proved to be a mightily successful managerial revolution which was to run the Royal Navy for no less than 400 years, and in so doing come to change the entire world.

The Navy Board's first spectacular success was the new British naval cannon, the so called 'Seed-Gun'. The old forged iron cannon that had been going to sea since the 13th century tended to blow up if fired too often (more than once an hour) or too far (a couple of hundred paces). Bronze cannon were better – but very expensive. Henry couldn't afford them so, under the supervision, and at the expense of the Navy Board, iron masters in the Wealds of Kent and Sussex were charged to experiment with making cast-iron cannon. They succeeded spectacularly so that by the time of the Armada (1588) the Royal Navy had far superior guns to the Spaniards, guns that could fire further and ten times as often as their Spanish equivalents. In fact the Dons never stood a chance – as the experts on both sides knew[1] .Drake and Howard's faster, more manoeuvrable ships (also products of the Board's ingenuity) held off from the enemy fleet, pounded them from a distance and chased them into the North Sea from whence very few ever returned to Spain. Thanks to a committee Britain was saved, and not for the last time. Incidentally those big guns were Britain's first successful heavy industry.

When Hitler came to power in 1933 the Brits began to worry about invasion from the air. At the instigation of H. E. Wimperis, a civil servant at the Air Ministry, a 'Committee for the Scientific Survey of Air Defence' was set up in 1935 under the chairmanship of Professor Henry Tizard. In no time the promise of radar had been established and Air Marshall Dowding (who was later to head Fighter Command in the Battle of Britain) persuaded the RAF to fund its immediate development. Thus was born the crucial weapon that would enable Britain to concentrate and conserve its slender fighter squadrons against the mighty Luftwaffe. It was neither the Spitfire nor the Tally-ho public school types of popular legend that played the primary role in repelling the Messerschmidts and Heinkels in 1940 – but the Tizard Committee.

And that was by no means the end of it. Tizard again set up the Maud Committee out of which the Atomic Bomb was born. (The Americans had to be later persuaded by members of that committee that the Bomb was feasible at all.)

Committees don't just have to be advisory like the ones above, they can be executive as well. On a day to day basis Britain ran its Second World war through The Chiefs of Staff Committee made up of the heads of the Army, Navy and Air Force. The most important decision ever taken by Churchill and Roosevelt was to set up, between their respective sets of military commanders, The 'Joint Chiefs of Staff Committee' which met every three months or so to make the most momentous decisions which controlled the war (The politicians of course liked to take the credit, but only when things were running well). For instance at the outset the Combined Chiefs settled on the 'Germany First' strategy and at Potsdam in 1945 it was they, not Truman or Churchill, who decided to drop that bomb on Hiroshima.

Committees, committees, committees – journalists don't like committees because they don't make good copy, and so they try to personalize, and in the process trivialize, complex matters which individuals probably could never solve on their own. Once again in that same war, allegedly dominated by Churchill, his cabinet had no less that 400 separate sub-committees which formed and dissolved as needs demanded, and which, serviced by over 500 civil servants, met 8000 times.[4]

Like any senior scientist I have sat on many committees, both, national and international, indeed it is impossible to imagine Big Science running without them. For instance over 35 years I sat on three committees involved in developing and then exploiting the Hubble Space Telescope—one of the most innovative and difficult projects ever carried out by mankind. In each case when we sat round a table for the first time we had no idea how to accomplish the task we had been set, indeed not much confidence it could be done at all. But out of our collective knowledge on the one hand, and the clash of ideas on the other, ways were found that none of us foresaw or indeed could have foreseen originally. All three succeeded despite one or two rotten apples in each barrel, because the majority of members, the chairmen in particular, could see the bigger picture and put the common interest first. Determined committees can even disinfect themselves; thank goodness Tizard's committee dissolved itself and then reformed without Churchill's pet 'Prof' Lindemann, one who could never see the merit in anybody's ideas beside his quirky own.

Why do committees work – especially in war? For four reasons think:

- First because they can bring more evidence to the table – and more evidence is what you need to reach a quick and sound decision. [Ch.5]
- Second, by averaging out the prejudices of individual members they are more likely to avoid the follies to which autocrats are often prone.
- Third ,because they should be harder to traduce, it being harder to traduce half a dozen than one.
- Fourth, perhaps surprisingly, because they can be more decisive than an individual. When six are convinced on the best course of action they are much harder to turn aside.

In British history committees seem to feature most prominently in times of war – with good reason. The decisions are more consequential, more urgent and more in competition with 'the enemy' on the far side of the hill. A society on the ropes cannot afford to let egotistical individuals cock things up – as they often do in peacetime. Think of Sir Fred Goodwin single-handedly ruining the Bank of Scotland, the world's biggest bank, or Bernie Madoff running up 65 Billion dollars worth of debt in some back office in New York. That's a lot of tanks!

We British so love committees that we've allowed one to run our country for 300 years – the Cabinet. And it hasn't done so badly either, seeing off any number of military genii from Louis the XIVth, via Napoleon to Hitler as well as presiding, or rather committeeing, over the invention of much of the modern world.

Cabinet government seems such an obviously good idea that one is forced to wonder why everyone else hasn't adopted it too. The Americans never have, neither have our chief continental rivals, and most of our newly independent colonies couldn't wait to abandon it, usually in favour of over-mighty and usually disastrous 'Presidencies' (Think Nkrumah, Idi Amin, Ayub Khan, Zuma, the Nehrus, Mgabe and so on and so on). That makes one think. Committees can only work in rather special circumstances which include:

- A determination by its members to work for some common good, not for personal or factional interests.
- A willingness to defer to majority opinion amongst one's fellow members (which may include supporting their majority opinion in public even when you disagree).
- A commitment to be honest in its dealings with itself, and with the higher authorities to which it might report.

But honesty, democracy and selflessness are rare and tender plants which cannot be relied on to flourish just anywhere. On the contrary. They are as much the outcome of high civilization as its protectors in times of war. They are a microcosm of the greater body which they serve.

The British certainly didn't invent committee government. Venice, to my mind the brightest jewel in all of civilization, was another maritime empire which lasted for over a thousand years. It was governed by a sort of parliament of 500 drawn from its merchant families, but real power resided in a Committee of Ten which they elected. The Doge (Duke) was an elected monarch, but his powers were largely ceremonial. With a fleet of over three thousand ships its wealth derived largely from controlling trade coming from the Far East along the Silk Road to the Levant and distributing it on at a handsome premium all over

Western Europe, the Russias and North Africa. This stream of gold only dried up when the Atlantic powers Spain, Holland France and Britain found better ways to trade directly with Asia using sea-going vessels developed originally by the Portuguese. But from about 800 to 1800 AD, when it was conquered by Napoleon, Venice sparkled like a jewel, leaving behind many legacies including Italian Opera (Monteverdi), the first Patent and Copyright Laws, Double-entry book-keeping (essential for Capitalism I'm told) and incomparable glass (out of which Galileo constructed his transformative telescope – not the first, but the best). Long before the British the Venetians lived for centuries by the ruthless use of sea-power. It is notable that two such long lived maritime powers had to rely on committees to run their complex naval operations

Committees have been both the offspring and the guardians of civilization – British civilization at least. Long may they flourish, particularly as it seems our many less civilized rivals will have to manage without them.

NOTES

1 One Spanish admiral wrote in advance: "*But unless God helps us by a miracle the English, who have faster and handier ships than ours, and many more long-range guns, and who know their advantage just as well as we do, will never close with us at all, but stand aloof and knock us to pieces with their culverins, without us being able to do them any serious hurt. So we are sailing against England in the confident hope of a miracle.*" [Quoted in "Safeguard of the Sea" by N.A.M Rodger Ch. 19]

REFERENCES

1 For a great history of The Royal Navy "*To Rule the Waves*" by Arthur Herman, Hodder, 2005.

2 For the Tizard Committee see "*Blackett's War*" by Stephen Budiansky, Knopf, New York, 2013.

3 For the bomb: "*The Making of the Atomic Bomb*" by Richard Rhodes, Touchstone 1988. A wonderful and most readable account .

All three fascinating books above have American authors so I hope I can't be accused of jingoism.

4 For committees in the Second World War see C.P. Snow :*Science and Government*, Mentor Books 1962 and *Churchill* by Andrew Roberts, Penguin, 2018.

5 *Venice* by Jan Morris. My favourite travel book,

HISTORY OF THE BRITS

CHAPTER 7.

PARASITES:

"...how small a part of the people work upon necessary labours, and Callings, viz how many Women and Children do just nothing, only learning to spend what others get? how many are mere Voluptuaries, and as it were meer Gamesters by Trade? How many live by puzzling poor people with unintelligible Notions in Divinity and Philosophy? How many by persuading credulous, delicate and litigious persons, that their Bodies, or Estates are out of Tune and in danger? how many by fighting as soldiers? How many by trades of meer pleasure, or Ornaments? And how many in a way of lazie attendance etc. upon others? And on the other side, how few are employed in raising, and working necessary food and covering? And of the speculative men how few do truly studie Nature, and Things"

John Graunt, , London 1662

They say that far more wild animals are killed by parasites than predators, and that even those that do fall prey have usually been weakened by parasites first. And as with creatures so with the societies in which we have lived. They mostly get eaten while still alive by parasites. The above is a nice eye-witness account of the matter by the founder of Statistics. By going through the records of the recently dead he compiled the first Mortality Table, including the occupations of the deceased and was shocked – though he was a Puritan

As far as I can see not much has changed. Over the ages the parasites may alter their disguises but their appetites remain as gluttonous as ever. If I define a parasite as one who takes significantly more from society than he or she puts in, then it is fair to say that most Britons either are parasites, would like to be parasites, or are in any case determined to see that their children become so.

If this is not obvious it is only because the secret of being a successful parasite is disguise, disguising it from your fellow citizens and, better still, disguising it from oneself. Almost by definition a successful parasite is invisible as such, for if they were not, any healthy society would strangle them before they stifled it.

Lets begin with some egregious examples of parasitism drawn from history:

- The Pharaohs, with their attendant priests, tricked a whole society into believing that they were gods who controlled the Sun and the Moon. The populance were recruited to build colossal tombs for the tricksters to enter the underworld with all their loot in tact. Parasites often leave megalomaniac memorials of their gluttony behind : Versailles, Topkapi, the Sultan's Harem in Istanbul, the Hermitage, Saint Peters, Sans Souci, the Taj Mahal, Blenheim Palace…… During my National Service I was trained at Eaton Hall, that tasteless extravaganza of the Grosvenor family who own much of West London. It had a replica of Big Ben – bigger than the original– and there were stuffed African Elephants in alcoves off the stairs.
- Rome itself, the great empire of crucifixion and slavery, couldn't resist being eaten away from inside once its relatively healthy republican government had been suborned by a long succession of emperor-tyrants who seized power and wealth – usually by force.[1]
- How come the whole of India fell to a bagatelle of British mercenaries employed by the East India Company? Because previously it was controlled by the parasitical Moguls, whose gross appetites can only be appreciated when you see some of the egregious monuments they left behind. In the Principality of Mysore – one of those princely states left by the British to be ruled by its Maharajah, we encountered evidence of breath-taking greed and vulgarity. Though no larger than an English county its maharajah had not one but dozens of colossal palaces, including a replica of Buckingham Palace – but three times life-size. Who but a monstrous parasite

stuffing his gorge, could possibly want several handcrafted, gold plated Rolls Royces? And the Caste System, which still throws a dark shadow across Indian society, was Parasitism enshrined in custom and law. No wonder most Indians welcomed the British in.

Now let's look at some modern parasites:

- The Saudi petrolocracy with their collaborators the Wahabi Sect (Funny how often governing and priestly parasites hang out together: it's a lethal combination). I had something to do with them through my student Salem – head of the bin Laden dynasty. He was a brilliant man and yet an example of literally insatiable greed. To my knowledge he had at least four European palaces, each with its embedded European mistress, and he had 28 private aeroplanes – which he piloted himself – in one of which he was bound to kill himself in the end (he did). He once did a slow roll in a jet airliner, with flaps and undercarriage down, as we were on final approach to Heraklion airport. He told me Arab rulers fostered hatred of Israel to fool their subjects into believing they were on the same side and thus to divert attention from what they were guzzling.
- Silicon Valley. The Americans didn't invent computers, nor have they been all that innovative since. [I can speak of this with inside knowledge because I have twice been at the cutting edge of this field myself.] But they cornered the market by a mixture of monopoly, government-subsidy, size, advertising, dodgy patent law and aggressive legal practices. Take Bill Gates who trousered 70 Billion dollars. He didn't even develop the ropey Disc Operating System('DOS') upon which his fortune was based. Ineptitude at IBM meant that every PC they sold gifted Gates $100. (When I worked at the Hubble Space Telescope if anyone mentioned Microsoft or Windows the whole room would burst into jeers of contempt and execration.) The fact is that in the computing industry necessity, not genius, has always been the

mother of invention. You could as well ask by how much Silicon Valley has delayed the progress of Data Processing, as advanced it.

- Post colonial governments – think of parasites like Nkrumah, Idi Amin, Ayub Khan, the Nehrus, Mobutu, Nyerere, Mugabe, Kenyatta, Zuma… the list is endless. They say 80% of foreign aid to Africa finished up in Swiss bank accounts. When I was in Kenya (1977) shortly after independence there was a surcharge of at least ten per cent on every financial transaction: it was called 'Mama Ngina's Share' (after Mrs. Jomo Kenyatta the President's wife).
- Big Pharma, with firms such as Pfizer. For example Ibuprofen is a wonder drug invented in Britain and still very cheap. Pfizer relabelled it 'Nurofen' and sells it back to the Brits at a mark-up of as much as 4000 per cent [Note 6]. And we buy it because of dodgy advertising and because you can be sure your pharmacist will give it a prominent place on the shelves – while Ibuprofen is hidden out of sight.

PARASITISM IN THE BRITISH CONTEXT

Historically of course we had the land-owning class which kept an iron grip on government until very recently. [Harold Macmillan, who had married into the Duke of Devonshire's family, appointed no less than 35 relatives to places in his 1957 Tory government.] They Enclosed much of the Common Land – which drove erstwhile free men and their families to near starvation in urban stews and many more(equivalent to 30% of the entire population) into emigration. Then (1815) they passed the Corn Laws to artificially raise the food prices and the land rents on which their idleness depended. [In 1914 about a third of recruits to the British army had to be rejected as suffering from chronic malnutrition]. They kept control of 'their' land by a mixture of intermarriage, primogeniture, inheritance and religious propaganda. But how did they come by that land in the first place? Apparently 60% of hereditary peers were, as late as 1970, the descendants of pimps and prostitutes ennobled by Charles II in return for sexual favours.[2]

Then there is the Church which is still a massive landowner – land acquired by all manner of immoral and rapacious practices – selling Indulgences for example to wealthy sinners so they could avoid the agonies of Purgatory. When Henry VIII dissolved the monasteries it is reckoned they owned a third of England's entire wealth. Priests have always been rapacious parasites – they still are. Look at the extravagant and ridiculous robes in which Cardinals and Archbishops adorn themselves to this day. Disciples of Christ? Pull the other one.

MODERN BRITISH PARASITES

It is always easier to spot parasites somewhere else in Space or Time, as we have been doing so far. But the parasites thriving here and now manage to get away with it mainly because they are successfully disguising their depredations from public gaze. So this next section is bound to be controversial. So it should be. Look at:

- Academics. My own and one of the most useless (with exceptions) and yet well-paid occupations in modern Britain. What they have managed to do is repeat the old trick played by the ancient monasteries. They guzzle by selling highly dubious tickets to heaven. The older lot sold "Certificates of Indulgence" to absolve the wealthy from the tortures of Hell. The modern lot mass-sell degree certificates to the young – supposed passports to a secular paradise here on Earth. Originally it was a clever trick based on 'grading', i.e. refusing to the un-anointed entry to the desirable professions. But they couldn't restrain their greed: 2 universities became 30 which then became 130 while every teacher became a professor – even those whose claims to scholarship are minimal (average salary £75,000). The trouble is that mass producing sustificates is as effective as mass producing paper money, and for the very same reason. The students are getting heavily into debt while much of what they are taught is worthless [Think Psychology, Business Studies, Management 'Science', Economics…..] And when the enormous bills come in from unpaid-off student loans [£12 billion at present but rising fast] who is going to pay? Presumably, as always, the industrious classes. The modern universities need to be cleaned out as ruthlessly as were the feudal monasteries. All they have done is replaced 'Holiness' with 'Cleverness'.[Ch.20 'Baducation']

- Doctors. Have you ever asked yourself why there are so many foreign doctors in Britain today? It cannot be because doctors are badly paid (even the average GP gets £90,000 a year, about 3 times the national average). It cannot be because British kids don't want to go to medical school – they are clamouring at the doors and need astronomical marks to get in. No, its quite simple; the British medical profession – through its trade union the BMA – has ruthlessly prevented more doctors from being trained in the UK – in order to keep up its high salaries. It's a dirty trick, as old and unprincipled as the hills, but fairly well concealed. But then successful parasitism has to be. I only learned about it because my dad was a hospital doctor in the Birmingham area – where there was, and still is, only one medical school between about 3 million people. In the 1960s he had a dozen assistants – all Indian or Pakistani – so it occurred to him and other colleagues that more British doctors should be trained and a second medical school be set up in the area. But the BMA successfully quashed the project – with the consequence which British patients are suffering today. There is nothing accidental about those long waiting times in A & E. They have been inflicted upon us by a bloody minded, coldly calculating trade union determined to maintain its exclusive status and high pay. The only question is why successive British governments, of both persuasions, have allowed such blatant parasitism to thrive.
- Once the nurses saw what the doctors were up to they naturally joined the freezing frenzy. Why shouldn't they too all have degrees, with emoluments to match? Then they could specialize and charge accordingly. So they did – with generally disastrous consequences for the NHS. Let one little anecdote tell the story. I broke both wrists in a cycling accident and was bleeding profusely from the face when admitted to the only A&E in Cardiff. There were half a dozen nurses on duty but no doctors (lunch-time I suppose). Next to me was a very old lady groaning in pain, and occasionally crying out for help. The 6 nurses, gossiping among themselves, totally

ignored us both. When I finally went up to remonstrate it turned out, so they claimed, that none of them was certificated to comfort an old lady, or clean a superficial wound. One was "a radiology nurse", one " a plaster nurse", one a "phlebotomy nurse" and so on. Eventually an uncertificated ward-orderly from Portugal, and a young doctor from Zambia, turned up to give us some (not very accomplished) treatment. You only need to spend a little time in an NHS hospital to see the consequences of outrageous restrictive practice in action. Where will it end? [NHS staff take off an average 14 'sickies' a year, as against 4 in the population as a whole]

- The legal profession have never been short of a thoroughly unearned bob or two [A lawyer with 15 years experience can expect to earn £180,000 pa] And with the government paying so many legal fees, boy what an opportunity! Whenever I hear a case reported on the news it usually concludes along the lines "the trial is expected to last 7 weeks".

    - Next to religion the oldest wheeze for extracting money from the helpless, or ignorant, is to claim some vital expertise. The possibilities are endless, but let me mention just two: Psychology and Economics. Although it (not the Nobel Committee !) awards itself pseudo "Nobel prizes" – what a fraud – Economics, as one can easily prove, is not remotely scientific, and never can become so.[See Chapt 14] Why not? Because there are an endless number of alternative explanations for every economic event – it's like dream interpretation. Thus Economics is prevented from using the Scientific Method by what Keynes called "The Principle of Limited Variety". Ditto Psychology, which is little more than a hodge-podge of private opinions, with no scientific basis whatsoever[4]. And ditto many other fields like "Management" which like to think they are sciences but which, for the identical reason, never can become so. ([Ch.20 'Baducation']. Bernard Shaw referred to the so called Professions as "A conspiracy against the laity"

- However all the depredations of other parasites are probably dwarfed by what the financial professions guzzle. I say probably because, by design, it is all but impossible to distinguish between what is legitimate and what is theft in the white-collar world. For instance every winter managers in the City of London award themselves £50 billion extra in 'bonuses' .That's £4,000 for every working family in the nation. Yes Banking provides an indispensible service to mankind. How otherwise could we buy a house, or save for retirement? But what would be a fair rate of return for such services – 3 or 4 % perhaps? But big bankers demand a rate of return on equity (their capital) of about 13% , quoting risk as their excuse for charging so much. But in practice there is no such risk because governments invariably bail out big banks at risk of failure [Gordon 'Pimco' Brown bailed out his Bank of Scotland – an incompetent crocodilian monster – during the 2008 banking crisis, which he had done so little to prevent]. Most of us accept burdensome banking charges principally because we have little option, and partly because what we will finally pay is well hidden in the small print. Buy a new car with a banker's loan and you will find out. Eventually. The whole art of financial chicanery is to muddy the waters , and financiers are very good at that. If you don't believe me try to find out what "Quantitative Easing" really means.

I admit to not having no real idea how much financial parasites steal from the modern economy – I don't think anyone does—but here are some figures to stimulate enquiry:

- Bernie Madoff stole 65 Billion dollars before anyone found out what the old fool was up to in a back room in New York (it was a simple Pyramid scam).

- LTCM, a whizzy financial scheme backed by two "Not the Nobel" prize winning economists lost so much money that it had to bailed out by a consortium of banks put together by the US government (1998). It has been estimated that it cost every man woman and child in the United States the equivalent of $3000.
- For his financial acumen a typical Hedge Fund manager charges his depositors " 2 and 20", 2 per cent per annum on all funds they deposit with him, plus 20 % of all subsequent profits those funds might make. Thus several of them clean out several Billion dollars a year. But the big joke is that research shows that such acumen simply doesn't exist – it was no more than temporary luck, and they will not 'beat the market' in the long run.

It has been reckoned that science and technology potentially deliver an annual increase of productivity of about 7%, and indeed the Chinese economy has been growing (so they claim) at that pace for the past 30 years. But in the Capitalist West we are lucky to manage 2% a year. So where does the other 5% go – 70 % of the whole? Most of it, I imagine, slides silently down the gullets of the financial sector. Look at their colossal skyscrapers in the City or Manhattan, look at all the luxury cars on the motorway, look at the egregious takings of MDs and CEOs. What alerted me to the breath-taking extent of the heist was a sailing holiday in the Med. Everywhere we encountered Super-yachts costing between 10 and 100 million pounds each, some as big as warships. Almost every one, and there were hundreds if not thousands, flew the Red Ensign, or a variant from one of those off-shore tax-haven dependencies of the British Empire such as the Cayman Islands. That's why so many of you have to work so hard for so little reward.

Can we do any thing about Parasites? Of course we could – but only after we recognize the literally sickening scale of their depredations. Until we do we'll be no better off than those ancient Egyptians who sweated their lives away building pyramids for false gods.

An alternative way to look at this matter is to ask what happened when there were occasional outbreaks of honesty. They're hard to find. But consider the huge economic advance made in Britain between 1750 and 1850. Historians invariable ascribe it to "The Industrial Revolution" and there is surely some truth in that. However it also coincided with the rise of Non-Conformist religion, a rare religion which actually practiced the scrupulous honesty which it preached. It may be a coincidence but so many of the great businesses and industries which started then were founded by Non-conformists and Quakers – whose word was their bond.[See nore 7] The landowning classes of course weren't interested and contributed little.

Economists, many of whom are paid to find excuses for gluttony, like to claim that Capitalism defeated Communism. But having spent some time in the FSU between 1986 and 1990 I don't think that is true. What happened was that the parasites hidden in the Communist Party (the so called 'Nomenklatura') choked their host to death before Western parasites succeeded in choking theirs – tho' they almost succeeded in 2008.

The history of any society must largely be an account of how it confronted its parasites. Most don't even try (viz Imperial Spain the once great superpower, strangled by its church and aristocracy[5]). Britain has struggled fitfully, but the more complex any society becomes the easier it is for parasites to hide away in its vital organs. In my opinion, for what its worth, we must all recoil from any intention of becoming parasites ourselves. But in any society somebody has to do the dirty work. Why don't we share it out, with everyone spending one day a week in the trenches? If you're outraged by that suggestion you are almost certainly a parasite yourself.

PS Parasites can be extremely devious. The *Toxiplasma* parasite causes host rats to run towards cats because it can only reproduce inside feline intestines.

NOTES

1 Read "*The Annals of Imperial Rome*" by Tacitus, or "*I Claudius*" a popularized version of it by Robert Graves.

2 Anthony Sampson : *The Anatomy of Britain.*

3 The Poldark novels by Winston Graham (13 of them) give an authentic and gripping account of the birth of the Industrial Revolution in Cornwall and the rise and effect of Non-conformist religion. The gentry couldn't believe that some religious people could actually be sincere practitioners of Christian principles .Most of them regarded the Church as a damn good way to keep the bloody peasants in their place.

4 Paul Masson's *Against Therapy*, 1978, takes the lid off the whole tawdry business. According to him Freud was a Fraud, Jung would be serving a long prison sentence today, therapists are little better than witch-doctors. He convinced me. The brain is far too complicated to be understood by simpletons.

5 *The Battle for Spain* by Anthony Beevor is about its awful civil war 1936-9. The first chapter gives an excellent potted account of its entire history up to that point.

6 '*Which*' magazine, from the Consumer Association. We never buy anything vital or expensive without consulting it first. An annual subscription will pay for itself dozens, perhaps hundreds of times over. Does anybody actually buy a new car after looking at an advertisement?

7 If one considers the Quakers alone, their contributions to British commercial history, enlightenment and progress are quite extraordinary, considering they made up only 1 in 500 of the population. For instance:

Abolition of Slavery: 5/12 of original Abolition Committee (1787)

Iron and Steel: Darbys of Coalbrookdale (Ironbridge)

Banking : Lloyds, Barclays, & most country banks.

First Railway: Stockton to Darlington (the 'Quaker Railway').1825

Bradshaw's Directory: the first national railway timetable. The Victorians' bible.

Chocolate : Cadburys, Rowntrees, Frys, Terrys. Originally as non-alcoholic drinks

Matches: Bryant & Mays

Self-sharpening plough : Ransomes (lawn-mowers today)

Shoes: Clarkes, Kendal's (K's)

Cornish Clay industry (Britain's biggest export).

Nantucket whaling industry

Western Union.

Science ; Meteorology (Richardson).

Pacifism (Richardson again)

www:quakersintheworld.org/quakersinaction/39/.Business/htm

www.leveson.org/stmarys/resources/cadbury0503.htm

And other far more numerous Non-Conformist sects, such as the Methodists were even more consequential. Honesty pays.

HISTORY OF THE BRITS

CHAPTER 8

CAN HISTORY HAVE A SCIENTIFIC METHOD?

"The most successful method of identifying, discovering and inferring facts is that of the natural sciences. This is the only region of human experience, at any rate in modern times, in which progress has indubitably been made. It is natural to wish to apply methods successful and authoritative in one sphere to another, where there is far less agreement among specialists."

Isiah Berlin wrote in his "*Proper Study of Mankind*" 1997, p18:

I have claimed that a scientific background is almost indispensable to writing history with insight. Here I try to make good on that claim. I will argue that the most controversial propositions in history are so because of conflicts in the evidence which bears on them. So in history, as in science, a systematic and transparent method for weighing conflicting evidence is an absolute necessity. Without it how is one to distinguish serious history from mere propaganda or polemic? I will claim that there is a Scientific Method for weighing conflicting evidence and that it may be applied to historical arguments, albeit with some significant reservations.

To get a measure of the problem let us begin with a selection of contentious historical proposition, or hypotheses, some of which we will discuss later in this book.

TABLE(8:1): CONTENTIOUS HISTORICAL PROPOSITIONS

1 The Romans held back European civilization by almost two millennia.

2 Throughout history Christianity has predominantly been a force for harm.

3 The British Empire was a glorious episode in British history.

4 The Jews have been persecuted largely because they have consistently practiced racism themselves (not marrying out).

5 British colonialism was good for India.

6 The defeat of Napoleon was a tragedy for the majority of British people.

7 Scotland would have done better outside the Union.

8 The strategic bombing of Germany was a foolish waste of Allied resources.

9 The Allies were right to A-bomb Japan.

10 America has been Britain's worst enemy.

I hope you agree that all the above hypotheses are both momentous and contentious. Certainly there are strong arguments both for and against each one. How could we come to a rational conclusion about them? In other words is there a proper 'Historical Method'(HM) ? Some historians have sought help from Science: thus Isiah Berlin in the quote heading this chapter. But can Science oblige? The problem lies in defining The Scientific Method itself. The distinguished zoologist Peter Medawar wrote: *"Ask a scientist what he considers the scientific method to be, and he will adopt an expression that is at once solemn and shifty eyed; solemn because he feels he ought to declare an opinion; shifty eyed because he is wondering how to conceal the fact that he has no opinion to declare"*. People, even some deluded scientists, imagine that scientists have a peculiarly logical and mathematical way of thinking that is both objective and effective. Indeed there is a whole subject area in academia called "The Philosophy of Science" centred on the matter. But practicing scientists keep well clear of it, feeling that what they do is more akin to a trade such as plumbing, than a branch of philosophy. And as for Mathematics it can have little to do with the matter for it knows nothing of Cause and Effect – the very heart-blood of Natural Science [Mathematics is about logical consistency – an entirely different concept]. In any case what have ethologists (who don't use maths) studying gorillas in the cloud forest got in common with physicists smashing atomic particles (who do) ?

Medawar went on to write: *"The day to day business of science involves the exercise of common sense supported by a strong understanding …."* while Einstein averred that *"Science is no more than a refinement of everyday thinking…."* I agree, but how does that everyday thinking work? It is so vital to our survival, and always has been, that, like our anatomy and physiology, it must be inherited almost entirely from our animal ancestors. If that is so then the crucial question to ask is "How do animals think?" . As far as I can see, we all, humans and animals alike, think primarily by using "The Association of Ideas". We have an idea and then our curiosity leads us to seek for clues bearing on (associated with) that idea – both for and against it. Each clue has to be weighed, and when their combined weights come down decisively on one side or another we make up our minds and act. Gambling is involved because we can rarely be absolutely certain that an idea is right (or wrong). The best we can hope for, be we chimpanzees, detectives, scientists or historians, is that the Odds, either for or against, are persuasively high. That is Common Sense Thinking or CST for short.[Note 1]

To incorporate a new clue, or piece of evidence E_1, into our thinking about some hypothesis H, we can use the Gamblers Rule:

$$O(H|E_1) = W(E_1|H) \times O(H). \qquad (8:1)$$

which simply updates our Odds on H, given E_1 from its previous value O(H) before incorporating E_1. $W(E_1|H)$ is simply a number called 'The Weight of E_1 as it bears on H'. Strong clues must be given high Weights, weak clues low, while clues unfavourable to H must have fractional Weights. It's up to you to assign a Weight to each clue.

Obviously the Gambler's Law can be applied over and over again, as each new clue turns up. And because it is multiplicative, high Odds can be reached, either for or against, if the clues generally weigh in the same direction. Eventually they may become high enough in combination for a decision to be reached about H – is it true or is it untrue.

Let's look at a simple example:

EXAMPLE

Take a crime which a detective is trying to solve, with H being 'X is the murderer'. There are only 7 feasible suspects so the detective assigns dispassionate Prior Odds on X's guilt of 6 to 1 against, i.e. O(H) = 1/6. Then there are 3 clues to each of which she assigns a Weight so that her thinking process can be summarized in an 'Inference Table' as follows:

INFERENCE TABLE (8:1) FOR 'X is guilty'.

Clue (E)	W(E|H)	O(H)	O(H|E)
Prior Odds		1/6	
Motive	2	1/6	2 times 1/6 = 1/3
Opportunity	4	1/3	4 times 1/3 = 4/3
Forensics	1/40	4/3	1/40 times 4/3 =1/30

The evidence conflicts but the overwhelming Weight of the forensic clue results (for now) in presumed innocence (Odds of 30 to 1 against guilt).

Note that this algorithm (recipe) is simple (i.e. it breaks down into identical steps, one for each clue); it is multiplicative (so that a small number of clues pointing in the same direction can potentially lead to decisive Odds) and it is Provisional (further clues can always be factored in at the bottom. It feels like a process that animals could employ step by step or in one step – our chief requirement for CST.

Also note that only very rough-and-ready Weights could be set on clues such as Motive (sexual jealousy here) and Opportunity – but that is no good reason to ignore them; on the contrary. For many significant clues Weights cannot be specified to a precision better than a factor of 2. Note also the overwhelming Weight of the single forensic clue. But suppose it is unreliable? Or put more broadly: 'How are we to deal with Systematic Errors ?' (See later)

At the heart of this process of thinking lies the assignment of values for the Weights of each and every clue. And here comes an absolutely crucial refinement to this process, which I call the PAW – the 'Principle of Animal Wisdom':

> "The only Weights permissible in Common Sense Thinking are:
> W(E|H) = 4 'Strongly in favour of H'
> W(E|H) = 2 'Weakly in favour of H'
> W(E|H) = 1 'Neutral'
> W(E|H) = ½ 'Weakly against H'
> W(E|H) = ¼ 'Strongly against H' "

Where does the PAW, which we didn't use in Table (8:1), come from? Animals who have to use CST to make survival decisions cannot afford to be misled into rash actions by single false clues, or single ill-judged Weights. If they did so they would quickly become extinct. The PAW is a precautionary measure which places the diversity, reliability and concordance of evidence above sheer tonnage or precision. Without such a constraint, a single clue, a single argument if you like, even it were unsound, could carry the day. [As it happens the forensic clue in Table (8:1) was wrong and led to the criminal escaping.] And that would be beyond foolish. So the PAW is just as vital to Science, and to History, and indeed to any usage of CST, as it is to survival out on the Serengeti.[See Note 1 for references to Common Sense Thinking]

To see how our scheme for CST, including the PAW, might work in the context of History, we shall apply it to one of the controversial proposals in Table

(8:1). Rather arbitrarily we pick Proposition 7 “Scotland would have fared better outside the UK”; at least it is topical and certain to rouse debate.

INFERENCE TABLE (8:2)

HYPOTHESIS: “Scotland would have fared better outside the UK”

CLUE	WEIGHT	ACCUM. ODDS
1Been governed locally (mixed blessing)	2	2
2 Spoken Gaelic not English	¼	½
3 Gone bankrupt in 1707 (Darien scheme)	½	¼
4 Kept control of its fish	2	½
5 Kept control of its Oil	4	2
6 Prob conquered in Counter Reformation	½	1
7 Prob conquered by Napoleon	½	½
8 Conquered by Hitler	1/4	1/8
9 Less opports for talented Scots abroad	½	1/16
10 Less trade with Eng. (eg shipbuilding)	¼	1/64
11 Been no part of Brit. Empire	½	1/128
12 Gone bankrupt 2009 (BOS)	½	1/256

Table (8:2), which shows my own attempt to tackle that proposition, illustrates both the strengths and the weaknesses of CST. Its main strengths are:

(a) It is transparent. My arguments, and the Weights attached to each, are laid bare for criticism and amendment.

(b) It stimulates broad research , because with PAW- Weights being so low, many different clues may be needed to reach conviction either way

(c) It is provisional, leaving room at the bottom for new clues to be incorporated, if they turn up. My mind is not closed to new arguments, but they will have to be numerous and strong to overturn my existing Odds. (256 to 1 against)

Its main weaknesses are:

(i) I have had to select which clues to include, and which to omit. (I discarded several as too equivocal to weight).

(ii) There is no logical justification for the value of most Weights. They largely have to be a matter of intuitive judgement – which could of course be wrong.

Nevertheless, in this case at least, my Odds finish up so high that I feel confident in my final judgement – as it happens against the proposition.

At the same time the discussion highlights the treacherous nature of 'What If' debates in History. If, as I am suggesting, an independent Scotland would not have remained independent for long (because it has 6000 miles of remote coastline to defend) it might have been invaded by France during the Counter-Reformation (~1700) and forced into Catholicism; or turned Republican by Napoleon, or Fascist by Hitler. Most likely of all it would have been invaded by England (as in essence it was) to prevent all those other threatening incursions into the home isle. Selectively picking out those few arguments, like Oil, favourable to its cause, as the Scottish National Party is inclined to do, is either extremely naïve, or downright dishonest. Would most Scots really have preferred to be Gaelic speaking subjects of France, or the Vatican or latterly Nazi Berlin? Somehow I doubt it. Invasion and control by England may have been, by some way, the least bad of alternative *feasible* fates.

Scotland aside I would argue that the approach here used to reach a conclusion has much to recommend it when it comes to discussing historical problems in general. It is open and frank. However ill-judged they may be at least the various Weights are declared and frank. And at the end there are combined Odds, no doubt imperfect, on the outcome being right. And who seeks perfection when the Odds become so decisive? One doesn't care whether they be exactly 100 to 1, or 500 to 1, instead of the 256 to 1 against, that we actually estimated here. On the other hand had they been as low as 5 to 1, or even 10 to 1, I would regard them, and the debate as a whole, as inconclusive – at least for now, and in need of more and better evidence. But that itself would be a fruitful conclusion.

The most innovative part of the suggested scheme is the PAW. It is vital to prevent a single but misguided argument, or a single strong but unsound piece of evidence, from carrying the day. All of the following unsound arguments, or clues, have misled humankind, sometimes holding back progress for centuries, sometimes causing untold misery and death:

HISTORICAL ELEPHANTS IN THE ROOM

The Pharaoh controls the Sun and Moon.

The Earth is flat.

The Sun goes around the Earth every 24 hours.

The world began in 4004 BC

Black people are sub-human

We Germans (British, Chinese…) are a superior race

The Hottentots (Aborigines, Jews ..) are inferior

It must be true; it's in the Bible (Koran……).

Self-government is always better than colonial rule.

You can tell a criminal by the shape of his head.

Women are weak and inferior.

---------s don't suffer pain like we do.

The IQ test is a measure of Intelligence.

The Communist Manifesto is Scientific, therefore indisputable

The communion wine is actually the blood of Christ.

Of course continents can't drift.

Evolution simply isn't true

Our German army wasn't defeated in 1918

The weak must starve because there's not enough food to go around.

It's their own fault if they're poor.

Diphtheria (Small-pox….) is caused by witches

Certain old women are possessed of the devil

Abortion is murder

Blood transfusions/ Euthanasia..… are against the will of God

ETC ETC

At various times all the above beliefs have been held by humane and intelligent people. In crucial debates such Systematic Errors, as we call them in Science, have often proved to be the weighty but fatal Elephants in History's room. Sometimes we cannot know whether this one or that of our cherished beliefs is actually an unsound Elephant. What we can do, by employing the PAW, is to dampen the effect they can have on our actions and decisions and thus limit the amount of unnecessary harm they could do. The PAW deliberately shrinks Elephants, sound or unsound, to roughly the same size as the other clues in the scales. PAW also makes CST so much easier to use, and so much more agreeable between individuals, because assigning clues to one of only five categories is vastly easier than assigning them specific Weights – which is what statisticians so often misguidedly try to do.

All I am recommending is the same form of codified CST that most successful scientists (and wise people in general) appear to use. It is by no means fool-proof, it involves gambling (choosing clues and setting Weights) and it will by no means work as well in History as it does in Science. Why not? For two significant philosophical reasons:

(a) In the natural world important 'Principles of Uniformity' [David Hume 1738] seem to obtain, rendering Science much simpler than History – indeed they are the main reason for Science's success. Thus we can assume: 'All Oxygen atoms are (nearly) the same'; or 'The geological processes acting in the past were no different from the ones we can observe in action today'; or 'The Laws of Nature are everywhere and everywhen the same'. We cannot prove these principles of uniformity, but assuming them appears to lead to very fruitful results. But that is no good reason to apply them to say history. For instance, all human individuals are not the same; the historical past is not exactly like the present, and so on.

(b) Keynes' 'Principle of Limited Variety' (PLV) asserts that CST will only work if there are a limited number of hypotheses to choose between. The interpretation of dreams is futile because there is an infinitude of possible interpretations [I would argue, for the same reasons that Psychology and Economics are futile subjects]. In an historical investigation there may be a limited number of hypotheses to choose between. If there are then, by all means use CST in an Inference Table. If there are not, then don't try. One might for instance use the PLV to argue that there were too many alternative scenarios in the Scottish Independence discussion above to make the application there of CST reliable, and perhaps that is so. All I would conclude with any confidence is that, because of its immensely long coastline, Scotland would be, and remains, highly vulnerable to invasion. Remaining independent for long was therefore never a practical option. The prefix 'Mac' to so many Scottish names is a reminder that it has been invaded time and again from Ireland, which is a mere hour or so's sail upwind.

History can never be an exact science, and we should not pretend that it can be. But by employing Inference Tables and assigning Weights according to the PAW, we can sometimes do a lot better than much of the stuff which has passed for History in the past; and still does. If nothing else it should be transparent.

NOTES

1 The paperback account of Common Sense *Thinking for Ourselves* by me on Amazon (Kindle Publishing) 2020

2 The massive intellectual footprint of the Scots is described in '*How the Scots invented the Modern World*' by Arthur Herman (an American). [England's appalling universities at Oxford and Cambridge were self-proclaimed seminaries dedicated to strangling the Enlightenment; see Ch.20] Had you sat at a meeting of the Oyster Club in a tavern in Edinburgh in the 1790s you might have encountered the greatest collection of intellectual gunpowder ever gathered on this planet, including Joseph Black (founder of both Chemistry and Thermodynamics), James Hutton ('the father of Geology') ,David Hume (arguably the world's greatest philosopher, though he thought of himself as a historian), Adam Smith (founder of Economics), James Watt (steam engine).... all arguing with one another. No wonder Edinburgh was called 'The Athens of the North'. But 'Athens' didn't do it justice; in my opinion Athens was never in the same league.

3 Recent accessible accounts of History's ambitions, methods and failings include: *What is History?* By E. H. Carr; *The Uses and Abuses of History* by Margaret Macmillan

HISTORY OF THE BRITS

CHAPTER 9

WHY MEN HAVE HAD TO FIGHT.

History is war; and war history. We may deplore that fact, even despair of it, but we cannot avoid it. Anyone who is interested in history cannot but be fascinated by war.

The ancient Greeks may be thought of as the founders of Western civilization. We can celebrate the glories of Greek philosophy, architecture, sculpture, literature, mathematics and so on but when you read their history, especially history written at the time, you come to realize those were all side-shows compared to the real business of a Greek man – which was fighting. Their founding myth was the Iliad – that Homeric glorification of war. Heroism, fortitude, gallantry these were the virtues praised and valued far above cleverness and learning – and perhaps we should be grateful for that – very grateful. For without their military prowess the stirrings of what eventually became European civilization would have been crushed by the mighty Persian Empire. The anonymous Greek warriors who died at Thermopylae and Salamis did as much for us as Euripides and Plato. It would be a travesty to admire the flowering of Periclean Athens without understanding where its wealth and hubris came from.[1]

The British obsession with classical learning concentrated more on its military than it philosophical aspect. At school in the 1950s we had to read Caesar's *Commentaries on the Conquest of Gaul* in Latin, while all our impositions consisted of learning by heart hundreds of lines of poetry celebrating the stands of heroes such as Horatio on the bridge, or Sir Richard Grenville on the deck of his *Revenge* as it was shot from under him by the dastardly Spanish Dons. And why not? If the two previous generations of British schoolboys hadn't been prepared to give their all, Western civilization could easily have gone under. Look at the French: they collapsed abjectly in 1940 rather than fight. Most of the French troops evacuated off the Dunkirk beaches in

1940 elected to go straight back to become prisoners of the Nazis rather than help liberate their own country. Whether we like it or not civilization and military prowess walk hand in hand; neither must let go of the other – especially, as we shall argue – in the Atomic age. Many intellectuals would prefer otherwise. But history, at least grown-up history, is not about preferences it is about facts. And the very first fact of history is that wherever we look across the time-scape men have fought – the British very much included.

But why do men fight? Most of us sensibly shrink from the prospect – after all we might get killed or maimed. The only explanation which makes any sense to me is that men have to fight, and they have to fight for a mathematical reason that is by no means obvious – but none the less compelling for that. Imagine a square island [Fig (9:1)] once upon a time divided up amongst a number of tribes, each dwelling within its own square territory. From time to time disputes would erupt—which might lead to fighting. All other things being equal the population of a tribe would be in proportion to the area of its territory, but the length of its borders would be in proportion to its diameter only (and therefore to the square-root of its area). Thus the larger a tribe the greater the amount of resources it can devote *per mile of border*, to either defending or expanding its boundaries (this is true irrespective of shape, the square shapes here merely make it easier to analyse). The long term outcome seems inevitable. The larger tribes must expand at the expense of the smaller until there is only one nation or empire left occupying the entire territory. Whether they like it or not bands must unite into clans, clans into tribes, tribes into nations, nations into empires. Any pacifist leader must see that by remaining small he is condemning his own people to eventual conquest and possible enslavement by force. Better to take up arms now and hope to grow at the expense of your smaller neighbours than wait for some other less peaceable tribe to grow and engulf you.

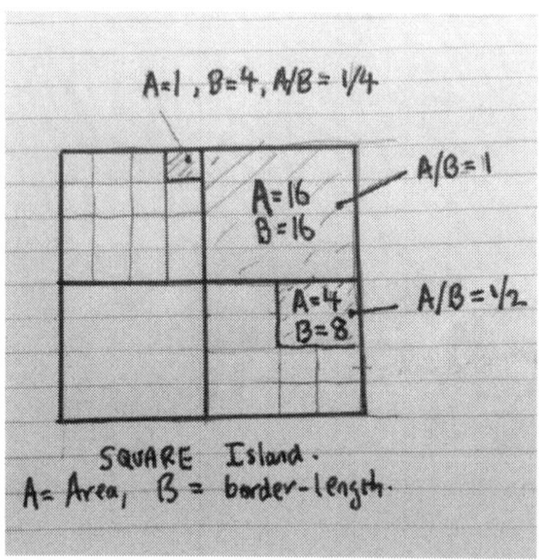

Fig (9:1) Our imaginary Square Island divided up into square territories by tribe; A's are areas, B's border-lengths. Note that as territories increase in size so their ratios of Area to Border increase. If population densities are everywhere much the same that implies that larger territories can afford more border soldiers per mile of border than smaller ones, and are likely to grow at the expense of them This is true irrespective of shape, its just easier to see in this simplistic square model.

Thus the waxing and waning of mighty military empires probably has little to do with economics, aggrandisement religion or culture. It has been forced upon us all by something far more fundamental – the goading of mathematics. Once a military nation begins to grow it can grow even faster, thanks to the tyranny of mathematics, until it swallows everyone else up, or is brought to a halt by other quite different factors – such as geography or internal dissension. History is littered with the mushrooming and subsequent decline of conquest empires – for instance the Assyrian (900 BC), the Persian (600 BC), the Alexandrine (300 BC), the Roman (200 BC), the Arabic (700 AD), the Mogul (1500), the Russian (1800), the American (1850) and the Zulu (1850). The proximate causes and courses of each are less important than their mathematical inevitability. Thus the Ancient British tribes found themselves on the margin of the then mighty Roman empire (50 AD) and were swallowed up, their culture so thoroughly obliterated that today we cannot know what their lives were like except through biased eyes[1A] There is no point to the anger which I sometimes feel when I come across the remains of an Iron-age Welsh village like Flimston on the coast of Pembrokeshire, because its defeat and probable enslavement were *inevitable*. If it hadn't been the ghastly Romans it would have been somebody else equally Big and possibly, if that were possible, even worse. The Square –Linear Law [See Box] has been the chief force for change in history. Like gravity it is neither good nor bad – just ineluctable.

THE SQUARE-LINEAR LAW OF HISTORY.

The population of a tribe will generally grow with the area it can occupy, but the length of its border will only grow with the diameter of its territory, and thus with the square-root of its area. Thus there will always be pressure for a tribe to grow at the expanse of its neighbours. It cannot afford to remain static or shrink. Thus men must fight for mathematical reasons, whether they want to or not. This has been the deadly driving force of history.

What the Romans added to this mix was *citizenship*. Once a tribe was overrun *selected* members of it were invited to become citizens of the Roman enterprise, to serve in its legions, to fight its wars, and thus to extend its boundaries even further (the rest were enslaved and often worked to death).

It follows from all this that if any society is to survive for long enough to become sophisticated it must be able to fight, and fight well. This will not be easy because fighting well is an extremely challenging task requiring far more than raw courage. *This is why civilization and military prowess can only march forward together, each depending umbilically on the other.*

Since they fended off the Armada (1588) the Brits have been in innumerable wars, four at least existential [1701-1715, 1796-1815, 1914-18, 1939-45]. We have learned much from them and they have moulded us in all manner of unforeseeable ways. For instance without WW1 female emancipation might have been delayed by half a century, while without WW2 the Welfare State might never have come at all. Only the stunted stature and lamentable health of so many army recruits in 1914 brought home to our greedy ruling class that they had been systematically starving their fellow citizens for a century. That belated realization in WW1 at last brought about a proper diet for our poor, improved ironically by nation-wide rationing in the Second. Peace sounds great – and it is for those in possession of status and wealth. But for those suffering at the bottom – generally a much larger number – peace may only defer any hope of real change. War may be miserable, and it is, but a society unchallenged by war is quite capable of inflicting horrors of its own – the chief of which is Parasitism (Ch.7).

Military science is every bit as complicated as the civilian variety. Having been both a military officer and a senior academic I can say with confidence that a modern major-general has to know far more, and know it better, than any Vice-Chancellor. He may become responsible for the lives of 20,000 soldiers in circumstances which might be alien, unpredictable and largely out of his control. He has to know about Intelligence, about enemies and allies, about man-management, logistics, artillery, air-defence, infantry cooperation with air, signals, anti-tank defence, medical support, topography, liason with nearby and cooperating units, river-crossings……. A Vice-Chancellor running a university has a paltry task by comparison; paltry!

Over the centuries the Brits have come to learn a great deal about war, and in the process become pretty good at it. It was they who planned and organised the D-

Day landings[2] – the most complex endeavour ever undertaken by mankind and very largely successful.

Such skills are based on centuries of experience, tradition and learning. Time and again the Brits have learned to beat their adversaries by outwitting them. Three examples:

In the Peninsula War (1807-1814) Wellington was faced by much superior French forces commanded by a succession of Napoleon's most brilliant generals. But he out-manoeuvred them in turn by better exploiting a combination of Spanish and Portuguese topography, local peasant allies and much superior logistics until, in 1814, he crossed the Pyrenees and defeated Marshal Soult at Toulouse, shortly after which Napoleon abdicated. It was a triumph of skill, guile, discipline, humanity and organisation.

Everyone got bogged down in the awful trench warfare of 1914-18. Only the British, with their Commonwealth allies, devised the weapons and evolved the tactics which would overcome machine-guns and barbed-wire, sending Ludendorff's huge army into headlong retreat towards Berlin[3].

And in the WW2 the crucial and quite awful battle was fought out of sight and sound in the storm-tossed North Atlantic by desperate men on both sides trying to save their families back on dry land from starvation. Neither side had prepared for the death-struggle, upon whose outcome the future of civilization hung. That outcome lay in the balance for 3 years during which time 5000 vessels and 100,000 lives were lost. Nothing in all of military history remotely compares with it. But gradually, tempest by tempest, idea by idea, sinking by sinking, convoy by convoy a mixed bunch of British and Canadian amateurs and professionals – fighting in tiny escort vessels entirely unsuited to the atrocious conditions – overcame the U-boat men, every bit as brave as they. They never got the recognition they deserved because no journalist, no politician made it out there to see what Hell our men endured, storm after storm. Forget Trafalgar, Thermopylae, Stalingrad and Waterloo: the Battle of the Atlantic, in scale, ferocity and consequence, dwarfs them all.[4,5,6]

Those who can't fight well must suffer the consequences: the French, humiliation and Nazi occupation after 1940; the Italians agony between '42 and '45; the Americans disgrace in Vietnam[7]. Any fool can deplore war – so do we all, but historians must understand that sometimes it is unavoidable. And the consequences of war are not all bad. We have mentioned some of its recent fruits including female emancipation and the Welfare State. But in a more general sense war may be the acid test for progressive civilization. If it is a highly sophisticated business, as we argue, then there must be a big premium in favour of the more progressive side. Germany got into and then lost the FWW largely because it was a dictatorship and the second because of its barbarity. Had it respected its Jewish scientists , or treated humanely instead of murdering, the downtrodden peoples of Poland, Russia and the Ukraine who it liberated from Stalin, it might just conceivably have won. But of course it was far too primitive for that[8]. War found it out and delivered the inescapable verdict, just as war had earlier found out the papist armies of Phillip II (1588) and Louis XIV(1715) which tried to put down the Reformation.

But how relevant is all this in the atomic age? Oddly enough more relevant than ever because societies which cannot or will not defend themselves by conventional means will be all the more likely to wipe themselves out, and perhaps the rest of us, by resorting to nuclear weapons. Those countries of Eastern Europe, including Germany, who are presently unwilling to pay the price of standing up to Putin's Russia, are asking for trouble. Are they expecting us instead to go in with nuclear weapons to defend them? They'd be mad to ask, and we'd be mad to respond. It was never more important to be defence-capable than it is today. Failure in the past merely meant enslavement; today it could bring about utter annihilation. I worry far more about weak countries such as Pakistan or Israel resorting to nuclear weapons than stronger ones like Iran – who don't need to.

We all came close to nuclear Armageddon in 1962 because America did not possess conventional forces capable of enforcing their Munro Doctrine over Cuba. If

Britain hadn't been able to retake the Falklands by conventional means it's just possible that it might have resorted to atomic bombs.

Liberals who effect to deplore war (who doesn't?) should realise that their liberty was earned, from Marathon to Normandy, by wiser men than they, who had to fight and sometimes die. And that fight will never end so long as tyrants rule. Creatures like Stalin and Mao, Putin and Chi, know that so long as liberalism thrives anywhere, their own people might see through them.

NOTES

1. *The Peloponnesian War* by Thucydides 450 BC.

1A. *The Agricola and the Germania* by Tacitus who lived near Newport for a year. What the Romans thought of us so called barbarians. A lot of people still teach this twaddle today.

2 From a letter to *The Daily Telegraph* from Nicholas Young, London, June 2019: (I haven't checked the detailed numbers)

"As we approach the 75th Anniversary of the D-day landings, it is time to correct Hollywood's view that Britain's role was minimal.

Strategic plans for the Normandy landings were actually conceved and developed by British general, Frederick Morgan. True, the Supreme Allied Commander, General Eisenhower, was American, but all Allied forces on the ground were under the command of General Montgomery. In addition, the Deputy Supreme Allied Commander, Arthur Tedder, was British, as were the Allied Air Commander in Chief, Trafford Leigh-Mallory, and the Allied Naval Commander in Chief, Bertram Ramsay.

On D-day itself, British and Canadian forces put 75,215 troops ashore over three separate landings and 8,500 paratroopers; the US landed 57,500 troops over two landings and 13,100 paratroopers. Of the 1,213 warships taking an active part in the assault, 892 were British. The Royal and Merchant Navies provided 137, 824 personnel, the Americans 52,899; and of the 4,126 landing craft involved 3,261 were British while

805 were American. In addition, almost half of the 11,590 aircraft involved were flown by the RAF, while 1,800 RAF personnel were also landed on D-day.

Bletchley Park had broken the latest German Enigma code some six weeks before the invasion, and false information about Allied inventions, including the fictitious "First United States Army Group" conceived by (British) Colonel David Strangeways, misled the Germans into believing the invasion would take place at Calais.

All those, of whatever nationality, who took part in the D-day landings deserve our eternal respect and gratitude. America's contribution was indisputably substantial; but it was certainly no greater than that of Britain and Canada. Lest we forget."

3 John Terraine. *To Win a War,* 1978, Sidgwick & Jackson. A blow by blow account of how the German army was defeated in the trenches in 1918.

4 John Terraine, "*Business in Great Waters*", a magnificent account of The Battle of the Atlantic. Magnificent.

5 Roskill, Steven; *The War at Sea"* 3 Vols. The definitive account of the RN in WW2.

6 Disney M, J, 2020, *Strangle,* The *scientific* side of the Battle of the Atlantic in novel form.

7 Max Hastings, 2019, *Vietnam.*

8 Quote taken from p 89 "*Science at War*", Crowther J G and Whiddington R., HMSO 1947, 2 shillings & 6 pence, (Amazon £8):

"What conclusions are to be drawn from the British and the German stories of radar? That the British found a far better method of organisation and collaboration of scientists, military users and industrialists. That enabled them to see further, and solve deeper problems, thus enabling them to provide our forces not only with more potent weapons, but with more profound ideas as to how they should be used………… The real German scientific defeat, surprising as it may seem, was in the field of organisation. They organised production and the Army superbly; but in the field of radar they failed to organise teamed collaboration between scientists, fighting men and industrialists. The reader will decide for himself how far that fundamental failure arose from the nature of

Nazism and German social tradition, and how far our success arose from the practice of democracy."

HISTORY OF THE BRITS

CHAPTER 10. BRITAIN IN THE SECOND WORLD WAR

" *Honour is what no man can give ye…and none can take away. Honour is a man's gift to himself.* " Rob Roy in the film of that name.

What will become of us as individuals depends to a great extent on our self-confidence. Some of that may be in-born but most, I suspect, derives from the events in our lives, and the stories we tell ourselves about them. Successes improve our life story, increase our self-confidence and that leads to higher ambitions and more successes in turn. Failures diminish our story, shrink our ambitions, and generally, though not always, shrivel our lives. In that sense life is, as scientists say, "a highly non-linear process". That is why we parents try so hard to get our kids off to a good start.

Note the crucial role of story-telling here. It's all too easy to get the story wrong; for instance to attribute failure to ill-luck rather than ill judgement; or take the credit for good fortune, or other peoples' efforts. In the long run bad story-telling will only lead to bad consequences, so faithful story-telling, about ourselves at least, is an essential life-skill. And as it is for humans so I believe it is for nations. Nations that cannot or will not get their own stories right may suffer fatal consequences. Thus the Athenians who, in alliance, had repelled the Persian invasion, boastfully arrogated all the credit to themselves, Their infuriated former allies, led by Sparta, turned on Athens and destroyed it.

If it is hard for individuals to tell themselves the truth, it is far harder for nations, which are often riven by factions with different, self-serving, stories to tell. Young nations in particular often float on a wind-bag of lies, lies which can lead to bellicosity and self-destruction.(Athens,Germany,Italy,Ireland ………)

The century to come is going to be so difficult that it must be doubtful whether civilization, or even life on Earth as we know it, will survive it. We simply cannot go on as we are – on a direct collision-course with Nature. But how are we going to change course? The only practical hope that I can see is that one nation will set an example of sustainable, and happy living – then others might follow. And that nation, as I shall argue later, can only be Britain. After all we invented the modern world, this industrialized, globalized world – with all its good, and also alas its unintended fatal consequences. So it is up to us to lead a way out of it. After all we did that once before: the Industrial Revolution was very largely our response to the Firewood Crisis. But that is going to require a vast amount of self-confidence. Are we up to the immense challenge? If we are a diminished, second-rate power, as so many appear to think nowadays, then presumably not. The purpose of this chapter is to look at the last occasion on which Britain's mettle was really tested and ask ourselves what is the true story we should tell ourselves about it.

If there is one bit of our history we Brits know something about it is the Second World War (SWW). The usual version goes something like this:

"Gallant little Britain stood up to mighty Germany almost alone. There was the miracle of Dunkirk; our Spitfire boys winning The Battle of Britain; the Blitz where we bravely stood our ground. Finally the mighty Russians, and the even mightier Americans came to our aid and secured the day for civilization." Here is a particular example of that myth from the military journalist Max Hastings:

"Britain's salvation was achieved overwhelmingly through the actions of her enemies in forcing the Soviet and the US into the war, not by any military achievement of her own, save that of defiance in the face of hopeless odds"

In almost all important respects I believe that myth is wrong. Britain did play a crucial role in the SWW – indeed the crucial role – but it was more complicated and far more interesting than the popular myth.

As I see it Britain held nearly all the strong cards which would lead to the eventual defeat of German as surely in the SWW as they had in the First. She was still an island – though the bomber had made an island less of a safe haven. The Royal Navy still ruled the waves and would starve Germany out by blockade just as ruthlessly in the second bout as it had in the first. Indeed, as nations become more sophisticated and industrialized they depend more on crucial imports than ever. Germany would either be starved or have to strike out East in the hope of escaping strangulation. In particular as air-power became ever more vital where was she to find her aviation fuel if not in the oil-fields of the Caucusus or Persia – thousands of miles away in the East?

And this increasing sophistication played into Britain's second strong suit – Committee Government. The Germans never lacked in scientific or military genius, but they never possessed the governmental sophistication to exploit that genius effectively. In consequence, as we shall later see, they lost battles over crucial techniques such as radar, cipher-breaking and nuclear physics. Indeed Germany's eventual defeat was so inevitable that she would, if she had been able to think straight, never have gone to war. But Germany didn't have a faithful story of her recent history – she fell instead for Ludendorff's Lie – namely that she hadn't been defeated comprehensively in the FWW – but had been betrayed by her own politicians who had " stabbed our invincible army in the back". For those Germans who wanted revenge for their suffering and humiliation following 1918 it was a comfortable lie to believe and the real secret of Adolf Hitler's astonishing rise to power. But it was a lie none the less, and the prime source of Germany's undoing. By the end of that first war Germany was slowly starving at the hands of the RN (her civilians were barely existing on 1000 calories a day) whilst in 1918 her army had been smashed in front of Amiens and thereafter retreated backwards unceremoniously towards Berlin. Its navy had run away at Jutland (1916), though the Kaiser claimed otherwise, never came out again, then, in 1918, mutinied at Kiel . Had it not signed the Armistice when it did Germany faced total occupation.

Britain's third strong suit lay in her allies. The German's had Mussolini's Italy. Britain had the Commonwealth and Empire, though not France this time, and hopes at least of recruiting some help from America, which Germany could not – because of the blockade. And if America remained aloof – as it effectively had in the first encounter, Britain had the resources, and the banking reputation, which Germany had not, to buy American munitions.

So to the dispassionate historian of 1939 the Odds on Germany winning must have been 10 to 1 against. Like the defeat of Napoleon victory might have taken 20 years, or it might have taken 4 as with the Kaiser. Of course there were to be surprises -- of which the greatest was the abject capitulation of France. That made life very much more difficult for the RN which had to cope with U-boat bases directly on the Atlantic shore, as well as air attacks throughout the Mediterranean which made the holding of that vital seaway very much more expensive than they had anticipated. Nevertheless the Navy (just) managed to hold out. They kept the Western entrance at Gibraltar caulked [Franco never dared risk an RN blockade] while its base at Alexandria guarded Suez and the Middle East beyond. And although Rommel's Afrika Korps made a bold bid to capture North Africa Hitler could never supply his army properly so long as Britain was determined to hold on to Malta as a base for its submarines and aircraft.

Hitler's only other real hope lay in the defeat of Russia, but there the mathematical logistics were completely against him [Ch. 4]. It was true Russia collapsed in the FWW but the appallingly incompetent Czarists were no longer in power while the cunning option of introducing a second Lenin into the Soviet Union to poison its political wells couldn't be repeated. And even here the RN could play a powerful role in escorting the Arctic convoys – which supplied Russia with 4 million tons of absolutely vital supplies, including 5000 tanks and 7000 aircraft.

Even without America Britain would have won eventually, though it might have taken years longer and cost far more in Commonwealth blood and gold. US mass production of welded ships (Kayser), landing craft, tanks, electronics, explosives and aircraft was invaluable, though her military forces were not noticeably effective because they had not the commanders, the know-how nor the tradition

to fight well. The US Navy abruptly pulled out of the Battle of the Atlantic in March 1943 just as it was reaching its crux, while on D-day off Omaha Beach it turned and ran, leaving all its amphibious tanks to drown and its poor infantry to be mown down by unopposed machine-guns in the bloody surf. It incompetently lost its vital Mulberry harbour to a storm off Normandy while the 8th USAAF's high altitude bombing campaign over Germany was brave but disappointingly ineffectual, in part because American bombers couldn't carry decent bomb-loads. The myth that America won the war was just that—a myth. You cannot mass-produce effective fighting forces overnight without years of training, know-how and above all tradition – none of which America possessed. As Admiral Cunningham said after he had lost a dozen precious warships evacuating the Allied army from Crete "It had to be done; it takes only 3 years to build a warship; it takes 300 years to build a naval tradition." When the Americans had to fight on their own, as they did in Vietnam, they made a complete hash of it. Fortunately, at the outset of their collaboration, Churchill and Roosevelt set up a Combined Chiefs of Staff Committee which saw to it that America's hot headed and ignorant commanders were restrained by wiser heads like those of General Alanbrook (The Chief of the Imperial General Staff) and of Admiral Dudley Pound (the First Sea Lord). The American Chiefs wanted to open a Second Front as early as 1942 – which would have been foolhardy, even suicidal (as the Dieppe Raid by the Canadians was to prove).

Many Americans simply didn't want to be in a war, and you can't blame them for that, especially when so many had German, Italian or Irish roots. So Churchill, with his half-American ancestry, had to butter them up, first in 1941-5 , then later in 1947-50 to keep them in Europe facing the Russian threat. He had to do the latter because in 1946 the US had passed The McMahon Act, effectively stealing the Atomic Bomb which the British had induced them, and largely taught them how to build. It was a foul act of treachery because it left Britain and Western Europe at the mercy of Stalin's Russia. Of course we couldn't say that at the time, but it was and is true none the less.

It is interesting to speculate what would have happened if there had been no Pearl Harbour and America had remained neutral. She would still have sold munitions to Britain, as she had in the FWW, because there was so much profit to be made. And so long as banks had confidence that Britain would eventually win, the money would have been somehow raised. Britain and Canada would then have exploded an A-bomb by 1948 or earlier and Germany, one way or another, would then have had to capitulate, even if Russia had collapsed beforehand. We know now (as the British government did then, thanks to cipher-breaking) that the Germans never got anywhere near building a bomb because they had handed over the project, not to a committee, but to a Supremo (Heisenberg) – who made a fatal error in calculating the Critical Mass of Uranium -- thus leaving him to conclude that the bomb was impractical.

If we compare the roles played by the three Great Powers in WW2:

1. Only the British entered with noble motives (to protect Poland).
2. Only Britain did not massively profit from its participation. Indeed it was drained by its efforts and had to pay off war debts amounting to at least 3 years of GDP (It was still paying America back in 2006].

3. And yet Britain had done significantly more than either of the other two to bring victory about. In particular Britain:

- Held out after France fell and Russia had conspired with the Nazis to dismember Poland.
- Imposed a relentless naval blockade on Germany from day one which it continued throughout. That left Hitler with little choice but to strike out East in search of strategic necessities such as oil.
- Had effectively hounded Italy out of the war early on (At Taranto and in Abyssinia).
- Gained a decisive upper hand in all the main scientific and technical struggles including: magnetic mines; radar (the Cavity- Magnetron); cipher breaking (Enigma, Colossus and Tunny); aero-engines (asymmetric gear wheels); Operational Research; anti-biotics (with US aid); HF/DF (high frequency direction finding – crucial against U-boats), Proximity Fuses (did for the V1 missile), Window (blinded German radar……
- Kept Soviet Russia in the war by convoying vital armaments (mostly American) through the Arctic against crippling Odds and supplying crucial Intelligence (e.g. at the Battle of Kursk, the greatest tank-battle in history, the Russians were told the German plans in advance, and so could build a gigantic tank-trap…) .
- Controlled the Mediterranean seaway, thus preventing Hitler from getting to Middle-Eastern oil via the Southern route.
- Used strategic bombing to pound German cities into rubble, thus preventing the Nazi armament industry from ever reaching more than 20% of its full potential (Critics who argue that German output scarcely

diminished, miss the entire point. Britain's equivalent output increased by 5 times over the same period).

- Planned and largely organised the D-day landings, the most complex operation ever undertaken by mankind.
- Raised and led a huge Anglo-Indian army [with 2.5 million Indian volunteers] which kept the Japanese out of India (thus saving an estimated 50 million Indian lives,) and eventually drove them out of Burma too.
- Before anyone else, recognised the potential of nuclear weapons, and devised the technology to make them practical (gaseous diffusion), then persuaded the US to build some (the threat of bombing prevented the safe operation of gaseous diffusion plants in Britain).
- Above all, with their Canadian allies, won the Battle of the Atlantic, the most momentous, and the most titanic battle in all of history (lasted 6 years, cost 5000 plus vessels sunk, and 100,000 lives). For reasons tactfully unexplained the US Navy pulled out of it abruptly in March 1943, just as the climax was approaching.

These are not fashionable claims to make – but as careful analysis will show – they just happen to be true. The Intellectual Left would rather portray the war as an avoidable folly, visited upon us by the old ruling class (through Appeasement) and then largely mismanaged by ham-fisted Blimps. But then they would wouldn't they? And of course it conflicts with Russia's and America's own self-glorifying myths about the war, and their emergence afterwards as the only two 'Superpowers'. But as time would show Russia was still a backward political behemoth whilst America was, and still is, a ramshackle affair crippled by its primitive constitution and its appalling racial history. The former certainly had 10,000 tanks and the latter 20,000 nuclear warheads (one may well ask why) but neither was, or is, a remotely fit model for the post-war world.

That brings us back to the question of who is, and in particular which nation might have the wherewithal to lead mankind out of the ecological nightmare which is growing about us with every passing day? Certainly Britain is no longer a naval or industrial colossus and, thank goodness, no longer drags a vast overseas empire in its wake. But so what? None would help one jot when it comes to completely redesigning a state for a sustainable and happy future. That will require political maturity – which we uniquely have, moral purpose, enterprise, scientific and technical ingenuity, social cohesion, diplomacy, and a willingness to try innovations and then change our minds when they fail : above all, the self- confidence to go it alone; in summary a very high degree of civilization.

The question really is "Who else is capable of giving the vital lead if Britain does not.?" The USA? Putin's Russia? Xi's China? The EU? World government? Dream on.

HISTORY OF THE BRITS
CHAPTER 11
BRITISH EMPIRE – ACHIEVEMENT OR CRIME?

Far-called, our navies melt away;
On dune and headland sinks the fire
Lo all our pomp of yesterday
Is one with Nineveh and Tyre!
Judge of the Nations, spare us yet,
Lest we forget –Lest we forget!
From '*Recessional*' by Rudyard Kipling.

At school (1950s) we were taught to be proud of the vast British Empire. at university (1960s) to be ashamed of it. In neither case were the given reasons convincing.

I never thought about the matter much again until the 1990s when my wife and I spent 3 months working at the Raman Institute in Bangalore India. Confronting us in the canteen was a six foot-two-inch, bull-knecked, broad-shouldered American lady in a sari:

"You Briddish" she said "Ought to be of ashamed of what you did here in India. You know your government cut off the thumbs of all the weavers in Madras—to stop them competing with your Lanka Shire cotton industry?"

We were shocked. Nobody at school had taught us that – but they wouldn't, would they? I consulted my friend Radhakrishnan who came from Madras: "Not heard it." he said "But next month we have a distinguished historian coming to do research in our library. Consult her."

Until she arrived, I frantically enquired after other brutal crimes which we Brits might have perpetrated in India during colonial times. But when she came the historian laughed:

"Of course it's not true. It was a canard put about by the Congress Party to win votes in an election."

Relief! But by then we were ourselves in research mode, hoping to find out what impressions the Brits had left in India. What other crimes had they committed? We got some surprises. For example while exploring the jungle near Kevalur Observatory we came upon the most delightful village in a clearing. The houses were painted startling white and pale blue with gourds flowering upon the thatched rooves. The women were washing their luncheon pots in the stream, the men squatting in the shade of a tree talking solemnly; the children were jumping with screams out of a tree into the village water-tank. When they saw us the men sent for the postmaster, the only villager who spoke English:

"You must be coming back to my shop for cups of tea." that friendly gentleman smiled: "There is a velly old lady here who remembers the English."

When that matriarch arrived, distinguished by her stunning long white hair, she knelt at my wife's feet and kissed them. Not knowing how to react Nino burst into tears.

"What's this about?" I asked the postmaster.

"She is remembering the British Collector who came each year to collect our taxes."

"Hardly cause for celebration I would have thought?"

But when raised to her feet and questioned the grand dame was emphatic:

"She is saying that the Collector saved us from the velly greedy zamindars." Zamindars, it emerged, were the parasitical landlords who had owned everything and squeezed everybody. The Collector had put them in their place and saved the villagers from starvation.

Later in Bangalore we met an old gentleman who had served as an army officer with the British defending India against the Japanese at Imphal and later in Burma. He said:

"Our present government doesn't want to acknowledge that there were 2.5 million of us Indian volunteers. We're not even allowed to wear our medals on parade. Instead they want to celebrate the small Indian National Army which sided with the Japs."

"But why?"

"It boosts that nonsense about their heroic fight for independence from the British. Judging by what they did elsewhere, if the Japs had got into India they would have killed at least 50 million of us. Under the British we defended ourselves while those Congress wallahs were sitting on their fattee bums. They don't want anybody to remember that. The British were fine soldiers, especially Sir Bill Slim our commander-in-chief."

"If you want to understand India" Radh said "Be sure to visit Mysore." So we went.

Mysore is one of those princely states, left to be governed by their own Maharajahs. It turned out to be a beautiful but ghastly reminder of the Moghuls who had governed India before the British came. Though no larger than an English county, the Maharajah had a dozen glittering palaces, one an exact replica of Buck House, but three times life-size. Its museum contained one ohis gold-plated Rolls Royces. We reckon he must have guzzled at least 80% of his states' output. No wonder so many Indians had welcomed the Europeans in.

When it comes to judging any colonial administration, such anecdotes illustrate how hard it will be to separate fact from myth and propaganda. At the very least one has to know what preceded it, and what happened after its demise.

There is neither the space nor ambition here to write a history of the vast, rambling and incoherent British Empire. Why does it matter anyway, now that it's all over? For two reasons I believe. First because certain outsiders want to make us feel guilty about it in order to get their own way (e.g. blackmail us into granting them immigrant status); and second because certain unsavoury Brits try to win arguments by branding their opponents as 'racists' or, almost as bad, 'Fantasists for Empire', which is a proxy for the same scurrilous charge. For instance at the recent Hay Festival I heard a rascal called Danny Dorling boosting his polemic against Brexit entitled "*Rule Britannia*". As far as I could make out from his spittled diatribe we Brexiteers are all obese, elderly 'Empire Fantasists'. Obviously he didn't have a good argument for 'Remain'. So the limited ambition of this chapter is to investigate the proposition *"Brits should be ashamed of the British Empire"*. To do so we will adopt the Scientific Method of History (SMH) outlined in Chapt. 8 , i.e. use CST in the form of an Inference Table, to weigh the evidence, both for the proposition and against. I don't know how else one would rationally proceed. However, before beginning, a few preliminary remarks are in order:

1 The Empire was never planned nor did it ever have a coherent purpose. Many British governments were dubious about both its morality and cost . Someone wrote that "It was acquired in a fit of absence of mind". It would be better said that it fell piecemeal into British hands because her all-powerful navy ruled the oceans for 350 years. During every European war bits and pieces of other peoples' empires, after they were cut off from their European roots, fell into her hands.

2 Napoleon described the Brits as "A nation of shop-keepers", and he was right. Its government at least was far more interested in trade, which could create wealth, than imperium, which cost. Thus the empire had to run on a shoestring. Very few troops or officials were funded to run it, so it wouldn't have worked unless the vast majority of its subjects acquiesced in its rule. The main objective of the RN was to keep the world's sea lanes open for everyone (bar Britain's immediate enemies in times of war) to trade upon.

3 Most subject peoples were far too poor to yield much tribute to their masters in any case. All they could do, with investment and initiative from Britain, was produce commodities which the British could not readily produce at home [West Indian sugar, Virginia tobacco, Newfoundland cod, Assam tea, Indian cotton textiles, Malayan tin, Burmese oil…..] – which were paid for largely by exporting manufactured goods, often shoddy because that was all the natives could afford.

4 It came to an end because cheap dive-bombers and cheap machine-guns rendered the old ways of policing it obsolete. Anyway nobody much wanted it or needed it any more, least of all most Brits. For over a century it had been a heavy drain on their resources. What purpose did it serve beyond keeping the seaways open, a role the Americans were eager to assume.

Now let's weigh the Odds for and against our proposition:

TABLE (11:1)

INFERENCE TABLE TO TEST PROPOSITION:

"*BRITS SHOULD BE ASHAMED OF THEIR EMPIRE*"

	CLUE	WEIGHT	ODDS
1	2.5M African slaves transported	4	4
2	But victims first enslaved by Africans	½	2
3	Britain enforced Abolition alone	¼	½
4	Britons treated locals as inferior	4	2
5	There were some very bad episodes[1]	4	8
6	Most native pops expanded enormously under British rule	¼	2
7	Better law/health/infrastructure und B. rule	¼	½

8	But things might have improved anyway	2	1
9	Minute force employed[2] :Acquiescent pops.	¼	¼
10	Brits usually left peacefully	¼	1/16
11	Brits left owning nothing locally	¼	1/64
12	Most colonies absorbed funds[3]	½	1/128
13	B rarely interfered with local religions	½	1/256
14	Preceding situation usually far worse[4]	¼	1/1024
15	Succeeding situation usually far worse[5]	¼	1/4096
16	Most conceivable alternatives much worse[6]	½	1/8192

Notes on Table:

1 Episodes that come to mind: The 'Missionary Trick' practiced on North American Indians by whites who gave them blankets infected with deadly diseases; Amritsar Massacre (1919); Chinese Opium Wars; Boer War….

2 In India tens of thousands of British troops controlled hundreds of millions of Indian citizens: one for every ten thousand.

3 Once a few Mogul baubles had been nicked how was a very rich nation like Britain to squeeze wealth out of a very poor nation like India? Only by enterprise and investment, such as smuggling tea out China and replanting in India; or taking rubber from Amazonia and cultivating it in Malaya.

4 The Moghuls; Suttee (the burning of widows); Thugee (ritual murder of travellers); Caste system with the rich taking all; Tribal warfare and enslavement in Africa and elsewhere; Chaka, king of the Zulus used to have 5000 people thrown over a precipice one by one for his after-dinner entertainment; regular famines; necromancy; plagues and tropical diseases; Cannibalism in Polynesia and Borneo; …….No picnic at all.

5.Think only of: Nkrumah (the 'Great Redeemer' in Ghana); Idi Amin (Uganda); Apartheid (South Africa); the Nehru dynasty; Nyerere (Marxism in Tanzania); The Biafran genocide (Nigeria); Bashir (Sudan); Mbeki (AIDS); al Sisi (Egypt); Mugabe (Zimbabwe); Burma (goons); Jamaica (violent gangs); Ayub Khan (Pakistan); Kashmir; Tamil wars (Sri Lanka), Zuma (S Africa)………………

6 For instance India might have been colonised by France instead, which has a far more violent colonial record than Britain[5]. Think: Algeria, Indo-China (Vietnam), Madagascar,……

It seems that the Odds *against* the proposition that the Brits should be ashamed of their Empire are overwhelming. Of course they are my Odds only. But they *are* so overwhelming that it is hard to see how they could be overturned. To get the same Odds, but in *favour* of the proposition, one is going to have to discover no less than 13 *strong* new arguments in its favour

CONCLUSIONS

We argued in Chapter 9 that most 'nations' are agglomerations of parts brought together, often quite recently, mostly by conquest or coercion. So what is is an empire, and what is not, is to some extent a matter of convention. Germany was confected out of about 50 principalities by Bismark as late as 1870; and could well be called The Prussian Empire. Likewise Italy which is scarcely older or more homogeneous; France has been only speaking French in comparatively modern times; Spain, the United Kingdom,….. Russia is certainly an empire and so definitely is the US, a hundred Indian nations brought forcibly and brutally under the heel of Washington as late as the late nineteenth century. The uniqueness of the British Empire lay only in its far-flung extent – a consequence of Britain's island geography and attendant preoccupations with maritime trade. In that respect it most resembled the Hellenic Empire dotted all over the Mediterranean in Classical times. For both, trade-winds were far more important than military roads.

I would hazard that something like the British Empire was inevitable anyway. Thanks mainly to Moon-power [Chapt. 2] and Printing European civilization shot ahead between 1300 and 1900. The Portuguese first, then the Spanish, Dutch, French and English ventured overseas in search of spices[1], trade and lucre. The imperial side of things arose more from rivalry between them than from intent to conquer poor indigenes – though they did that too. In the short term some terrible things happened, principally plagues such as Influenza, Small-pox, Potato-blight[2] and Phylloxera[3]. But in the long run we nearly all benefitted. Subjects of the British Empire probably did so with less oppression than most. We can hardly be proud of what was inevitable. But we don't have to shrink from it either.

NOTES

1 After the Khans died out (~ 1400 AD) the overland Silk Route from the Orient broke down. But spices like pepper had become *absolutely essential* to preserve meat in the days before refrigeration. Without such preserved meat European populations starved over winter. Thus it was literally vital to find a sea route to the Orient! This is what induced the Europeans, led by the Portuguese, to explore South and East. It took them a century to get around the southern Cape of Africa but not long after for Vasca da Gama to reach India (1498). It was all about trade-winds and Coriolis Forces. But why and how did the tiny state of Portugal transform the European diet and thus transform world history? There are some fascinating mysteries here. See "*Lodestone and Evening Star*" by Ian Cameron, Hodder & Stoughton, UK, 1965 .

2 The importance of plagues in history is well covered in Jared Diamond's fascinating *Guns Germs and Steel.*

3 The coming of the steam cargo ship (1840s) brought some unintended but catastrophic plant plagues such as the Potato Blight, which lead to famine in Ireland, and the even worse Phylloxera which all but wiped out wine production across all of Europe at a time when a third of the peasants were employed in producing it. Wine was not a luxury but another cunning way of preserving perishable calories through long European winters; thus an absolute necessity. [*Phylloxera*, by Christy Campbell, Harper Perennial 2004]. *The Story of Wine* by Hugh Johnson is one of the finest history books I have ever read. Do yourself a treat.

HISTORY OF THE BRITS

CHAPTER 12:

ESCAPING ITS PRIESTLY CHAINS

"Religion is an insult to human dignity. With or without it you would have good people doing good things and evil people doing bad things. But for good people to do bad things, that takes religion." Steven Weinberg, Physicist.

The awful dying curse which Rome imposed upon its subjects was the Church. The story goes that on his deathbed (337 AD) the emperor Constantine, seeking absolution for the murders of both his wife and his son managed to find priests fraudulent enough to grant it – in return for earthly power. Thus the ghastly blight of Christianity settled all over Europe (and beyond), a miasma which blotted out the Sun for 1500 years. Britain's history over the past five centuries is largely defined by attempts to throw off this ancient curse. We have succeeded at least to the extent that we are now the most atheistic population on Earth.

The difficulty for the historian is that one cannot know what the alternative to Christianity might have been, and whether it would have been better, or even worse. When one looks at other empires for enlightenment – for instance the Chinese, Mughal, Aztec, Inca, Ottoman, Zulu…they are not reassuring. So a case can be made, and has been made ad nauseam, that Christianity was the best of a very bad lot.

Any priesthood survives by expunging all trace of its predecessors and rivals. Thus it has been found that the yew-trees so often found in British graveyards are older than the churches built on top of them. Since the yew was an icon of the pre-christian Druid priesthood we can only suppose that Rome's chosen were exploiting and then obliterating even earlier superstitions. It is notable that Christianity died out almost immediately after the Romans left. It was reintroduced from Ireland 2 centuries later.

The Christian fairy story is so childish, so unlikely, and so lacking in corroborating evidence that one must wonder how discerning adults ever fell for it. The penny dropped for me when I visited some of the few remaining painted wooden churches (in the FSU). They are covered, inside and out, with gruesome depictions of the torments of Hell. The newly dead are put on a trolley and moved from torturer to torturer. First their eyes are plucked out by demons. Then their tongues wrenched out with hot pliers and so on and so on. All you have to do of course is obey the priest and you will instead go to heaven to be with the angels. How pathetic, and yet how effective if you can keep your congregation in ignorance. Then again all cultures are fatally sensitive to propaganda – as we know to our cost in the 21st century. The Roman church depended on keeping its congregations in ignorance. Constantine's successors ordered the destruction of the great library and centre of Hellenic learning in Alexandria and the execution by torture of its then female head Hypatia (415 AD). After all the influential local Saint Augustine of Hippo (354 - 430 AD) had written: "*There is another form of temptation, even more fraught with danger. This is the disease of curiosity…….It is this which drives us to try and discover the secrets of nature, those secrets which are beyond our understanding, which can avail us nothing and which man should not wish to learn.*" Even today much of the Church's hocus pocus is conducted in Latin, a deliberately befuddling trick no doubt adopted from earlier successful witch-doctors.

And that reminds us of the very worst and most malignant feature of any religion – its seizure of education. No religion can afford or survive for long an enlightened and enquiring citizenry. Look at the chaos today in the Mohammedan world. Look how quickly Tony Blair, a closet Catholic, (with his Protector Rupert Murdoch) foisted us with "Faith Based Schools".

Anyone who doubts the malignant effect of religion on British education should pay a visit to Oxford or Cambridge. Inspect the buildings and ask yourself whether you are looking at a university devoted to learning – or a seminary. Wonder where the colossal wealth came from to erect such edifices (from the sale of Indulgences, i.e. fast track passports to heaven for the filthy rich). Find out when scholars not in holy orders were first allowed to teach there. Find out why they never taught science, or allowed women students, until very recently. Ask why there were no other universities allowed in England until the nineteenth century! The fact is that the two seminaries almost succeeded in strangling the life out of English higher education – they even controlled entry into the medical schools in London. Far from being the beacons of progress they pretend to be they have been bastions of privilege and reaction which contributed almost nothing to the rise of science, industry, egality and commerce going on in Glasgow, Birmingham, Manchester and London. As late as 1920 Robert Clifton Bellamy, who had held the post of Professor of Physics at Oxford for 50 years, wrote only one significant paper during that time on the grounds that "research betrays a certain restlessness of mind". But the propaganda for Oxbridge goes so successfully on and on that large numbers of British parents still want their sons (and even more astonishingly their daughters) to study in institutions steeped in religious prejudice, reaction and snobbery. Personally I find that hilarious. At least it should remind us Britons, like our continental cousins, that we are still struggling against the blood sucking tentacles of Constantine's death-bed curse. They are so all-pervading that it is often impossible for us victims to recognize their existence.[See Ch.20 'Baducation']

The Channel though has helped the British to gradually tear off those tentacles one by one. Without it our still benighted neighbours would have re-imposed our Catholic yoke. Phillip II of Spain tried to do just that with his Armada in 1588. And later, without the Royal Navy, Louise the XIVth of France might have stifled the Protestant Reformation. [If you ask me Tony Blair is so upset about Brexit because he saw the EU as a way of keeping us chained within the Catholic fold.]

Protestantism (Luther 1517 started it) was of course still religion, but at least it encouraged independence of mind. That, and another German invention – the printing press (Guthenberg,1450, Mainz) – were to lead the way out of the dark into the Enlightenment. See how rapidly some crucial steps followed one upon another:

1543 Copernicus revives classical heliocentric hypothesis

1570 Invention of telescope. England, Leonard Digges – as a natural development of his previous invention the Theodolite. Imprisoned by the Catholics.

1600 Microscope invented in Holland

1600 First modern scientific textbook: *Die Magnete* by William Gilbert.

1600 Giarduno Bruno burned in Rome "for imagining other worlds"

1602 First Scientific Society: *Academia Linceii*, Rome.

1605 Francis Bacon's "*Advancement of Learning*" proclaims that "knowledge is power".

1606 "*On the motion of the Blood*", William Harvey.

1609 Galileo sees with his spyglass that the planets are for sure other worlds orbiting the Sun (Heliocentrism confirmed).

1609 Kepler's Laws of Planetary Motion, based on Tycho's observations of Mars' orbit (Denmark).

1633 Galileo imprisoned indefinitely by the Church for heresy (Heliocentrism).

1637 Steno's *Prodromo*, the manifesto for Geology (Denmark)

1665 Hooke's best selling '*Micrographia*' illustrates the microscopic world for the first time.

1666 Newton splits white light into colours then recomposes them.

1676 van Leeuwenhoek first sees his 'animalcules' (bacteria).

1687 Newton's *Principia* convinces us that the world is a predictable machine, not a plaything of the Gods.

1695 Newton forced to leave Cambridge because he refuses to take holy orders in pursuit of promotion.

1696 Huyghens (Holland) sketches out 'The Scientific Method'.

After 2000 years of Roman-imposed stasis we were finally on our way again. But it was a near run thing. In torture chambers and dungeons the Church snuffed out science in Italy, while it never evolved in Spain. But Northern Europe, and island Britain in particular, were now beyond its strangling reach.

One is still left to wonder how such a childish fairy story bewitched so many for so long, and whether Christianity was an accident – or deliberate fraud. [According to the recently discovered Dead Sea Scrolls there were, a century before Jesus, hundreds of prophets being crucified in the Middle East for claiming to be scions of God.] My own suspicion, for what it is worth, is that it had to do with the insecurities inherent in settling down to an artificial and unnatural way of life – farming. Hunter-gathering man moved on. Having no sort of control over the environment or the future he probably didn't worry overmuch about either. But once he settled down to grow crops, uncertainty began to grip his very soul. Would the rains come in time? Would robbers come to steal his harvest or rustle his cattle? Why did the seasons roll around and the constellations change from month to month? What would happen to his family, and to himself, after he died? Uncertainties plagued his days and tormented his nights. He became an easy prey for any charlatan who offered comforting fairy stories and easy answers. All he had to do was propitiate their Gods and things would go well. In a very uncertain and lawless world a little certainty was worth a tithe. It is noticeable, even today that the most secure societies are those least likely to be priest-ridden.

Then there was another more intellectual reason why anyone might be taken in by the idea of God – "The Argument by Design". How did the eagle get his wondrous eye, or the Rainbow Lorikeet her gorgeous plumage – if not for an intelligent Creator? There was no other plausible explanation until Charles Darwin and Alfred Russell Wallace came up independently, in 1858, with "Evolution by Natural Selection".

To my mind the publication of Darwin's '*Origin of Species*' in 1859 marks the high watermark of human history. Although its immediate effects were not dramatic, nothing would be, or could ever be the same afterwards. There was no longer the need for a designing Creator. Man no longer sat on the Right Hand of God to have " *dominion over the fish of the sea and over the birds of the heavens and over the livestock and over all the earth and over every creeping thing which creeps on the earth"* (The book of Genesis). If Man could think at all it was because he had inherited that skill as a survival mechanism from his hairy forbears. Morality, if morality there was, must come from Earth and not from Heaven.....on and on and on and on......the implications were endless. All culture, all philosophy would need to be re-examined from its very foundations – a revolution which the Establishment, including an

Education Establishment built on Greek Philosophy and Abrahamic Religion, largely tried to avoid.

It is vital to understand how 'Evolution by Natural Selection' came to be accepted by an influential section of society at a time when there were apparently insuperable *scientific* objections to it. For instance how could manifestly related large animals dwell on continents separated by oceans far too wide to swim? Acceptance came because of a fundamental but ill understood philosophical principle called 'Ockhams Razor' (or 'Parsimony'): if there are two explanations for some phenomenon Ockham urges us to always prefer the simpler. Why? First because it is more likely to be right; and second because, if it is wrong, it will be easier to prove it so, and thus move on. Both have to do with pliability; the more complex an hypothesis is the more easily it can be bent to fit the facts. But if a simple hypothesis fits those same facts it can hardly do so by chance – and thus is far more likely to be right. In the context of 'All things bright and beautiful, All creatures great and small' Natural Selection is arguably a much simpler explanation than an all-powerful God. And one by one the insuperable scientific objections to it were removed by time. Thus, a century after Darwin, large animal cousins living oceans apart were explained by Continental Drift. (If Ockham's Razor is powerful enough to dispense with God shouldn't everybody aim to understand it? [Note 3]

So it was the British who first came to see that God was an entirely superfluous confection. They were able to do so because, being a secure island, they had developed a comparatively tolerant political and cultural tradition. And it was no accident that Wallace and Darwin came from the world's foremost maritime power. Darwin got his formative experience, serving aboard HMS Beagle for 5 years as a gentleman's companion, while Wallace couldn't have done without steamships (another recent British invention) to transport himself and his specimens around the tropics.

The great glory of enlightened thinking is its *provisional* nature [Ch.5]. It is always willing to change its mind in the light of sufficient new evidence. But to religion, any religion, that has to be anathema. So putting religion behind it is the indispensible step any priest-ridden society has to take before it can join the modern world. To my eye it may be centuries before most Muslim states are able to so. It is telling that Sultan Erdogan has just prohibited the teaching of Evolution in Turkish schools as he tries to force that country back into the benighted past. (By the way the Muslim world banned the printing press for 200 years – which explains a lot.)

MODERN PRIESTS

I define a Priest as someone who lays unjustified claim to special knowledge and hence authority, not only of God. Modern varieties include Economists, Psych***sts, Communist Party officials and many titled Academics. They're all dangerous.

NOTES

1 To get some idea of how Darwin came to his transformative ideas his *Voyage of the Beagle* is a popular account of his adventures and wonderments on a 5 year voyage around the globe in the 1830s. The final chapter of his *Origin of Species,* entitled *Recapitulation and Conclusion* is, in my opinion, the most important document ever written [the rest of the book I found hard going).

2 Darwin usually gets all the credit [after all he was a member of the Establishment and a millionaire by marriage; his wife was a Wedgewood.] but Alfred Russel Wallace a poor plant collector with a far more adventurous life, got the same idea of Natural Selection quite independently. Indeed if it hadn't been for Wallace, Darwin might never have dared to publish his ideas (he was even more fearful of being pipped by Wallace than of his wife's reaction to Evolution. She was very devout). *Wallace, a Life* by Peter Raby tells his engrossing story. Wallace's crime, apart from being working class and half Welsh, was his Spiritualism, which he used to keep in touch with his younger brother who had died with him out in Amazonia.

3 Ockham's Razor is discussed at length in my book '*Thinking for Ourselves*' Amazon, 2020.

t

HISTORY OF THE BRITS.

CHAPTER 13: THE BALEFUL SHADOW OF AMERICA

I argued in Chapter 5 that Britain was the most progressive nation on Earth. I believe it still is. If that conclusion is sound then it is important because it means Britain has a special responsibility to try and lead us all back from the ecological disaster towards which the presently leaderless human race is marching as a rabble.

To reach my conclusion I have to explain why America, although it sometimes appears like a colossal superpower, is still a second-rate affair quite incapable of assuming that vital leadership role. To do that I will argue:

- America never joined WW2 'to save Western civilization'. It was suckered into Pearl Harbour by the KGB.
- Apart from revenge against Japan its main intent after that was to drag down Britain and assume her leading role in the world – which she did. Britain beat Hitler but Roosevelt and Truman picked her pockets while she was lying weakened on the battlefield.
- The Brits (Churchill in particular) reacted naively. They wanted to believe that America was an ally and not a ruthless adversary. So Britain won the war but comprehensively lost the peace.
- Even so, rich as it became, and bristling with dangerous weapons, America is, and will remain, incurably second rate.

Lest I be accused of Anti-Americanism let me say I regard myself as one quarter American. I owe America a great deal, including most of my professional training (as an astronomer and Space scientist). I have lived over there three times (Arizona, Ohio and Baltimore), my only child was born there, and I have camped right across her beautiful wilderness areas "from sea to shining sea". I have even stood at Cape Canaveral with my American colleagues, tears streaming down my cheeks, singing their national anthem, as we watched the Shuttle lift off carrying our instrument, with its attendant astronauts, into orbit. But this is not a history of the Yanks but of the Brits. And there is little doubt in my mind now that America did its best to bring Britain down in the war so as to assume its leading role in the world. And why not? The USA had no obligation to Britain. And if the Brits were too deluded or too exhausted to realize that they were being robbed then, arguably it served them right. But it is necessary now to put the record straight.

1 PEARL HARBOUR. Historians since Liddel-Hart {1} have puzzled over America's ultimatum to Japan in 1941, which was bound to lead to P.H., or something very like it. In my naivety I imagined it was cooked up by a cunning Roosevelt to drag his reluctant citizens into the war to save Liberal Democracy at Britain's side [See Note 4 on prehistory of PH]. Apparently not. It appears that R disliked B, and conspired to put an end to, or even hi-jack her empire.

The man who actually originated and composed that ultimatum to Japan was a minor functionary in, of all places, the US Treasury, called Harry Dexter White. As early as 1943 White was fingered as a KGB agent by two fellow conspirators but it wasn't until 1948 that the FBI questioned him, after which he immediately 'died of a massive heart attack'. Fifty years later publication of decrypts from the Venona Project to break Soviet diplomatic codes, leave little doubt of White's treachery.

Suddenly Pearl Harbour makes sense. The major and perhaps only beneficiaries were the Soviets who were reeling from Hitler's assault on Russia. But Stalin had a large army locked up in Manchuria facing the Japanese. After

Pearl Harbour he could safely transport it across the USSR on the Trans-Siberian-Railway and put it into the field against the Wehrmacht. Its winter offensive saved Moscow.

There is no incontrovertible proof that America was duped. However, after the USSR fell, several high level KGB defectors testified to its veracity. I am inclined to believe it because no other explanation for Pearl Harbour makes any sense. Although Churchill long afterwards claimed otherwise, Pearl Harbour nearly ruined Britain which now had to fight on two fronts ten thousand miles apart. Her Australian allies pulled out of North Africa to defend their own country – which later led to the fall of Tobruk. It resulted in the immediate loss of Hong Kong, Malaysia and Singapore, which were to have fatal post-war consequences. And she had to raise a vast Anglo-Indian army, including 2.5 million Indian volunteers, to defend that vast sub-continent.

So Stalin was the sole beneficiary [Note that the US didn't declare war against Germany, it was the other way round; Hitler declared war against America 3 days after PH. What would have happened if instead he'd been smart enough to declare war against Japan? Intriguing.]

American historians are as reluctant to concede the KGB plot as I was; but of course they would be wouldn't they. It makes America look foolish and discredits any claim she has to be the saviour and leader of the West.

2 LEND-LEASE

Even before P.H. Churchill crossed the Atlantic to discuss the future course of the war with Roosevelt. One outcome of their deliberations was Lend-Lease, a program which would enable Britain to *purchase* huge amounts of American munitions, without having to pay for them *immediately*. It sounds like charity (Churchill called it "the least sordid act in history") but actually it was a cunning trap into which he walked. It took him years to learn that Roosevelt was a political chameleon who would, and did, say anything to anybody if it suited his immediate purpose [Only at Yalta three years later did Roosevelt show his true colours when, on most important matters, he sided with Stalin against Churchill with dire post-war consequences, notably for Eastern Europe, including Britain's ally Poland]. In fact the L-L treaty, when it emerged in full, contained the notorious Clause VII in which Britain, in return, had, among many other obligations, to give up Imperial Preferences, the whole basis of its successful interwar trading strategy. This wasn't pick-pocketing; this was a smash and grab raid on the British Empire, America's supposed ally. Churchill gagged but Britain, after leaving all its heavy military equipment at Dunkirk, had to surrender its wallet. Had Churchill been more honest with them L-L might not have passed his Members of Parliament.

3 BRETTON WOODS

In 1944 the Americans held a huge conference at BW New Hampshire to lay down the post war international financial settlement. It was organized, and largely presided over, by no less than our old KGB friend Harry Dexter White, who started planning it not long after P.H. There could be no doubt that this time he intended to sucker the Brits by pretending that the conference was based on the ideas of their Economics panjandrum John Maynard Keynes. But this was complete bamboozle. The intention was to erect, over the grave of sterling, the almighty dollar as thc world's only convertible currency in place of gold. And so it came to pass. America would become rich beyond its wildest dreams while Britain, as its reward for resisting the Nazis, faced beggary. Keynes, chief of the British delegation, should have walked out of Bretton Woods, but he was either too flattered by the bombast, or too weakened by heart disease, to see the trap. The result was an absolute post-war disaster for Britain and its Empire. [If you think this is a conspiracy story cooked up by me, please read the Postcript to this chapter.]

4 POSTWAR DEBTS

If America ever intended to pay its fair share of the cost of the war (its GDP more than doubled between 1939 and 1945) how come it emerged so humungously rich, while Britain emerged so raggedly poor? At the end Britain's National Debt (owned principally to its citizens who had purchased War Bonds, and to the US and Canada as loans) amounted to between 2.5 and 3 years of total GDP. Add to that war damage, probably as much or more again, and she was in hock for 5 to 9 years of her future income (imagine that personally). If the government budget (taxes) was something like 1/3rd of GDP then the entire budget for something like 20 years ahead would be entirely committed to recovery. No wonder Britons would have to live on thin rationed gruel to pay for a war that had made America fabulously rich. Fortunately, some of that foreign debt could be deferred [B paid off the last instalment of its WW2 debt to the US – £83 million, in 2006.] And by the way the much vaunted Marshall Plan, was a mere drop in the ocean. Britain's share of it (26%) amounted to just over 1% of its total war-debt including war damage.

In defence of America Britain had in 1934 defaulted on its huge loans from the USA in WW1. But it finally paid up (£3.5 Billion) in 2015.

4 BRITAIN'S SUBSIDY TO US SCIENCE AND INDUSTRY

Before the war US industry was good at mass producing technology of intermediate sophistication such as cars, trucks and tractors. Afterwards it became the global hub of super–sophisticated industries such as armaments, electronics, aircraft, computing, rockets, drugs, nuclear weapons and reactors………. How did that come about? In no small measure through picking Britain's brains, while denuding it of the capital Britain itself would have required to exploit them. Here are some instances:

- The Cavity Magnetron, invented by Randall and Boot at Birmingham University, was "the most valuable product ever to reach America's shores". Able to generate short wave electromagnetic waves with thousands of times the power of its valve-based progenitors, Taffy Bowen carried it with him to America in his "suitcase full of secrets" (1940) and showed the Americans how to build sophisticated radar systems. [You have one in your microwave oven]. We know now that the contents of Bowen's suitcase was literally priceless, for it was to entirely overturn the world, not to mention Britain's and America's relative positions in it {Buderi}.[See Note 5]

- Less well known was the silicon crystal rectifier refined at Bristol University by H W B Skinner. Until America adopted it US radar sets were hopelessly uncompetitive. Shocked, the Americans put thousands of PhDs to work on silicon crystal devices at Bell Labs and elsewhere, which eventually led to the transistor. {Buderi}.
- Jet engine technology – which it took Frank Whittle over 20 years to develop, was sold to America for a song (£800,000). The chief American engineer who was tasked in 1940 to come over, pick it up and take it back, told me of his shame at how Britain was fleeced. He also told me a fascinating story of, as he put it "The real technical secret that won the war." Apparently a humble engine fitter in the Midlands, whose job it was to service worn out Merlin aero-engines, noticed that their gear-wheel cogs always wore out asymmetrically. "Why" he wrote in a note he put in the factory 'Suggestions Box' "Dain't we build 'em with asymmetric gears in the first place?" Fortunately a Rolls Royce engineer read and understood. The first engine so built produced no less than 30% more power! This revolutionised Merlin became the basis of most of Britain's successful war planes including the later Spitfires, the Lancaster and the Mosquito. Daimler Benz never

caught on – after which the Luftwaffe didn't stand a chance. [According to Anthony Fokker {1938} the engines are usually the real secret of successful aircraft] . As for America it was good at mass producing aircraft, less good at designing them. The exception was the P51 Mustang, perhaps the outstanding aeroplane of the war. But even it was a lemon until its 800 Horsepower Allison engine was replaced by a 1670 HP Merlin built with asymmetric gears.

- Among other things Britain also shared (generously or foolishly depending on one's point of view) its secrets in antibiotics, cipher-breaking, computing and Operational Research (OR) which last was pioneered by British 'boffins'[Ref 14 Budainski]. OR has never received the public attention of the other three (presumably because of the maths), but was just as crucial to winning the war and far more important to expanding production afterwards. Using quantitative ideas to analyse and improve complex operations, it was crucial to the Battle of the Atlantic [for example see the Convoy Equation in Chap.4] while US Admiral Rickover claimed it had reduced the time to develop the Polaris submarine missile system from 9 years to 2. Getting Man to the Moon on time would have been impossible without it. The management of Space projects is driven by CPA (Critical Path Analysis) a simple but ingenious branch of OR developed in the States. (I use it to do our cooking. Try it.).
- How and why America became such an overweening nuclear power is, to my mind, still a puzzling and disturbing conundrum. Was it a sinister plan, or just ramshackle government? But there is no doubt where it originally got its nuclear know-how from. Again from Britain, again from Birmingham University{Rhodes}.Two

exiles from Germany (Peierls and Frisch) working in Mark Oliphant's group there, calculated the critical mass of Uranium 235 needed to set off an explosive chain reaction (10 kilograms as opposed to the 10 tons calculated by the Germans), while in the wider Maud committee the gaseous diffusion process needed to separate out the deadly isotope (of which there is only 1% in natural Uranium) was worked out and found feasible, if very tiresome.

Britain decided (cipher breaking) that such a bomb would come too late to affect the war in Europe but in 1941 Oliphant went around Physics labs in the States, who were highly sceptical originally, to persuade them to build the bomb instead. Thus the almighty Manhattan project started as a joint venture between the two allies. {Rhodes}.

As we all know America dropped two Atom bombs on Japan, but she shouldn't bear the sole responsibility for that. The decision to do so was taken by the Joint Chiefs of Staff in Potsdam with Churchill and Truman in attendance. Apparently there were no dissenters. [Had they not been dropped, the bloodthirsty General Curtis Le May might instead have burned half the Japanese to death in their highly flammable cities.]

What should worry us all though was the way the American nuclear program grew so grotesquely out of proportion afterwards. Tens of nuclear bombs would have sufficed; they manufactured tens of *thousands*! And they threw out Britain (Macmahon Act 1946) leaving Western Europe entirely at the mercy on the one hand of Stalin's vast tank army based on the plains of Germany, and at the whim of the United States on the other. To my mind it was a foul act of treachery, but the victims were in no position to complain at the time (instead poor old Britain had to quickly cobble together a Bomb of its own which it could ill afford).

Possession of the bomb appears to have gone entirely to America's head. What they had in mind with their vast nuclear arsenal it is impossible to fathom. How we so narrowly evaded a nuclear holocaust over Cuba (1962) was a miracle when *all* of the American chiefs of staff wanted to 'Nook the Soveet Union'. Such stupidity is beyond belief, but a symptom of their Hollywood-cowboy mentality. [However I went deep into the Soviet Union in 1986 and there spent considerable time talking with their presiding nuclear genius Jakov Z'eldovich. What I found out makes for a story far better than any spy novel.[See Note 1]

5 AMERICA'S SECOND-RATE STATUS

When discussing the progressiveness of societies (Chapt. 5) America just scraped in to the bottom of the second rate class. But that was judged on performance over the past century. Surely with her recent superpower status she will do much better today? Let's see:

TABLE (13:1)

RELATIVE PROGRESSIVENESS OF STATES

Quality	USA 100y	USA today	Ancient Greece	Ancient Rome
Curiosity	3	5	4	1
Literacy	5	5	5	2
Democracy	2	3	3	2
Honesty	3	2	(3)	(2)
Tolerance	2	3-4	2	2
Adaptability	4	3-4	4	2

Score	720	1800	1440	32
Class	II	II	II	IV
Class I	>3125			
Column No.	(1)	(2)	(3)	(4)

Modern America [col. (2)] certainly scores higher than it did, notably because of increases in Curiosity (Science) and Tolerance (Black emancipation). But it still falls well short of first–class status (> 3000) because of poor scores for Honesty, Democracy and Adaptability. Since these scores are mine alone I should explain how they were reached:

(A) HONESTY .

Casual dishonesty is so widespread in American public life that is difficult to know where to start or end. For instance:

- The Wright Brothers never made mankind's first powered flight from Kittyhawk (1903).[Note 1] .Go to https://tinyurl.com/y9kgj844 for my case on that Good example of using CST to sort out conflicting evidence, an essential skill for all historians.
- Admiral Peary, who claimed to be first to the North Pole, never got anywhere near it (1912).
- The promised US army finally reached France in mid 1918 – but with no field-guns, so it couldn't fight. Moreover General Sherman refused to fight under Allied Command, which rendered the US contribution more or less useless. It was mainly show{Terraine}
- The petroleum and motor industries knew very well that the lead they needlessly introduced into petrol was highly poisonous but they fought

successfully for over 40 years to deny it. The harm, particularly to children, was horrendous.

- Ditto US Tobacco. By the 1940s it was known, first in Germany then Britain, that smoking killed millions. It took 20 years for the US tobacco industry and the US Surgeon General to grudgingly admit the truth. They should have been strung up like war criminals.
- Selman Waksman stole the credit, and the Nobel Prize for discovering Streptomycin, from his assistant Albert Schatz, whose career he deliberately wrecked 1944. Never exposed as a thief during his lifetime. {Meyers}
- In the Vietnam War senior US officers routinely lied to the politicians who routinely lied to the people {Burns & Novick ; Hastings}.
- Sixty per cent of US hysterectomies were carried out by doctors for money, against the interests of their patients.
- Large armament contracts are routinely won by putting in artificially low bids , then jacking up the prices to make enormous profits.
- Big Science in the US is often betrayed and undermined by systematic lying about project costs in advance. [See The International Space Station – a complete boondoggle costing $100 Bn. ; the Texas Supercollider (cancelled in the end by a furious Congress) and now the James Webb Space Telescope whose costs have escalated by a factor of about 40 !!!!!! while its launch has been delayed a dozen times. It may never do science but JWST keeps a lot of people in well paid jobs, while preventing better projects being funded.]
- Kennedy never admitted that détente over Cuba was only reached after he bowed to Russian pressure to remove equivalent US missiles from Turkey [But thank goodness he did. John Wayne would never have approved.].

- The US Atomic Energy Authority has never admitted that its Pressurised Water Reactor design (now used all over the world except in Britain which uses much safer gas-cooled reactors) is fundamentally unsafe.(The PWR was developed to produce enriched Uranium for bombs, and for nuclear submarines).This is an *absolute tragedy* because we might have had far safer and cheaper Liquid Thorium reactors instead, making us no longer reliant on the poisonous hydro-carbons that are dangerously heating up the globe {Hargraves & Moir, 2010}.
- The perils of anthropocentric Global Warming have been covered up in the US by a cabal of sinister ex defence-scientists who knew nothing of the real matter, but who have used every dirty trick to deceive the people, the scientific profession and the planet {Oreskes & Conway}.
- The 2008/9 Financial Crash was the direct result of US white-collar dishonesty: Toxic Mortgages, Opaque Financial instruments such as CDIs, auditors in cahoots with dodgy clients, over-leveraging by greedy banks…..
- US Big Pharma routinely lies about the safety and effectiveness of its products. The Opiode crisis, now killing more than 50,000 poor Americans a year, is only the latest example. But boy is it profitable! The recent Theranos scandal illustrates how Big Money and Big Law can defy honest attempts at investigation {Carreyrou}

Need I say more?

(B) DEMOCRACY

America's appalling written constitution means that the presidency is little better than a succession of ramshackle absolute monarchies. Each president enters office with his own retinue of courtiers and toadies, his own list of obligations to powerful backers, and leaves with all the presidential papers in his private keeping. And no matter how inept, feeble or dishonest he is it is practically impossible to drive him out of office. (even hereditary monarchies can do better than that; viz mad King George and the Regency). Thus:

- Mrs Woodrow Wilson locked her stricken husband out of sight in the bedroom and effectively ruled America from the White House for 17 months (1919).
- Nixon was a traitor who stole office by first sabotaging the Vietnam peace talks in Paris.{Burns & Novick}
- Reagan claimed, (and probably believed) he'd been a soldier who had liberated Nazi concentration camps when in fact he'd spent the entire war profitably acting in Hollywood. He would often take important decisions after consulting Mrs. Reagan's fortune teller.
- If George Washington "Couldn't tell a lie" Franklin Roosevelt could barely tell the truth. At best he was enigmatic; at worst a shyster. [see Note 3].
- Truman is thought of as a decent little man who developed into a pretty fair president. But his fellow senators would barely speak to him because he'd been crookedly shoe-horned into that august body by T.J Prendergast, who was subsequently sent to gaol (even in America!).{McCulloch}
- The absolute nature of a monarchical presidency means that a president can fill all the powerful offices of state (including the Supreme Court) with unelected and often incompetent cronies. Thus FDR filled the headship of the Treasury with a dimwit confidante called Henry Morgenthau. Morgenthau galvanized the Germans to go on fighting for another 6 months by openly calling for Germany to be reduced to a rural peasantry,[FDR's unilateral call for an 'Unconditional Surrender' was a similar idiocy which cost millions of unnecessary lives].And it was Morgenthau who hired and promoted Harry Dexter White, the KGB agent who caused so much trouble.

- Then there is the shameless gerrymandering that goes on in Congress. Once elected senior politicians are in office they are rarely voted out afterwards. Why? Because they gerrymander the boundaries of their constituencies so as to cheat the voting public.

If that is 'Democracy' then I am a Dutchman.

(C) ADAPTABILITY

is as essential for a nation as it is for any organism. But, thanks to its sclerotic Written Constitution, America is almost powerless to change itself, or its leadership. Thus:

- It couldn't join the League of Nations or declare war voluntarily to save democracy (because its powerful minorities, the Zionists and the Irish in particular, would never allow it to take sides with Britain.)
- It couldn't impeach Nixon (who was finally ousted not by the Press, as they liked to claim, but by Deep Throat who croaked.)
- It cannot outface the Gun Lobby.
- It cannot provide a minimum of decent health care for its poor.
- Its legal system largely exists to protect the rich and powerful against the poor and helpless {Carryrou}.
- For every elected congressman and congresswoman in Washington there are 50 Lobbyists employed there solely to look after the interests of the entrenched, of big banks and corporations, of monopolies, hedge funds and of billionaires and of influential minorities like the Zionists. Much of the mess in the Middle East can be attributed to the influence of these last.

No wonder the US often seems paralysed: it *is* paralysed much of the time. It is beyond me to imagine that it could decisively reverse its stance on say

Global Warming let alone lead the world on any enlightened crusade. Thus I maintain that its poor standing in the Progress Table is fully justified.

6 AMERICAN CULTURE – GLAMOROUS OR GLUTINOUS?

Perhaps the most crippling effect of Britain's post-war impoverishment was the dramatic loss of 'Soft Power' that came with it. American films flooded our cinemas; British television screens and living rooms were inundated with US programs, our radios and record-players with American music. American advertising for American products bellowed and blasted everywhere. Then US tycoons like Rupert Murdoch operated, only half behind the scenes, manipulating Britain to their own sinister ends (Blair was a Murdoch puppet). The combined effect of all this was overwhelming, to the point that an American future came to seem both glamorous and inevitable. But in truth it is neither. One probably has to live over there, as I have done three times, to recognise that the American lifestyle, compared with Britain's, is, all-in-all, second rate. By comparison it is transient, insecure, materialistic, bland, unhealthy, hyper-competitive, work-obsessed, friendless – and generally not much fun. When I found that half of my colleagues felt obliged to come in to work on Christmas-day I knew that America was not for me. Yes America is full of brilliant individuals, but by and large they're not having a good time. They don't know that, because they've got no comparison, and so Hollywood cannot know it either. But it is so. You can drive 4,000 miles across the United States and never get anywhere. By aping America, without real understanding, post-war Britain, in my opinion, undermined its own self-confidence, and in doing so did itself, and its future, much unnecessary harm.

CONCLUSIONS.

1 If one nation could lead the world away from its approaching collision with Nature it ought to be the US. Like no other country it has the combination of land, natural resources, secure borders, wealth and technical know-how to do so convincingly. If only it could! But as I have tried to argue the US is not a Great Power and probably never can be. Thanks to its appalling Constitution, its polyglot and therefore divided population and its pervasive public dishonesty, it is alas, and will remain, a second-rate power. Trump's ambition "To Make America Great Again" is therefore not only dangerous but impossible; it *was* never Great. Liberals on both sides of the Atlantic like to imagine that he is a temporary aberration. On the contrary. Trump is a pretty fair representative of America's delusions, ambitions, weaknesses and limitations. We all have to recognize that and move on.

2 If America cannot lead us back from the environmental brink then, I am suggesting, Britain must try. However, one of the many obstacles to that is the perception, particularly among its own intellectual classes, that, beside America, Britain is second rate and irrelevant. Yes in terms of wealth, weaponry and empire she certainly is. But as I tried to argue in Chapter 5 on 'Progress', those are *not* the factors which count when it comes to Civilization. Britain was laid low economically by its huge (and thank goodness successful) efforts in two world wars while America made itself filthy rich out of them, largely ``(and dishonourably) at Britain's expense. But Britain has gradually recovered its finances, if not its self-confidence—and that largely because of the baleful shadow which Mighty America appears to cast across the Future. The White House, the Pentagon, Hollywood, Wall Street, Madison Avenue, Cape Canaveral, Silicon Valley, Amazon.... these are the icons which constantly dominate world news. But look more closely. The world wars which made America so rich are long over. An economy based on hydrocarbons hasn't got much future. Unless it can resort to nuclear missiles, which of course it cannot,

America has a pretty feeble military footprint. Manufacturing is a fragile basis for national income because it can always be imitated and then be undercut, either by cheaper labour or by currency manipulation (viz China). Monopolies such as Silicon Valley and Hollywood are long term unsustainable. And while the Moon Landing was spectacular, Big Science probably won't thrive for long in a climate of pervasive dishonesty.

3 If then somebody is going to lead us out from the approaching darkness, back into the receding light, and it cannot be America, then who can it be if not Old Britain? Yes she took a fearful battering in two world wars, and made the fatal mistake of trusting America. But she's back on her feet again, all the wiser one hopes for her misfortunes. Like the old she-elephant who has led her herd through droughts and perils innumerable, she may totter a bit, but only she has the mix of experience, curiosity, self-honesty, flexibility and wisdom to lead the way. Pray that she still has the will, and the self-confidence, to try.

POSTSCRIPT

I found this a very difficult chapter to complete, principally because some of the conclusions are so surprising and so personally unwelcome to me. While I always suspected there was something dodgy about the Pearl Harbour story I never expected it would be the KGB. And I was brought up to believe that America was Britain's closest ally, not her treacherous pick-pocket. But any decent historian, or scientist as I am, must be prepared to change their minds when the evidence comes down otherwise. Readers will of course make up their own minds but before doing so I urge them to read in particular "*The Battle of Bretton Woods*" by Benn Steil, *The Weapon that Won the War*, by Buderi, and Budianski's *Blackett's War*, all much praised works of American scholarship, which certainly startled me.[References]

NOTES

NOTE 1. When my wife and I were crossing the Atlantic in 1968 a tiny warbler landed on our ship during a storm in mid ocean. That he could have flown so far seemed to us miraculous. We got him to within smelling distance of Long Island but he dropped dead trying to make the final lap. In tribute to his gallantry I decided to get to the bottom of avian aerodynamics, a fascinating endeavour which, among other things led me to become a glider pilot. It turned out, much to my amazement, that the range of any flying machine is *independent of its size*. If a Jumbo or a goose could do it, then so could a warbler.

The Wright brothers had always been heroes of mine, I'd even been to their workshop in Ohio. But when I applied my equations to their famous Flyer things simply wouldn't work out. I assumed of course that I'd made a mistake. Then why did every other calculation work out exactly, including that of Bleriot who first flew the Channel in 1909. So then I looked at the historical evidence for the famous flight at Kittyhawk, and piece by piece it came apart. If you don't believe me go to to the link on p 114. It's telling that no replica of the Flyer with a 12 Horse power engine like theirs has managed to take off. Yes they did fly after 1903 – but only with the aid of a massive catapult. Unlxt.ike Bleriot's, their design was all wrong, something they never remedied. They left no legacy.

NOTE 2. In a trip deep into the FSU in 1986 I unexpectedly ran into my hero Jakov Z'eldovich, one of the finest astrophysicists and greatest minds of the 20TH century – and incidentally the brains behind the Hydrogen Bomb. He told me many fascinating things – for instance of the imminent collapse of the Soviet Union, and for reasons I have never heard anyone else mention. But that's another story. He also led me to believe that both Russian and American scientists, at great risk to their lives, had been sharing their bomb secrets throughout the Cold War because neither lot trusted their own politicians to keep the peace. I later found evidence to support his claim, but which, in all conscience, I cannot reveal. Anyway why should he lie? His own life was on the line. Right from the beginning some bomb scientists have felt the same way.

The Venona Project revealed that one young American scientist called Theodore Hall had gone to the Russian Embassy in Washington and spilled the beans on the Manhattan project as early as 1945(He afterwards settled in Britain as a bio-physicist). One could argue that Klaus Fuchs and Nunn-May were not so much traitors to Britain as heroic saviours of mankind. With a Hollywood Cowboy like Curtis Le May in charge of the US Strategic Air Command it was vital to prevent him imagining 'We got an edge'. Incidentally Kariton and Z'eldovitch had worked out the critical mass of Uranium 235 in 1939, even before the British. There is much more on this in my 'novel' *Crouching Giant.* [Note 6]

NOTE 3: Roosevelt was a highly successful US political animal – which means he was almost unprincipled. He would and did say almost anything to anybody if it would further his immediate political ends. Let me just give one instance. In 1940, against the strong advice of his senior admirals, R insisted on stationing the Pacific Fleet at Pearl Harbour. Thus the subsequent disaster was largely R's responsibility. So what did he do? He sacked those same admirals and ordered an inquiry into their conduct (which conveniently didn't take place until after the war was over and R was dead). Worse still, far worse, he appointed in their place a drunken incompetent he dug out of the US Navy's 'Elephant Graveyard'. Admiral Ernest J. King, who had no command experience, was invariably in a drunken rage (his daughter's testimony) and had a sulphurous hatred for the British, the Royal Navy in particular (was that his attraction for R?). At least four times King almost lost the Atlantic war: failing for six months to introduce a convoy system off the US East Coast; failing to turn off the city lights there with the result that British oil-tankers were silhouetted against them, perfect targets for waiting U-boats; failing, against the direct orders of the Combined Chiefs of Staff, to deliver a handful of Very Long Range Aircraft to help close the notorious Atlantic Air gap where allied shipping was most vulnerable to U-boats;

and then in March 1943, without warning or excuse, entirely withdrawing the US Navy from the North Atlantic just as the fateful battle there was reaching its very climax . He might as well have been a Nazi.

NOTE 4 The timeline of events leading up to PH makes for interesting reading:

1930s: Japan occupies Manchuria

1937: Japan attacks China

1939: US embargoes export of steel scrap and av-gas to Japan

1941 Jan.: US closes Panama Canal to Japan.

26/7/41: US freezes J assets in America.

1/8/41: US cuts off all oil exports to Japan (which gets more than 80% of its oil from there). A sabre thrust to the guts.

26/11/41: Ultimatum from US Secretary of State Cordell Hull (prepared by Dexter White) contains the notorious Sect. 2 Clause 3: "The Government of Japan will withdraw all military, naval, aviation and police forces from China and Indo-China."

7/12/41 Pearl Harbour attack.

Any way you read that, Japan had no recourse but to military action. Roosevelt's subsequent thunderous denunciation of the attack: "A day that will live in infamy,", has more than a touch of hypocrisy about it. Whether PH was a consequence of cunning, foolishness or KGB manipulation then becomes a very good question.

Roosevelt was an enigmatic chameleon who somehow managed to control the US press – never very sharp. The US public was, for example, never to know that R was completely crippled by his Polio, nor that, besides his wife, he kept a mistress in the White House. Perhaps we can forgive Churchill for being so completely taken in. Everyone else was.

NOTE 5. THE SUITCASE FULL OF SECRETS According to Buderi (p27) inside Bowen's suitcase: *" ..lay nothing less than the military secrets of Britain, virtually every single technological item the country could bring to bear on the war. Had some freak accident burst the lock off the chest, the platform would have been awash in blueprints and circuit diagrams for rockets, explosives, superchargers, gyroscopic gunsights, self-sealing fuel tanks and even the initial germs of the jet engine and the atomic bomb."* All the Brits asked in return was the Norden bomb-sight, which Roosevelt personally refused to them "on political grounds".

NOTE 6: I have spent much time living in the US, principally working on the Hubble Space Telescope program for over 30 years. It was a very exciting time mixing with many exciting, colourful people, full of adventures and misadventures. For those interested I have just published a series of 4 self-contained novels covering that experience between 1964 and 2012 . You can look them up on Amazon. Titles, in chronological order: *Against the Fall of Night, The Whispering Sky, Crouching Giant* & finally *Beyond the Western Stars.*

REFERENCES

1 Buderi, Robert, 1998 "*The Invention that changed the World*" (Abacus). This is the fascinating story of radar, especially as it developed in the US after Taffy Bowen arrived there with the first Magnetron (1940). He shows for instance how many subsequent Nobel Prizes (including for the Transistor) were won by US physicists who cut their teeth perfecting microwave radar. Likewise immense fortunes. Thus IBM got its foothold in computing when it was awarded the contract for SAGE, a computer designed by MIT radar scientists to coordinate the information from a chain of radar stations in the Arctic.

2 Burns & Novick; 2017, *The Vietnam War*, a series of 10 films (shown by the BBC). This is a masterful, moving epic of a tragedy in which 3 million

Vietnamese and 50,000 Americans died to no discernable end. The perfect antidote to hubris, Hollywood myth-making and dishonesty. If only some German film-maker had made a film as honest as this about WW1 we might have avoided Ludendorff's Lie, Hitler and WW2. But the American media at the time were both supine and superficial (I lived in Arizona 1968-70). How could citizens come to know the truth? You can't make successful war on the basis of lying; I swear you cannot.

3 Liddel Hart, Basil, 1970. *History of the Second World War*, Orion Books, Google. Distinguished war historian expresses his own doubts about the Pearl Harbour story.

4 Steil, Benn; 2013, *The Battle of Bretton Woods*, Princeton University Press. This is a magnificent example of American scholarship which changed my mind about so many topics dealt with in this chapter, notably: Roosevelt's attitude towards Britain, Harry Dexter White and the KGB, Pearl Harbour, Maynard Keynes.....

5 Fokker, Anthony; 1938, *Flying Dutchman.* Penguin Books. The man who designed so many fine aeroplanes, particularly for the Germans in WWI, writes about the secrets of his trade. There's nothing magic about it. Engines are crucial.

6 Rhodes, Richard; *The Making of the Atomic Bomb*, 1986, Touchstone Books. History, Science, Politics, Biography....this book works magnificently at all levels. One of my favourite reads of all time.

7 Oreskes, Naomi & Conway, Erik, *Merchants of Doubt, 2010,* Bloomsbury Press. Anyone with doubts about anthropocentric Global Warming must read this carefully researched account of how a cabal of eminent US defence-scientists, with no special knowledge in this area, used general ignorance of The Scientific Method to traduce the whole public discussion of the matter in the US. What their motives were or are nobody knows.

127

8 Carreyrou John; *Bad Blood*, 2018 ,Knopf. The story of how a very young fraudster raised billions to finance a non-existent medical 'invention' and then used the money to pay lawyers to silence her critics.

9 Terraine, John; *To Win a War, 1918 The Year of Victory*; 1978, Cassel.

10 Meyers, Morton A; *Prize Fight*, 2012, Macmillan. Gripping account of some of the filthy tricks in medical science.

11 Hargraves & Moir, 2010, *Liquid Fluoride Thorium Reactors, American Scientist*, 98, pp 304 to 313.

12 Hastings, Max. *Vietnam,* 2019, Penguin, gives a blow by blow account of that tragic war which showed America up for second rate.

13 David McCulloch, *Harry S Truman.*

14 Budianski. *Blacketts War*

HISTORY OF THE BRITS

CHAPTER 14

HALF BAKED ECONOMICS; THE MODERN RELIGION

"Economics was invented to make Astrology look respectable."

J.K Galbraith, Historian of Economics

1 INTRODUCTION

The gods my change but there will always be priests offering Certainties to those who refuse to acknowledge that the adult world must always be uncertain, in constant need of reflection and re-appraisal. Look at the poor bloody Marxists. As Josh Billings opined : *"It ain't what a man don't know as makes 'im a fool; it's what he do know as just ain't so."*

If we define a religion as a body of irrational beliefs that can cause the faithful to behave in unnatural and often self-destructive ways then I want to argue here that the modern religion is Half Baked Economics (HBE for short); that it has already caused the Brits (who invented it) untold harm, and that its modern priests are literally undermining the very world they think they understand; indeed that HBE is a debilitating blight, spreading everywhere, and causing unnecessary ruin wherever it goes. The great news is that it is not malignant. With a little insight we can halt HBE dead in its tracks. Let's think about it.

2 THE FALLACY THAT ECONOMICS IS A SCIENCE.

The essential skill of any kind of science is hypothesis-testing. In Chapter 5 we illustrated how that could be done using betting Odds, and in Chapter 8 by the even more basic method of Categorical Inference, Common Sense in fact. But both methods – which turn out be identical under the skin—suffer from one fundamental limitation. Neither will work unless the number of possible hypotheses (to explain the evidence) is finite, and indeed very limited in number. Thus dream-interpretation can never become a science because the number of possible explanations (hypotheses) for any dream is unlimited. But if there were an infinite number of possible hypotheses then the initial Odds on any one of them being right would have to be infinitely small, and no amount of subsequent evidence can make something infinitely small finite – that is the obvious logic. Philosophers call this "The Principle of Limited Variety" (PLV for short). The Greeks, the Romans and the biblical Jews were all big on dream-interpretation, but now that we understand the PLV we have (except for psychologists) given the dodgy practice up.

So what about Economics – can that be a science? For Economics to claim that it is, or could become a science, it must demonstrate that the Principle of Limited Variety applies to it. But how could it do that? Take the recent financial crash of 2007/8. Practically nobody foresaw it, but dozens of books and thousands of learned papers have been written about it since, pointing to different culprits which *include*: greedy bankers, toxic mortgages, opaque financial instruments, over-leveraging, vast international imbalances (China saving versus US borrowing), auditors in cahoots with the companies that paid them, Fanny Mae and Fanny Mac (you don't want to know), the scuppering of the 1944 conference on international banking at Bretton Woods[Chap. 13], Nixon refusing to back the US dollar in the aftermath of the Vietnam War (1971), over-saving, poor wealth distribution, flash trading, inadequately financed pension funds going in search of unrealistic returns, poor or non-existent supervision of the system by financial supervisors, the Euro, hubris following the collapse of Communism, a naïve belief in 'perfect markets', the inappropriate use of 'The Normal Distribution' by financial 'Quants', insurers ignoring the possibility of correlated market movements, extremely foolish advice given by the actuarial profession, dishonesty on the part of politicians willing to buy votes by offering unaffordable utopias and raising government debts, house owners foolishly believing they were rich because house prices were rising…..and so on and so on. When I read and try to understand the various hypotheses, they all carry a degree of plausibility to me. Moreover they can interact with one another in a whole variety of plausible and dramatic ways. Thus H_1 plus H_2

plus H_3 is really a new hypothesis H_{88}, so the hypothetical possibilities are uncountable—or nearly so – abrogating the Principle of Limited Variety.

Thus it must be true that Economics is not, *and never can become*, a science! The Nobel Prizes they award themselves are a joke; dunces' hats in fact [Note 1].

There is another way to look at the matter. Imagine that Economics *is* a science capable of generating reliable predictions. Suppose that it predicts that farmers will make more money from selling beef than selling milk. Then smart farmers will switch from dairying to beef production. Through scarcity the price of milk will rise; through oversupply the price of beef will fall. The very prediction of the allegedly sound Economic theory has proved to be *self-defeating* ('reflexive' in the jargon). And it seems to me that any 'science of human behaviour' would be self-defeating in the same way.

Thus *everybody* needs to understand that Economics is a church built on quick-sand. However much one might wish it otherwise, nothing can ever be done to recue that situation. This argument is so simple that one has to wonder why Economists themselves do not understand it. Perhaps they don't want to.

Galbraith was right. Economics is indeed half baked.

3 THE FOLLIES OF FREE TRADE.

If there is one thing that nearly all economists believe, and preach, it is the benefit of Free Trade. As a result all Britain's great industries have either closed down, or are in the process: coal, steel, ship-building, cotton mills in Lancashire, woollen mills in Yorkshire, cars, motor-cycles, bicycles, trucks, clocks and pottery in the Midlands, white goods, aircraft, computers, electronics,…….going, going, gone. But it isn't just Britain. Youth unemployment in France is 25%, 40% in Italy and Spain. And look at America: its great manufacturing centres such as Pittsburgh, Detroit, Cleveland….. are now part of that broken rust belt which rose in despair and voted for Trump. What have we all done to ourselves? I will now demonstrate that what the academic economists proclaim is so good for us is actually a deadly poison.

An imported commodity may be dramatically cheaper at the point of retail sale than its domestically produced equivalent. Unfortunately though imports can also have large Sunken Costs arising from losses in domestic employment, investment and profits. And none of us can afford to ignore such hidden costs because we will all have to stump up for them in the end in the form of extra taxes to pay for unemployment benefits, retraining and relocating workers, lost capital and wasted infrastructure (factories, roads, schools, shops, hospitals….). And that says nothing of the misery involved in breaking up communities, families and friends. All that should be obvious; but not apparently to our Economist friends.

What needs to be made, commodity by commodity, is a calculation of the benefits of a particular Free Trade set against the Sunken Costs which we will have to be borne by the wider community as a whole (i.e. the importing nation). That shouldn't be too difficult – and it isn't. I won't bore you with the algebra (which is rather simple) but you can follow it all up in detail via the links provided (Note 2). The results though, which are both dramatic and shocking, are summarised in Table 1:

TABLE 1 : COST ADVANTAGES REQUIRED OF IMPORTS TO OFFSET THEIR SUNKEN COSTS

T_W	1	2	3	4	5		8
Years							
T_0							
1	28%	36%	44	52	60		84%
2	37%	44%	51	58	65		86%
3	46%	52%	58	64	70		88
4	55%	60%	65	70	75		90
5	64%	68%	72	76	80		96
8	91%	92%	93	94	95		98

The Table illustrates how much cheaper an imported commodity has to be (in %) *at the point of retail sale* compared to its dometsic equivalent, for the benefit to the importing nation (as a whole) to exceed its sunken costs. [The Parameters T_0 and T_W, measured in years, along the margins refer respectively to different types of commodity (industry) and different kinds of society. Take for instance a motor-car [$T_0 = 4$ years], imported into Britain [$T_W = 3$ years]. According to the Table it will have to be 64% cheaper than its domestic equivalent to be a bargain. Sixty Four Percent ! Most of the foreign cars on Britain's (Frances's, America's…..) roads are thus an absolute disaster for the importing country as a whole because the Sunken Costs far exceed the benefits. Ditto for many other countries and other commodities (though bananas will still be welcome in Britain). The more sophisticated a country is in social terms the less it can afford to indulge in Free Trade because its sunken social costs (mostly investments in people) are so high – by definition. FT makes far more sense for unsophisticated countries because their people-investments are (equally by definition) so much lower. [China for instance barely has a social welfare system so, by the same argument, it benefits from a wide variety of free trades.]

I couldn't believe this calculation when I first made it in 2016. But it has been checked by several other people with far more commercial background than I. It's right. But please check it out because it is so important for you and your family[Note 2].

So why do Economists still preach the nonsense they do about Free Trade? I'm sorry to say that it's chiefly because Economists appear to be too simple-minded to recognize the fallacies underlying their own profession. Unfortunately the harm they have done already is almost incalculable [below].

N.B. My argument above is NOT Economics, merely accountancy [Note 2]. The distinction is that Economists have to make assumptions about how humans will react. I have not.

4 ASSORTED EPISODES IN BRITISH ECONOMIC HISTORY.

A) In 1798 the Revd. Thomas Malthus, a don at Cambridge, published his highly influential "*Essay on the Principle of Population*". In it he argued that an unrestrained population would always multiply faster than its food resources, leading inevitably to starvation, to misery, and to a "struggle for existence". In his own words this struggle entailed ".....every cause, whether arising from vice or misery, which in any degree contributes to shorten the natural duration of human life. Under this head, therefore, may be enumerated all unwholesome occupations, severe labour and exposure to the seasons, extreme poverty, bad nursing of children, great towns, excesses of all kinds, the whole train of common diseases and epidemics, wars, plagues and famine".

Malthus' well-intentioned but naïve argument, was that while population increases exponentially (like flies breeding), food production increases only linearly. It was almost puerile because it ignored the fact that hungry people can often find ingenious forms of alternative sustenance – thus displaced crofters founded the mighty Scottish herring fishery. But many influential people chose to believe Malthus' essay, with absolutely tragic consequences for the British poor. It excused: work-houses, forcible land Enclosures, the transportation of juvenile petty thieves, Highland clearances and so on and so on. The rich used it as an excuse for land grabs, the poor were emiserated, deprived of their livings and their homes, and even of their dignity as human beings. The equivalent of 30 % of the entire British population was forced to emigrate. Never did so little algebra generate so much unnecessary misery. It should have been a warning to all: '*Beware economic theorists.*'

B) 1814. At the end of the Napoleonic War, Parliament introduced the Corn Laws, which effectively prevented the import of cheap corn. Prices and land-rents soared. Landowners and clergymen (through their tithes) became even richer while the poor, unable to afford bread, either starved, became industrial slaves or had to emigrate. The injustice of the whole affair, particularly after the Reform Bill of 1832, which entitled many more men to vote, lead to agitation and eventual repeal of the Corn Laws in 1846. This repeal was portrayed by its advocates as a holy crusade for Free Trade, which ever since has seemed inviolable. [Thus, even today, one of my newspapers *The Economist*, which was founded in 1843 as part of the repeal movement, treats any discussion of Free Trade as an assault on its religion and not the intellectual issue which it actually has to be.] What with Malthus and the Corn Laws the nineteenth century, which should have been a triumph, was a tragedy for many powerless Brits. So much so that in 1914 a quarter of the volunteers for its Army had to be rejected on the grounds that their constitutions were irreparably damaged by malnourishment.

C) The rich however grew so rich that they didn't know what to do with their surplus wealth. So they invested it abroad in all manner of risky ventures such as Argentinian railways. Many bombed, with the loss of humungous amounts of British capital. It has been estimated that of every pound earned by Brits in the nineteenth century 50 pence was thus wasted abroad[1]. At the beginning of the century British GDP per head was more than twice as high as in the next richest nation. By the end of that 'triumphant' Victorian century, and by the same measure, Britain ranked twelfth.

D) In 1925 Britain went back on the Gold Standard with generally disastrous consequences for British industry because its traditional exports, such as coal, became too expensive to sell abroad. To compensate, coal owners forced the wages of their miners down – which led to the General Strike of 1926. The Chancellor of the Exchequer Winston Churchill is often blamed but, apparently, he was acting on the unanimous advice of professional economists in the Treasury and Bank of England.

E) In the 1930s Keynes wrote his famous treatise suggesting slumps, of which there have been a dozen or more in British history (e.g. 1763,1772,1792, 1796,1819,1825, …………1884,1890,1896,1901……1929….2007), are the result of over-saving and that for governments to end them they should spend liberally on infrastructure.

F) At the Bretton Woods conference in 1944 Britain was forced to end its system of Imperial Preferences. Its huge war debts would take decades to pay off. [Chapt. 13.]

G) The coming of the container-ship in the 1970s meant that exports could move around the globe at minimal cost [A 20-ton container can get from Asia to Europe for less than a thousand dollars]. The last restraint on ruinous Free Trade was thus removed and advanced countries such as Britain began to suffer catastrophic de-industrialisation as their manufacturing started moving to relatively backward countries in Asia.

H) In 1973 Britain joined the Common Market in the hope of defending itself against Asian competition. But all that did was accelerate ruinous Free Trade among the countries of Europe, to their mutual disadvantage; Europe stalled.

I) From 1980 on all the previously advanced countries faced massive de-skilling and de-jobbing by unrestrained globalization.

J) Thatcher adopted Reaganomics based on the Economic theories of Milton Friedman who wholly rejected Keynes' ideas. Friedman is the arch-high-priest of Half Baked Economics [Note 4]

K) 2008. The huge banking crash, mainly brought about by dishonesty in America and half- baked economic mismanagement at home, halts all growth in real wages for ten years while the government bails out failing banks with tax-payers money. [Note 3]

L) 2015 - 19: The Brexit debate is dominated by HBE arguments. But they do not fool the majority of a population who are experiencing the misfortunes of Globalization at first hand.

5 SOME TRAGI-COMEDIES OF BRITISH CAPITALISM

- Between them husband and wife now have to work more hours a week to support their families than did their grandparents. And this despite the wonders of modern machinery and automation.
- There are no less than 400 different models of new car now on sale in Britain (anywhere).
- Many citizens have to commute for hours every day to find work.

- Many of us don't get out of education much before we are 25, and even then we are not guaranteed a secure occupation. It's getting worse.
- During manufacture some car components travel back and forth across the Channel over 30 times before they are built into a vehicle.
- It takes 17 tons of scarce Peruvian water, and a 3-week refrigerated voyage, to deliver just 1 kilo of avocados to the British market.
- Every winter, shadowy 'managers' in the City of London pickpocket 50 Billion pounds in 'bonuses', about £4000 for every working family in Britain.
- Job insecurity and mass immigration are forcing more and more poor devils into mega-hives such as London. They, and their children, will never be able to afford proper homes to live in.[Ch 16]
- We are relentlessly bombarded from all sides with advertisements to buy things we do not want and cannot afford. Thus we are kept in totally unnecessary debt, whilst becoming ever more tolerant of lies. [The *Financial Times* publishes a tasteless monthly supplement called '*How to spend it.*' Anyone who doubts how fat white-collar parasites are becoming should read a copy of it or of '*1843*' an analogous give-away from the *Economist*. They both make me vomit.]
- Many of us nowadays are going to universities to learn skills, of which many were redundant decades ago. Moreover universities cannot teach Common Sense Thinking, which is what we really need, because they have no idea what it is. [Chap.18,20]
- The gigantic multinational Amazon has a turnover in Britain of over 11 Billion £ but pays only £ 200 million in taxes (2%). 'Smart' accountancy allows it to move its profits to low-tax regimes abroad such as Ireland. So the rest of us have to pay them instead. Its founder Jeff Bezos is the richest man on the planet.
- Many universities have set up Business Schools because they are extremely lucrative (as much as a thousand dollars a week in tuition fees.) But would you expect self-proclaimed ivory towers to be sources of commercial acumen[2]? (By the way

universities are where so many of those wretched HB Economists hang out. The University of Chicago, Friedman's Church, is a particularly poisonous nest.)

- Crude oil is transported around our coasts in VLCCs (Very Large Crude Carriers). As large as the Empire State skyscraper they each weigh three times as much, take 20 kilometres to stop, 15 minutes to turn, have one engine, one propeller and no effective anchor. They are far too clumsy to be safe. They are uninsured (no insurance company will insure them, they are too dangerous) and are registered in banana republics. So none of the huge tanker disasters, from *Amoco Cadiz* (1978) to *Sea Empress* (1996) was remotely an accident. They were bound to happen and will happen again because Western governments are either unwilling (the UK) or unable to regulate them. Smaller, safer tankers would add less than a penny to the price of a litre of fuel. But no.

And so on..............

But just because much of modern capitalism is a joke doesn't mean we have to become Marxists instead, that is an egregious example of a 'false dichotomy'. In my experience of the FSU, Communism was an even more egregious failure, an even more tragi-comic paradise for parasites. Look how many of their Mega-parasites escaped with their loot to the West, particularly to London, much of which they now own. [70% of high value London homes are now sold to foreigners]

6 SOME IMPLICATIONS

If my reasoning about Free Trade is sound then it has widespread and profound implications, and not only for British history. If ! I suggest therefore that readers first satisfy themselves about that reasoning before proceeding further. [Note 1]

As far as I can see Section 2 employs nothing beyond Common Sense, Section 3 nothing beyond simple accounting.

A degree of diffidence might be expected of an astrophysicist delving into a subject so far away from his home territory as macro-economics. All I can say is that in the history of the Natural Sciences the outsider's point of view has often proved indispensable to understanding and progress. Take Continental Drift, arguably the most important scientific discovery of the 20th century. It's founding father was the German *atmospheric* scientist Alfred Wegener (educated as an astronomer actually). To a man geologists and geophysicists mocked and hated him. But Wegener was wiser than they, if only because he was not immersed in their suffocating Group-think[1].

We certainly want to understand how wealth is both created and destroyed. However wanting to fly and being able to do so, are entirely different propositions. Predicting how tribes of human beings will react to complex stimuli is presently impossible, and is likely to remain so. Malthusian pessimism on the one hand, Marxist collectivism on the other, have already led to massive human tragedies. Therefore we need to be sceptical of naïve intellectuals who want us to follow them as they attempt to defy gravity with their HBE. Their obsession with Free Trade is very likely responsible for the de-industrialization and demoralization of the West. We can afford to go no further down that miserable trail, nor do we have to. Provided citizens are willing to think a little for themselves we can reverse this gadarene stampede towards Globalization. If Free Trade made any commercial sense then why isn't the European Union thriving? Instead it is the perfect illustration of how destructive cross-border trading between nations at equivalent states of development is. Moreover why has China grown so rapidly just as the West is stagnating? Until I did the FT calculation I used to suppose (as Trump now does) that it was due to sinister currency- manipulation

---

[1] Wegener wrote "*The Origin of Continents and Oceans*" in 1915 while convalescing from war wounds. Later he spent much time exploring East Greenland and in 1930 the winter came early leaving Wegener and his men stranded and short of food. Wegener died a heroic death trying to help his companions ,and is entombed in the ice. His ideas didn't take off until the 1960s when paleomagnetic measurements of the ocean floor showed that it was young and spreading apart at about a centimetre a year.

and the theft of IPRs (Intellectual Property Rights) by the Chinese. After all what skills or resources does China possess that the West does not? But the FT makes it clear that China benefits anyway because it provides almost no welfare to its citizens – they have to save 50% of their earnings against hard times·· So if one goes to Table 1 China's values are significantly lower than the West's , making many trades profitable to her which are far too sunken-costly for us. Both Americans and Europeans badly need to understand this before we all get embroiled in a bitter and unnecessary trade-war – which could then escalate to something far worse. The FT calculation reveals that the real trade war is not between nations but between importers and manufactures *in the same importing nation.* That should be relatively easy to fix. Yes we should impose tariffs, or Fair-Play Taxes as I call them, but we should regard them not so much as a weapon against hostile foreigners, as HBEs imagine, but as a way to level the playing field between our own entrepreneurs and citizens [Note 5]. This would not only be easy to do but almost everybody(bar unprincipled importers such as Sir Philip Green who cleaned out his employees' pension fund before slinking off to the West Indies) would benefit in the end. Even China will, because it will have to introduce a proper welfare system for its own citizens instead of unintentionally undermining ours.

That leads on to the whole difficult question of financial interdependencies between different nation states. They will always be much harder to manage, because they involve *at least* two governments, than equivalent interdependencies between citizens of the same state, which is often hard enough. *Shouldn't they therefore be eschewed as far as possible?* Why should the infections or misfortunes of one state be allowed to infect another? That can lead not only to unnecessary misery but to nationalistic hatreds, even to wars. We have already discussed the reasons why men have all too often felt themselves obliged to fight – because inequalities at their frontiers almost force them to do so [Chapt.9]. Shouldn't we therefore reduce international dependencies as far as we can? I believe so. Let me just give one instance. Because there is no social welfare system in China Chinese citizens are obliged to save over 50 per cent of their earnings against a rainy day. But where are they to deposit those gigantic savings? Not, if they are wise, in a Chinese bank, for there they will be under the control of Xi and his goons who are likely to waste them on prestige projects at home or abroad. When the Xi regime disintegrates, as such a primitive tyranny inevitably must, the savers will probably lose everything. So, in as far as they can, they invest their vast savings in Western securities, i.e. in stocks and shares. But those are the very securities we were relying on to pay our own pensions when the time comes; when foreigners buy our stocks and bonds their prices go up, and so their 'yield' i.e. their annual dividend as a fraction of their purchase-price, goes down. Thus pensions will become so much more expensive for the Brits to buy. You can imagine the righteous and explosive anger that will arise on both sides then; another egregious folly of the HBE Church. But the general point is that financial interdependencies that cannot be regulated could lead to unnecessary wars. This is a difficult subject but we need to think about it very hard and very fast; foreign trade shot up from 39% of world GDP to over 50% in the decade from 1990 to 2000 alone. All nations are going to have to cooperate to save the planet. The last thing we can afford is to antagonize one another unintentionally.

One could go on forever listing the manifold misfortunes of HBE. But the real point is that *they are not fundamental*, merely the outcome of a profound misunderstanding among "financial experts" who fantasized they were scientists. They are not, and they never can become so. But that is wonderfully liberating news! If we can think for ourselves, we can cast them aside, then rapidly put things to rights. Within less than a generation most of the follies listed above will seem like distant jokes. IF only we can screw up the self-confidence to think for ourselves once again……. That is the issue.

7 REFLECTIONS

The past five thousand years or so could be called 'The Age of Experts'. The world seemed too complicated – and was – for most of us to think it out for ourselves. Thus the priests who knew God, and could intercede for us, at a price, took over. For them it was a vainglorious, not to say a highly profitable undertaking. So they multiplied without limit: Witchdoctors, Soothsayers, Sybils, Zoroastrians, Delphic Oracles, Buddhists, Druids, Hindus, Jews, Christians, Mohammedans, Catholics, Protestants, Methodists, Christadelphians, Rastafarians, Marxists, Spiritualists Psychologists, Economists, Management Consultants, Councillors, Dieticians, Mumbo- Jumbo men, many Academics…… Now the Internet offers each one of us the chance to locate the specialised knowledge we may need to make wise and informed decisions ourselves. But to make use of it we will first need to find out just how Common Sense Thinking works [See Note 1].

If Economists really knew what they were talking about then how come China has a growth rate of about 7% per annum while the sophisticated West ,with all its Economic Philosophy, can manage only 2% ?

NOTES

NOTE 1: There is much about CST in this book but my other book *Thinking for Ourselves* [Amazon 2020] is entirely devoted to it. For instance Section (13:3) demonstrates in detail why Economics is not , and never can become, a Science.

NOTE 2. THE FOLLY OF FREE TRADE

As an astrophysicist I am used to discussing complex processes in terms of their significant timescales, and that is the only innovation I have introduced into accountancy here. But it is very insightful. Thus the whole issue of Sunken Costs and Free Trade reduces to the following 'Free Trade Equation' (FTE) which resulted in Table 1:

$$f_X T > T_0 + 0.1 + \left[0.9 - \frac{T_0}{T_D}\right] \times T_W \qquad (1)$$

Where $100 f_x$ is the quantity we are after (the percentage in the Table, '>' simply means 'more than', and:

T_D is the discount-time – the number of years after which investors in an industry expect to get all their money back, and

T_0 is the capital invested in the domestic industry in years of its Value Added.

T_W is the number of years of salary require to retrain and relocate workers made redundant by imports (including their families) and

T is what I call the 'Churn-time' , the number of years over which one could hope to make reasonably reliable forecasts ahead. As the world speeds up so T must fall. In the slowly changing mediaeval world T might have been 200 years or even 500. Now it is down to 10 years, or less. Note that f_x and T are coupled together on the left hand side of the Equation so that as T falls f_x *must rise to compensate* ! Thus a particular Free Trade, which may have been sensible in the past, could be absolutely ruinous today. This speed-up is the vital aspect of the matter which Economists seem to have missed. They're not astrophysicists. You can follow these arguments in detail on the website or at :

https://tinyurl.com/y2umz2bx

NOTE 3: BANKING DISASTERS: Consider the simple equation:

$$T_2 = \frac{100}{L(i - i_L)} \qquad (1)$$

which was certainly one culprit in the banking crash of 2007/08. An investment bank wants to double its money over a period of T_2 years. It has 1 million of its own money to invest and sees a promising opportunity to invest it in oil-tankers say at an expected rate of return of i = 5%. According to the equation (if we ignore L and i_L for now) that would lead to a doubling-time of 100/5 = 20 years. Too slow – far too slow. But what if the bank was to borrow L million dollars at i_L percent and put the whole lot into tanker operating. That's called 'Leveraging': you are 'levering' the effect of your original investment by a factor of L. The doubling time would be reduced, according to equation (1), if L= 10 and i_L = 3% to:

$$T_2 = \frac{100}{10(5-3)} = \text{ 5 years}$$

which is far more satisfactory. Indeed it's money for old rope – seemingly. Why not Leverage at 50, i.e. borrow 50 times your initial investment and get:

$$T_2 = \frac{100}{50 \times (5-3)} \approx 1 year \text{ !}$$

It seems like magic. The bankers are borrowing other people's money to double their own every year. Let the good times roll. They must be geniuses. They feel entitled to steal huge bonuses, buy yachts and erect vast skyscrapers.

Hey, but wait a moment – there's no such thing as magic. Where's the snag? The snag is right there in equation (1). What if the investment turns nasty? What if there is a slump – or too many tankers get built – a very likely result of such exuberance ? The return i will fall below the borrowing rate i_L and then T_2 is no longer the doubling-time but the halving-time on the original investment of 1 million. Suppose i goes to 0; the halving time become 100/150 years or only a few months. And i might easily become negative, say -5%, in which case the halving time falls to 100/(50 × [-8]) or about 3 months! The situation is disastrous. Somehow the bank has to off-load all its tankers on a falling market and pay back it's enormously leveraged loan of 50 million. It can't be done. The bank crashes. The loans default, panic spreads.

The point, as a simple approximate equation makes crystal clear, is that high leveraging is potentially profitable but also extremely dangerous. It is all about timescales. Had the banks been less greedy, and less ignorant, they would have had more time to adjust their affairs. Bank regulators are there to see that leveraging is held down to prevent greedy bankers from capsizing the entire system – which they will do, and have done many times in the past, if they're given the chance – after all it's *other people's money*. Alan Greenspan (US) and Gordon Brown (UK), allowed leveraging to rise from about 25 in 1995 to over 50 in 2008. Presumably neither of them, nor their economist advisers, understood simple algebra – which is all you need to devise and understand the Leveraging Equation. Gordon Brown, who had a PhD in Economic History, was arguably the worst Chancellor of the Exchequer in British history. After allowing greedy banks to go bust he then bailed them out with our money ; e.g. Lloyds was 'induced' to rescue the Bank of Scotland a wildly incompetent crocodilian monster. Next wee Gordon ordered two enormous aircraft carriers to be built in his constituency (even though we couldn't afford any planes to go on them).Then he wormed his way into the Prime-ministership; Then he lost an election. Now he advises a huge US bond concern called Pimco. How far hot air can rise!

(Note how often it is the comparison of timescales which leads to understanding)

NOTE 4: MILTON FRIEDMAN: CAPITALIST MUMBO-JUMBO MAN.

If you still have any illusions about Economics you should read '*Capitalism and Freedom*' by Milton Friedman "the most influential economist of the second half of the 20th century" (*Fortune* magazine). How this very bad book can remotely be thought of as 'science' defeats me. Near the beginning (p4) he writes, "….the great advances of civilization, in industry, or agriculture, have never come from centralized government". This is complete and utter nonsense, as factually wrong as stating 'The Earth is Flat'. [Think only of sewage systems, clean water, roads, computers, space-satellites, anti-biotics, astro-navigation, jet engines, radar, the Internet, broadcasting, machine-tools, anti-scorbutics, satellite navigation, and so on and on.] To call it 'naïve' is far too polite – either the author was a complete fool or a deliberate liar. Certainly he was an enthusiastic apologist for the worst excesses of Capitalism (Reagan and Thatcher were fans). And the fact that he was awarded a ' Not-the-Nobel Prize' in Economics highlights the fraudulence of that particular award. (That prize is *not* awarded by the Nobel Foundation, who were furious that the prestige of their own Prize, with its name, was misappropriated by the Bank of Sweden, who 'invented' the tawdry 'Economic' variety. It should be called "The Dunce's Crown" in honour of such a 'Confederacy of Dunces'.

NOTE 5: FAIRPLAY TAXES:

As is very apparent from Table 1 only imports in its top left corner are likely to be healthy *these days*. (In the past things may have been vastly different.) If a given import is being sold cheaper than its tabulated value then an Importers Tax or FAIRPLAY TAX, should be levied by the government to bring it up to that value *in order to see that that the Sunken Costs are paid by those who aim to profit from the sale,* not by other citizens . It is important to recognize that such taxes are not aimed as a hostile gesture against foreigners; they all about *fairness at home*. Without them importers get away with murder! Economists don't understand all this and point to tariffs as if they were poisonous darts; fair taxes play a vital role in binding societies together [Ch 26].

REFERENCES

1 *Economics for the Exasperated*, Gordon Rattray Taylor

HISTORY OF THE BRITS

CHAPTER 15

NUMERACY, THE SEVENTH PILLAR OF WISDOM

"Mathematics is a human activity and is subject to all the foibles and frailties of humans. Any formal, logical account is pseudo-mathematics, a fiction , even a legend, despite the element of reason." Morris Kline, "Mathematics, the Loss of Certainty" [Note 5]

1 INTRODUCTION

If there is one truth we have learned over the past 5,000 years it is that few matters are absolutely certain, absolutely right or absolutely wrong. As we have matured so we have come to decide "On the balance of probabilities", to advance towards the truth by a series of "successive approximations". As we argued in Chapter 5 Progress seems to require six qualities: Curiosity, Honesty, Adaptability, Tolerance, Literacy and Democracy. But there is one more and that is Numeracy. The weighing of Evidence in the scales is an essentially quantitative process – which is more and which is less. While it doesn't have to be done with actual numbers it is nevertheless a weighing process – to determine on which side of the argument the weight of evidence comes down.

Literacy has brought with it the ability to compound many more clues together. Numeracy enables us to weigh in with two new *kinds* of clues: numbers and measurements. Indeed some important arguments are of a purely quantitative nature (e.g. 'Civilization and Moon-power' Ch.2). Thus a language for describing and analysing purely numerical evidence has become essential to the modern thinker. Unfortunately many otherwise intelligent Brits find mathematics both unnatural and distasteful. They can only get away with it because so many of their fellow citizens are likewise afflicted. Thus they have tolerated a succession of innumerate prime-ministers where they would never have put up with an illiterate one. Numeracy, unlike flower-arrangement, is no longer an optional accomplishment; sometimes it is the only way to discern the truth.

Fortunately innumeracy is not a congenital deformity – it is invariably the result of a misunderstanding by the teaching profession that goes back over 2000 years. The Brits, if they wanted to, could easily put that right.

2 NUMERACY AND BRITISH HISTORY

Mathematics is not a national language but as this is a book about the Brits we might as well select our illustrations from their history:

(A) In 1619 John Briggs published the first Table of **Logarithms**. As he wrote in a preface: *"Logarithms are numbers invented for the more easie working of questions in Arithmetike and Geometrie... By them all troublesome multiplications and divisions are avoided and performed only by addition instead of multiplication and subtraction instead of division. The curious and laborious extraction of roots are also performed with great ease……… In a word, all questions not only in Arithmetike and Geometrie but in Astronomie also are most plainly and easily answered."*

Briggs' tables (mooted a decade earlier by John Napier in Sciotland) revolutionised Man's capacity to make the complex calculations vital to navigators, engineers, bankers, astronomers, insurers, surveyors, actuaries (pensions), shipwrights, architects, builders, gunners, merchants, cartographers, statisticians, taxmen……. Logs led naturally to Slide-rules (William Oughtred 1624) which no scientist or engineer would be without until the 1970s. Werner von Braun who, more than anyone else, got us to the Moon in 1969, never used anything else. It is likely that Logarithms speeded up human progress by a century – possibly two.

(B) In 1686 Isaac Newton published his famous '*Principia Mathematica*'. In it he demonstrated that the complex motions of the heavenly bodies could be explained by three simple Laws of Motion – combined with his Universal Law of Gravitation. The details need not concern us but the implication was startling – even if Newton did not recognise that himself. The heavens appeared to run like **a colossal clockwork machine**, utterly predictable from one century to the next. It followed that all the capricious gods of the ancients couldn't be meddling with it. Indeed there was no real need for a god in it at all. None of the priests and potentates could make a. mite of difference to it. What a colossal liberation that would come to seem. We were in to The Enlightenment.

(C) In 1707 Admiral Sir Cloudesly Shovell's fleet, returning home from Gibraltar, ran ashore on the Scilly Isles drowning 2000 prime seamen including the admiral. With no reliable means of finding their **Longitude** the navigators aboard imagined they were safely far to the West. In the tragedy's aftermath the Brits of course set up a committee – The Board of Longitude – empowered to offer a vast prize to the first who could come up with a practical and accurate (to within 30 miles) method for finding the Longitude of any vessel out at sea. The Board also had sums to support inventors with promising ideas. One such was a self-educated Yorkshire carpenter John Harrison who decided, at age 21, to build a marine chronometer so accurate and so reliable that it would win the prize.(The Latitude is easily found from measuring the altitude of the Pole Star)

Because the Earth rotates towards the East by 15 degrees every hour, finding the Longitude is all about measuring time. Local noon in Cardiff occurs 12 minutes and 43 seconds after it does at Greenwich, thus Cardiff is at a Longitude of 12 mins and 43 seconds West, which is, at Cardiff's Latitude, (51.5 degs. North), equivalent to 137.9 statute miles.

In Harrison's day there were thus two approaches to telling the time at sea—a marine chronometer of previously unimagined accuracy (a tenth of a second a day) or using the Moon as a clock-hand as it traverses its passage among the stars. But that 'Method of Lunars' would require tables of the Moon's sidereal trajectory to be calculated years in advance – as it happens a fiendishly hard task. Many men set out to win the Prize but only two succeeded. In Yorkshire, in a 40-year technical tour-de-force that has never been equalled in history, Harrison produced a series of ever more precise chronometers which eventually (1761) accomplished the task of navigating HMS *Deptford* from Portsmouth to Jamaica with a positional accuracy of better than 2 miles! In Germany the surveyor Tobias Mayor produced a table of Lunar positions of equivalent accuracy, and both eventually shared the prize, deservedly so for the two methods were complementary. For a practical seaman the chronometer was far more convenient, but every so often it would need correcting – using Lunars.

Astronavigation would change the world and Britain's place in it. So equipped Captain Cook (1768 -71) was sent out to explore the Pacific (and secretly to find a new supply of giant trees that could provide superior masts for the Royal Navy's biggest battleships). He found and mapped New Zealand, Australia and NW Canada, and 'claimed' all three for Britain (and incidentally found those masts on Norfolk Island). But, far more important, astronavigation made ocean-voyaging so much safer and therefore cheaper, that the whole world could now trade for basic commodities like wheat and wool, not just for slaves and spices. The Admiralty took on the task of charting the Seven Seas and publishing them for all to use.

(D) In 1864 a Scots physicist James Clerk Maxwell, first composed the equations which describe the discoveries of the experimental electricians Hans Christian Oersted (1820) and Michael Faraday (1831). His discovery was eventually to prove far more momentous than 'the discovery of ' America. Why? First because his equations argued, to general astonishment, that

electromagnetic signals should travel through Space at the speed of Light – indeed that Light itself was an electromagnetic wave. Second because they implied that there must be deep flaws in our understanding of Space and Time. After Maxwell the bulk of the modern world would be born – broadcasting, the radio-demagogues, television, code-breaking, computers, Relativity and smart-phones were all waiting in the wings of History. Maxwell's name is not as well known as other titans of Science such as Darwin and Einstein – but it ought to be. James Clerk Maxwell has probably changed your life more than any other figure from history.

(E) While the British climate is almost ideal, its **weather** is highly unpredictable – or rather it was. Nowadays we know to the hour when it is going to be fair or foul and can alter our plans accordingly. But how? Because a Quaker polymath from Newcastle Lewis Fry Richardson realised one could write down all the Partial Differential Equations describing the atmosphere, and then solve them numerically, that is to say by slogging them out with slide-rule or computer. Since there were no electronic computers in his day (1920) Richardson envisaged a huge auditorium filled with clerks with slide-rules. Each was to be responsible for a smallish cube of the atmosphere but would keep in touch with the clerks responsible for the 6 cubes abutting his or her own. Whilst serving as an ambulance driver in WW1 he actually carried out a trial calculation to prove its feasibility. After electronic computers became available in the late 1940s they were harnessed to the task, with ever increasing success.

(F) Thus far in this section I have been 'triumphal'. Now I will describe just one of the dire consequences of the innumerate British elite. In 1996 the 140,000 ton tanker *Sea Empress* ran onto the rocks at the entrance of Milford Haven in West Wales. Despite the best efforts of all the Queens tugs and all the Queen's men she couldn't be towed off before most of her cargo of crude oil had breached from her shattered hull to despoil beaches and murder sea and bird life for 50 miles around. It was an ecological catastrophe. Nobody wanted to take responsibility. Neither the ship nor its cargo were properly insured (they never are – it's too risky for insurance companies). The Port Authorities attempted to prosecute their own pilot. The subsequent government Inquiry was a white-wash which concluded that because the vessel's sea-worthiness certificate was up to date it was in no way to blame.

But it was. Entirely so! It was far too big and clumsy to be allowed anywhere near the rocky tidal coast of Europe, and yet it was only half the tonnage of a true 'VLCC' [Very Large Crude Carrier]. Such monsters are bigger than the Empire State skyscraper, weigh 3 times as much, take 20 kilometres to stop and 15 minutes to turn, have no effective brakes or anchors, cannot be controlled by tugs in any wind, and sometimes have to be crabbed at 45 degrees to their direction of travel to squeeze them into port against the tide. It's crazy!!!!!! One slight error of judgement by the crew, the pilot or a tug captain and they're on the rocks, with catastrophic effects for Man and for Nature (and yet they don 't save a penny on the price of a litre of fuel). Yes it is crazy!!!! When the *Amoco Cadiz* (1978) lost its steering engine in the Bay of Biscay even the most powerful tug in Europe couldn't turn its head a few degrees against the wind, and so prevent it crashing into the coast of Brittany with the spillage of 275,000 tons of crude oil. I got involved in the subsequent *Sea Empress* Inquiry but found it all but impossible to persuade educated but innumerate people that if you scale something up too far it can lead to fatal consequences. A VLCC, because of its sheer size, has no brakes, cannot turn out of danger, should never be allowed to carry oil, should always be fully insured, shouldn't be registered in a banana republic (as they all are), shouldn't be allowed anywhere near a rocky coast, indeed shouldn't be allowed on the high seas at all. But they are. The next *Sea Empress* disaster, the next *Amoco Cadiz* will happen any year now. It's simple mathematics, very simple. But our rulers simply can't do it, and what is worse, refuse to believe those who can. [Note 1]

When you scale any design up you usually change its properties in fundamental ways. Big trees have to be thicker in proportion than little trees – look around you. Men taller than 7 feet would be bed-ridden with crippled knees, ruptured discs, chronic constipation, shortness of breath and kidney failure. Turkeys cannot take off. Take a glass of tepid water and scale it up by a million. What would you have? A star like the Sun. **Scaling laws** are so ubiquitous that any adult ignorant of them is an ox blundering about in a minefield. We saw in Ch. 9 that men have had to fight throughout history just because of such a Scaling Law – 'the Square-Linear'. It is no exaggeration to say that any innumerate society equipped with VLCCs, Atom bombs , container ships and Free Trade will do for itself sooner or later. [Note 2)]

3 THE REWARDS OF NUMERACY

are as various and subtle as those of Literacy. Here are some:

Numeracy:

(a) Encourages us to grow up philosophically and away from the childish need to brand arguments as either "Absolutely Right" or "Absolutely Wrong" towards "Which is stronger and which is weaker" .Thus it encourages a measured (civilized) approach to both thinking and discourse.

(b) Is the face of Weighing and Balancing, the Common Sense method of reaching wise decisions.

(c) Introduces new categories of evidence into Common Sense Thought – Counting and Measuring.

(d) Constantly reminds us of the deep Scaling Laws which can dominate both social and physical worlds.

(e) Will be essential if we are to confront and overcome the environmental problems we have brought upon ourselves largely through ignoring numbers. For instance ‘How many people can a territory support sustainably? How many fish can we harvest from the sea? How much Carbon Dioxide can we vent safely into the sky? And how much will the sea level rise in consequence?’

(f) Enables us to break into new and unsuspected worlds, like Maxwell with his electromagnetic waves.

(g) Is the magic carpet which can transport the human mind to regions. where no other vehicle can – the centre of the Earth for instance (seismology), or the centre of the Sun where all our energy arises.

(h) Is essential to help us build and refine new tools, from bridges to airliners. Thus Heaviside’s simplified version of Maxwell (1890) speeded up telegraphy by a thousand times while Tsilkovsky’s mathematical analysis of the rocket (1903) foreshadowed Space travel.

(i) Is mandatory for any rational discussion of immigration and population. It. is far more about numbers than principles.(Ch. 9,16, 19)

(j) Expands and enlightens both the possibilities and limitations of commerce. Without Discounted Cash Flow Analysis we cannot make wise long-term investment decisions; without algebra estimate the Sunken Costs of Free Trade; without Calculus sense the peril of an arms-race (Ch. 4)

(k) Helps us to winnow significant information out of the vast streams of data recorded nowadays.

(l) And, not least, it should lend us the self-confidence to challenge all those ‘experts’ who seek to overawe us with their imagined numerical tech-wizardry. We’ve already outed Half Baked Economists [Ch.14] but the world is crawling with other simpletons and charlatans who would like to persuade us that they know better than we do – but who very often are deluding themselves – before deceiving us.

It is practically impossible for an innumerate person to become wise.

4 BUT WHAT IS NUMERACY?

Rather than arbitrarily writing down a syllabus of what the properly numerate adult ought to know I think it better to sift back through our history book and identify episodes that depended crucially on numerical arguments. For instance:

- The Square-Linear law of fighting (Ch.9).
- The ideal climate and the SLOT (Ch 1).
- Moon-power and civilization (Ch 2).
- Leverage and banking disasters (Ch. 13).
- The instability of Arms Races (Ch 4).
- Critical battles in WW2 (Ch.10)
- Common Sense and Odds (Ch 5).
- Oil-tanker disasters (Ch 15).
- Discounted Cash Flow Analysis (Ch.25)

And so on; readers can make their own selection. Then, from that selection, a numerate person could list the specific numerical skills we would all need to know. Without going into detail I conclude that:

(i) Numeracy must comprise more than just Pure Mathematics; it must include some fundamental scientific concepts including:

- The Laws of Motion
- Heat and Energy

- Dimensions and Units.[Note 4]

These matters fall under what is nowadays called 'STEM' (Science, Technology, Engineering & Maths)

(ii) Mathematically it must go at least as far as Ordinary Differential Equations and their solutions in simple cases. This means a fair amount of Calculus.

(iii) Since Common Sense Thinking involves gambling one needs familiarity with Odds, Probabilities, Permutations and Combinations.

(iv) Given that so many problems which cannot be solved exactly can nevertheless be solved numerically using electronic means, I would include some limited experience of approximations, algorithms and computer-coding.

Whilst a Numeracy Certificate should be the ambition of every school leaver, facilities for adults to pick Numeracy up should be paramount. We must all become numerate; for ourselves, for our society, and for our planet. And we could.

5 HOW TO BECOME NUMERATE

Many Brits are proud to own that they are no good at maths – as if it were a nerdy, rather grubby activity best left to inferiors [In its ignorance my *Economist* newspaper sometimes refers to numerates as 'pointy- headed wonks'] It obviously has nothing to do with their level of intelligence; even Churchill was innumerate – but that nearly cost us WW2. To make up for his deficiency Churchill formed the closest of bonds with Frederick Lindemann who thereafter became Lord Cherwell, "the most powerful scientist in history" [1]. Lindemann's trick was to perform lightning-fast calculations in his head – which impressed Churchill and the other innumerates around the Cabinet table. The trouble was that many of those calculations were wildly wrong – and nearly cost us WW2. Lindemann's scientific contemporaries knew they were wrong but because Lindemann was Professor of Physics at Oxford no less, and such an intimate of the PM, they weren't attended to. Lindemann almost scuppered the development of radar in favour of dangling bombs on wires in front of enemy bombers (The Tizard Committee had to dissolve itself to get rid of him). (Note 3)

The reason so many Brits are innumerate is because of a basic misunderstanding that arose amongst the Ancient Greeks 2000 years ago. Greek geometers were obsessed with 'Proofs', watertight deductive arguments as to why certain propositions, such as Pythagoras' Theorem, were true. They were so delighted with their discovery of this power of Deduction that ever since Maths teachers have taught their pupils deductively, even though Deduction is an unnatural mode of thought for humans, even for creative mathematicians. Instead we use Common Sense Thinking, or *Induction*. Maths teachers have mistaken the grocery bill for the groceries, legalism for morality (See quote from Kline heading this chapter0. Thus they have put off 80 generations of children who naturally rebelled. What a tragedy – almost on the same scale as Christianity [Note 5].

Once we recognise that misunderstanding it shouldn't be hard to put it right and help nearly everybody to become properly numerate. I know because I have taught higher mathematics deductively in a university Maths department – where it was almost a complete failure, and the *same mathematics* inductively in a Physics department, where it was almost a complete success. Once they could use their natural inductive methods of thinking students found they could get their heads round the toughest mathematical ideas (e.g. Vector Calculus and Maxwell's Equations – see above) because the reward (revelation) was more than worth the effort – far more. It was a pleasure to watch their faces light up, their young bodies literally grow in stature [By contrast the Mathematics students shrank and half of them failed to get Honours degrees. Ironically many of those 'failures' would go on to teach mathematics in schools, so handing on failure and innumeracy from generation to generation.]

Alas one is not going to change the mathematics profession, or its teaching methods, overnight. But there has to be a way. We cannot afford to remain innumerate in an ever complexifying world. Fortunately Mathematics is peculiarly well suited to on-line teaching. So I would propose:

(a) Issuing a national syllabus for what every properly numerate adult should be expected to know. (Note 5)
(b) Holding exams for a nationally recognized Diploma in Numeracy.
(c) Rewarding every individual (of whatever age) who obtains the Diploma an immediate cash award of *at least* £5,000, better £15,000.
(d) Reserving many plum jobs in government employment, and elsewhere, for those so qualified.

If you suppose that would be impractical recall that at present:

(i) British children attend school for a dozen years at a cost of about £5,000 per annum – and yet mostly emerge innumerate.
(ii) British university students pay about £30,000 each just in tuition fees and yet mostly still emerge innumerate.

So the average, and innumerate Brit, is still costing £75,000 to educate (half now go to university). If only 10 % are numerate now (optimistic) each one of those is costing society approaching £750,000. That of course is an exaggeration because there are other values to education – Literacy for instance. But if numeracy is something like one third of the aim then we are wasting over £200,000 per citizen at present. Thus even a cash reward of £15,000 per Diploma in Numeracy would be an amazing bargain.

6. BUT WHAT ABOUT NATIVE ABILITY?

The other obstacle to progress is the lazy assumption that only a few have a native faculty for mathematics whilst the rest are born dumb. In fact, given the right stimulus, all of us can numerise loud and clear. I've seen it as a teacher, have experienced a mathematical epiphany myself. As a child I suffered from two phobias: of Mathematics and Spiders – the last as the result of a horrific experience when I was 4. So, like many with a phobia, I read everything I could find about spiders, and poked under the bed at night before getting in, in case there was a monster there drooling in the shades. But then, at age 14 I came across an alleged mathematical proof that spiders could never grow beyond a modest size (it was a Scaling Law). Unfortunately I was hopeless at Mathematics (114th out of 120 in my year at school). But in the circumstances it did seem worth trying to understand the spider-proof. After a two-day struggle the penny dropped. Nightmare spiders vanished from my life forever and within weeks I was easily top of my entire year at Maths. Mathematics, you see, is an inspirational subject like music or poetry. You just need the right stimulus "… to hear the horns of elfland faintly play".

7 IN CONCLUSION

From the battles of Ancient Rome to modern banking disasters, from astronavigation to philosophy, we have seen what a powerful, if often unseen role, Numeracy, and its opposite, have played in British history.

Numeracy is the Seventh Pillar of Progress – or Wisdom one might say. [A useful mnemonic to recall them all quickly is 'CHANTL(i)D' standing for : Curiosity, Honesty, Adaptability, Numeracy, Tolerance, L(iteracy), and Democracy].

At a certain level (the 3 R's) Brits are aware of the importance of Numeracy. But, through a 2,000-year-old misunderstanding, they have allowed the maths-teaching profession to seriously muck up their children's education. If they want to they could easily put things right. To do so might cost £100 million a year. But that is a mere trifle compared to some large infrastructure projects which could never hope to electrify a whole society to anything like the same extent. For instance:

HS2 Rail	~	£88 Billion (2019
Cross Rail B.	~	15.4 Billion (2019)
Third runway Heathrow	~	£15 Billion (2019)
Enumerating an entire generation (30 years).	~	£3 Billion
Enumerating whole nation.	~	£6 Billion

NOTES

NOTE 1 You can see just how foolish allowing colossal oil tankers is by following the inquiry into the *Sea Empress* disaster. Once again the best way to analyse things is to look into critical timescales. To be safe any pilot, or indeed any safe driver, must have plenty of time to steer out of trouble. Driving too fast, or slowing down one's reactions with drink, can be fatal. Obviously. But the maritime authorities in Britain will not concede that. A VLCC pilot is expected to make every decision perfectly, every time. As I say it's madness. But the authorities can't see that. They're innumerate! Follow the story at https://tinyurl.com/y8a7aoqr.

NOTE 2 The Sun has been shining unabated for about five thousand million years! That seems miraculous until you realize, *gram for gram*, it is giving off no more heat than a tepid glass of water. How come then that it looks like a fiery furnace, not like a glass of tepid water? It's a Scaling Law! They're everywhere. They control every aspect of our lives. Do you understand them? Once you do they make life so much more interesting![See the book *Scaling* by Geoffrey West on Kindle]

NOTE 3 It was CP Snow[2], the famous novelist of science, who called Lindemann "The most powerful scientist who ever lived " and he was right. The 'Prof' as he liked to be called amongst his country-house friends, was both hero and villain. In WW1 he worked out why so many aircraft went into the death spins which killed one in 5 trainee plots. Then *theoretically only*, he worked out how to pull out safely. Then he had himself taught to fly. Then, without a parachute, he put his plane into a spin and lived to tell the tale; the first pilot ever to deliberately so do and survive. He was incredibly brave and all pilots have been grateful to him ever since; I know I am. Churchill greatly admired courage so that is why he made the Prof his most trusted ally and closest friend between the wars and during WW2. But Lindemann was also a dangerous man to associate with. He turned on almost all his family, his friends and his former associates like Tizard, who had originally got him his chair at Oxford. He wasn't much of a scientist but loathed anyone who disagreed with him. As such he did more harm to the British war effort than any other German bar Hitler; a fascinating but repellent character. You can read about him in *"Prof"* by Adrian Fort.

NOTE 4 UNITS. Scientists and Engineers continually make 'back-of-the-envelop' (BOE) calculations to see if some idea is feasible or not. They can be extremely crude, involving little more than the dimensions and units of the phenomenon concerned. Only if the crude calculation looks promising need one consider the idea any further. Thus such calculations are a first filter for separating good ideas from bad, surely something we *all* need. Consider a dramatic example`; the Industrial `Revolution worked only because a small amount of heat can generate a vast amount of mechanical energy. If you know your units (calories and ergs here) a BOE calculation reveals that the energy required to heat some water by only one degree Centigrade could instead lift it upwards half a kilometre! That is why very crude steam engines could pump out deep mines, power factories, drive railways and ships – but if you use the wrong units (which alas they teach at school and university) all this magic remains concealed. **Every wise person must be able to do back-of-the-envelope calculations on a daily basis.**

NOTE 5. Deduction plays an important role in Mathematics, because that subject has to be *self-consistent*, which is what Deduction is all about. Even so it can be greatly exaggerated. Mathematicians understandably like to have 'proofs' that what they are saying is unequivocally true. Unfortunately many such proofs have turned out to be flawed when examined by subsequent generations – who know more mathematics. So wise *users* of Mathematics expect no more absolute certainty in Mathematics than they can expect in the other arguments they have to employ. In other words the uncertainty involved in not having a definitive proof is often a quite acceptable gamble. Once that is conceded the necessity to teach mathematics deductively, which is so unnatural and so unsuccessful, evaporates. There is an enlightening and very readable discussion of this whole situation in Morris Kline's wonderful *"Mathematics, The Loss of Certainty*" 1986 OUP. In the following link I show how one very important mathematical result (All triangles contain two right-angles) can be taught either deductively or inductively, and you can decide which is best for yourself. See
https://tinyurl.com/yya7q8dk

.

HISTORY OF THE BRITS

CHAPTER 16

POPULATION & IMMIGRATION:THE NUMBERS

"Dear me, let us hope it is not true. But if it is true, let us hope it does not become widely known."

Bishop of Worcester's wife upon hearing of Darwin's Theory of Evolution.

1 INTRODUCTION

This whole area is so fraught with hysteria that I intend to divide the discussion into two. In this chapter I will stick exclusively to numbers, expressing no views as to whether this or that aspect of the issue has been, or is either good or bad for Britain – that will come later (Ch.19). If this seems like ducking the issue it is actually the numbers which turn out to be vital. Whatever our opinions might be about, say immigration, they will, and should be, informed by the numbers involved – over which, at present, there is almost total confusion – if not deliberate obfuscation.

Consider the following four statements:

a). 'The present immigration level is only half a percent a year.'

b) 'About 300,000 new immigrants are coming to and remaining in Britain every year.'

c) 'Incoming migrants are replacing every other native Brit who dies.'

d) 'The present immigration rate is so high that it is equivalent to 3 British mothers out of 4 having an extra child'.

Which of the above statements are true and which are not? Take a pause to think about the question, then ask yourself which of them might affect your opinions about immigration.

LONG PAUSE FOR THOUGHT

Whether or not any of the above statements is exactly true or not, the fact is that *they are all equivalent*. If any one is true so are they all. Although I am an experienced mathematician I found myself a little shell-shocked by that. Indeed, it took me weeks of calculation and reflection to arrive at that conclusion, and even more weeks to check that it is right. Demography, which is our subject here, is a profound matter, as well as a driving force in History. It merits some deep thought because it cannot but help dominate world and British politics for centuries to come – whether one likes it or not.

2 HISTORY OF THE BRITISH POPULATION

As I was taught it, we Brits are descended from waves of immigrants from the East, the North, the South, even from the West: Celts, Romans, Angles, Saxons, Jutes, Friesians, Vikings, Normans, Flemings, Huguenots, Irish …and so on. But modern evidence[1] reveals that 70% of our DNA is inherited from ancestors already living on the main island before 4000 BC. In other words we are nearly all Welsh. Just because revolutionary ideas such as agriculture and printing arrived from elsewhere does not mean that many farmers or printers did. Ideas can fly.

Reliable numbers are hard to come by, especially before 1800 A.D., but Table (16:1) gives what I hope is a fairly reliable, if not precise, account of the combined population of our main island from about 8,000 BC to the present.

Much before 8000 BC the climate was glacial while about 6500 BC Doggerland, which joined East Anglia to the continent, was inundated by rising sea levels, leaving Britain an island, hard if not impossible, to reach with Stone Age technology.

TABLE (16:1)

BRITISH POPULATION THROUGH HISTORY

1	2	3	4	5	6
Time	Population	Ratio increase	No. of generations	b	Life Expectancy.
8000 BC	100 - 1000				
		15	90	2.06	~ 35 y
5,000 BC	~ 5,000				
		200	150	2.07	, ,,
0 AD	~ 1 M.				
		5	50	2.06	~35
1600 AD	5 M				
		2.2	6	2.3	~ 40y
1800	11 M				
		4.5(6)[2]	5	2.7	40-60y
1950	50M(+15)[2]				
		1.3(1.08)	2	2.3(2.08)	65-80y
2015	67M(-13)[3]				
Averaged Overall		160,000	400	2.06	

NOTES :The raw data are contained only in columns 2 & 6. The other numbers are inferred from them.

Superscripts: [2] allows for the 15M Brits who emigrated during that interval while [3] subtracts the 13 M foreign-born Brits who have recently arrived. For b see (c) below.

Crude though it is, Table (16:1) gives much for food for thought. For instance:

(a) Some 400 generations (~33 years each) stretch from Doggerland days to the present (bottom line).

(b) If there were between 100 and 1,000 ancestors here in Doggerland days then each one has given rise to no less than 160,000 descendants today.(Bottom line).

(c) Over our entire history the average British mother has successfully raised – to breeding age 2.06 children (Col. 5) barely above the replacement rate of 2.00 (bottom line). How do we reconcile this 2.06 with the 160,000 above?

(d) That breeding rate (call it 'b' in future) only begins to rise significantly above 2.00 in 1600 A.D. (to 2.3) then rises significantly again in 1800 (to 2.8) before falling back again (2.08) since 1950. What conceivable reasons might explain these trends?

Let's with the question implied in (b). Since humans raise their young as mated pairs the population multiplier X from generation to generation is not b but b/2 , not say 2.06, but 1.03. Thus after 400 generations the British population will have increased roughly by a factor: $1.03 \times 1.03 \times 1.03 \times 1.03$ …. 400 times. According to my phone calculator 1.03^{400} equals 136,424! It is an enormous factor, almost the 162,000 we mentioned. Here we see the fatal magic of 'Exponential Growth' – so called because of the 'exponent'– 400 here. Multipliers only marginally above 1.00, when propagated over many generations, can give rise to immense numbers. This is the First Law of

Demography, the First Law of History, the First Law of Zoology, the First Law of Ecology, the First law of Biology, ...indeed the First Law of Nature.

THE FIRST LAW OF NATURE
Populations of things or creatures which grow (or decay) exponentially can have apocalyptic effects – unless checked after so many generations.

To see just how critical, how fine-tuned the multiplying factor X must be let us change it very slightly and see how X^{400} changes:

TABLE (16:2)

EXPONENTIAL BREEDING CONSEQUENCES

b	X	N	X^N	Population after N generations ; P(0)= 333
2.02	1.01	400	53	17,000
2.04	1.02	400	2,800	1 Million
2.06	1.03	,,	140,000	50 Million
2.08	1.04	,,	6.5 M	2 Billion
2.10	1.05	,,	3 Bn.	1 Trillion
2.75	1.37	,,	5×10^{54}	Popln, weighs more than entire Universe
1.98	0.99	,,		32 people
1.96	0.96	,,		extinct

No wonder that the average breeding rate b of British women over the past 10,000 years is 2.06 precisely. Had it been anything else this would not be Britain . At 2.08 a quarter of the worlds present population would be living here; at 2,04 only 1 million, while at 1.96 we would now be extinct! If one even tickles the mean breeding rate b, in the long run the result will be dramatic – either way. That is the nature of exponential growth (EG).

Precisely because EG is so dramatic one has to be extremely cautious in interpreting table (16:1) . It does *suggest* however, rather surprisingly, that nothing much changed Britain's gradual growth all the way through from 8000 BC to 1600 A.D – not agriculture, not iron , not plague, not invasion, not even the Romans, the Angles or the Normans. But then something changed around 1600 A.D. (when fortuitously our history book begins). First it rose from its archaeological value of 2.06 to 2.3, then it shot up around 1800 to nearly 3, before subsiding back again to 2.08 in 1950. Intriguing, it is all too easy to explain in multifarious, probably spurious, ways: in particular we have to be aware of the "Noise " introduced by the short epochs into which I have divided the table in recent times – into only a few generations compared to the 400 overall. Such temporary fluctuations may have occurred throughout the past– before being swallowed up, averaged out, in history (e.g. the Black Death 1350 AD) . All we can safely conclude is that typical Welsh mums and dads have left just a tiny fraction over 2.00 surviving children behind.

3 EXPONENTIAL GROWTH IN GENERAL

Quite apart from human demography, exponential growth (EG.) is such an important yet slippery mathematical concept to grasp that it needs discussing more generally, and in different contexts. For example:

- Money invested at compound interest grows exponentially: the more there is the faster it naturally accumulates each year.
- Virtually all wild animal population can grow exponentially because the more mothers there are, the more offspring .Thus to recover from a plague of rinderpest the wildebeest population of the Serengeti has

grown exponentially in recent decades to over one million[4] .EG is a necessary recovery strategy from dramatic setbacks and will continue until it runs into controlling factors such as disease, starvation, predation, parasites, warfare.... Some sort of balance is reached only when the various competing factors come into equilibrium. The only species I know of smart enough to control its own population is the Sulphur Crested Cockatoo of Australia. Very long-lived birds with few predators , they live in fiercely territorial bands of a hundred or so. If they were to breed freely they'd starve. Instead, within each territory, there are a small number of designated nesting sites; if a couple can't bag one that season, they don't breed.

- The most dramatic example of exponential growth is the atom bomb. From time to time Uranium (U_{235}) atoms split spontaneously, giving off much energy, and two free neutrons – each one capable of splitting another uranium nucleus. Providing you squeeze enough of them tightly together (a 'Critical Mass') a chain reaction will start– then Bang! That's EG, that's explosive growth if you like.
- Interfering in exponential growth is a tricky business– whether in bomb design or fishery control. Mankind has inadvertently screwed up the natural world time and again by interfering in it. Through killing wolves, he allowed deer to multiply and destroy much of the pre-existing ecosystem in both Europe and North America. By killing sea otters for fur, he allowed sea urchins to destroy the kelp forests off the coast of North America which supported so much else[4]. And by miscalculating how many fish could be taken, he recently (1970s) destroyed the Newfoundland Cod Fishery, one that had fed Europe for 500 years

The problem with exponential growth in general, is that tiny, initially imperceptible percentages, can, in the long term, have dramatic, even apocalyptic consequences. People who could not calculate those long-term consequences thus did much harm to themselves – and to other creatures. So rather than talk about 'Percentage growth' (Or decay) it is more helpful to think in terms of 'Doubling Times' ('Halving Times') , the time it takes for an exponentially growing population of something, be they fruit-flies or Sperm-whales, to double (or halve) in size. There is a useful relation between the two:

$$Doubling\ Time = \frac{70}{\%\ annual\ growth} \qquad (16:1)$$

Which generates the following:

TABLE (16:2A)

EXPONENTIAL GROWTH (OR DECAY)

Annual % growth (decay)	Doubling (halving Time
1%	70 y: Brit. Pop .incl. Immig.
2%	35 years: Brit GDP
3%	23y. Safe equities
5%	14 y: Stock Exchange
7	10 y: China GDP
13.5%	5 y: Banker's Equity

Historians like me who tell stories stretching back dozens, even hundreds of generations , must be exquisitely aware of exponential growth and how tampering with even minute rates of growth can have historic, even apocalyptic consequences.

4 THINKING ABOUT IMMIGRATION

One's attitude towards immigration is, or ought to be, informed by how much of it we think is going on. But what do we mean by "How much"? Describing immigration in terms of hundreds of thousands per year, and then comparing it with the existing population of about 67 million, is completely fallacious, because one is a rate, the other is a total. One has to compare either rates with rates, or totals with totals: that is *fundamental*!

So, what other rates are there for comparison with the roughly 300,000 migrants a year presently coming to stay in the UK:

There is the death rate ~ 600,000/Year

There is the birth rate ~ 600,000/Year ; (~ means 'Roughly equal').

So, in terms of rates:

- Immigrants are replacing ~ half of all Brits who die.

  OR

- For every two British babies born ~ one immigrant is arriving.

To my mind these are pretty startling comparisons – more than unexpected. They imply, at the very least, that the whole composition of the British population will be completely altered in a single generation or two, from largely Welsh to largely foreign.

If you don't like rates then the alternative is to think in total numbers, not numbers per year– but numbers arriving over a lifetime – which is about 80 years in Britain at present. 300,000/year then translates into 80×300,000 which is 24 Million, more than a third of the existing population (67 million) and almost half of the native born (54 million). Now the rates-approach, and the total- number-approach are tending to agreement. They both imply that in one lifetime the demographic composition of this island will change more than it has over the past 10,000 years. And who can say what the numbers will be in two lifetimes (160 years)? According to all the evidence, immigration rates tend to increase with the size of the existing diaspora, and so they accelerate spectacularly[5]. In parliamentary constituencies with a significant immigrant fraction MP's surgeries are already taken up 95% of the time by existing immigrants trying to get more of their relatives into the country[5].

When we scientists are faced, as we often are, with an awkward problem concerning rates and totals, we try to write down and solve equations which capture the *essence* of that problem, and thereby to understand, in an intuitive way, what is really going on. But Mathematical Modelling, as it is called, is as much an art as a science. Having been such a modeller for half a lifetime I ruefully admit that it is all too easy to fall in love with one's own model – and then to be led , and to lead others, into folly, even tragedy. Thus Malthus (1798) made his population model too simple, unwittingly condemning the Victorian poor to abject misery [Ch.14]. Thus the Club of Rome (1970s) made their world resources model too complicated and were betrayed into an egregious folly by a glitch in just one of their too numerous subroutines (algorithms).

The challenge of modelling is to capture the essence of the process, not the detail. With the essence grasped one can reach an intuitive and hopefully reliable understanding of what is going on, which can be tested against the evidence, and which can be used to predict what is likely to happen in future. At that point one can almost throw the model away and put into words what one has learned. And that can be convincing, as I hope you will find here. [Note 1]

Think of the average British man. In only 2 of his 80 years will he contribute to changes in the population: the year he is born and the year that he dies. Likewise think of the average British woman: in only four of her 80 years does she contribute to a change in the total: her birth year, her death year and the 2.06 years when she becomes a new mother. Now think of arriving immigrants: new ones arrive in *every one* of the 80 years in question. That is how they could swamp the natives in pretty short order.[Note1]

There is a less emotive way to look at the subject. Imagine there was no immigration, but instead the native Brits decided to expand their own population at the same rate as presently results from immigration. What proportion of British mums would need to have an extra child? Here, according to my model, is the answer:

TABLE (16:3)

IMMIGRATION RATE versus EXTRA BIRTH-RATE

Immigration rate/annum	Proportion of mums needed to raise an extra child
100,000	1 out of 4
200,000	2 out of 4
300,000	3 out of 4
400,000	All

It turns out, because only half the population can have babies, that to fully appreciate the implications of immigration you have to multiply the immigration rate I, not by the lifetime T but by *twice* that number i.e. by 2T (~160 years) and so reach $2\times 160 \times 300{,}000 = 48\ Million$ – which sounds pretty apocalyptic to me. If, without immigration the breeding rate is b per female per lifetime, with immigration it effectively rises to

$$b + \frac{2IT}{P} \quad \text{where P is the existing population.} \qquad (16:2)$$

So $\frac{2IT}{P} \sim 160\, I/P$, which we will call B, is the *immigration index* which leads to Table(16:4) below. In other words the intergenerational multiplier big X we used in section 2 now becomes :

$$X = 1/2\left[b + \frac{2IT}{P}\right] \qquad (16:3)$$

Then, if the breeding rate b remains close to 2.0 for the indigenes, the future population of Britain will be decided almost entirely by the immigration index B (= 2IT/P). So, if one looks ahead five and 10 generations then at the present rate of immigration (and if immigrants are assumed to have the same breeding-ratio as indigenes), we can expect:

TABLE (16:4)

FUTURE COMPOSITION OF BRITAIN v IMMIGRATION RATE

1	2	3	4	5	6
Immig. Rate	Im. Index	Multiplier	In 5 gen	In 10 gen	% Indigenes
I	B = 2IT/P	X	X^5	X^{10}	
25,000	0.067	1.033	1.2	1.4	83
50,000	0.133	1.067	1.4	1.9	34
100,000	0.27	1.133	1.9	3.5	22
200,000	0.53	1.27	3.3	11	9
300,000	0.75	1.37	4.8	23	3
400,000	1.07	1.53	8.5	73	1%

Any talk of Britain being "*swamped by immigration*" is usually dismissed as racist hysteria, but looking across the penultimate row, closest to the existing situation, in five generations time people of British descent, who make up 86% of the population now, could make up only 86/4.8 = 18% of the island's population of around 400 million by then. That sounds very much like swamping to me. And look down the last column for 10 generations ahead.

. These calculations are of course somewhat simplified – any useful model has to be so, but the only simplification I have made is to assume that the immigration-index will remain constant, i.e. that the immigration rate will rise or fall in proportion to the current population – after all you would expect a larger population would accept more immigrants in proportion, so that the ratio I/P , presently 0.5% per annum, will neither rise nor fall [In practice one would expect it to actually rise as the foreign diaspora took up an increasingly large fraction of the whole population, turning the immigration-laws to their own advantage[5].] So the estimated effects of immigration in Table (16:4) are probably underestimates, perhaps significantly so.

NB: Having seen in Table (16:2) the dramatic effects of tinkering with the breeding ratio b, we cannot be surprised by the dramatic effects of immigration. Equation (16:2) reveals that immigration does exactly that: 300,000 a year corresponds to a b of 2.75 and see row in Table (16:2) corresponding to that – a population heavier than the entire Universe !!

5 REDUCING THE POPULATION

Later, I will argue that to preserve any reasonable part of the world's ecosystems human populations everywhere will have to be dramatically reduced in the long run. So, if Britain is going to set an example it will have to reduce its own even faster. How fast could it realistically do so, and how would immigration/emigration affect the matter? The maths is almost the same as in the last section [Note 1] with breeding rate b (indigenous) now less than two, and the immigration factor 2IT/P being either positive (net immigration) or negative (net emigration). There has always been some emigration (at rate E pa.) from Britain– principally to join families in other emptier parts of the

Commonwealth such as Canada and Australia, and that could well continue. Thus the immigration index B will become 2(I-E)T/P (instead of 2IT/P)

So let us estimate future populations under different assumptions:

TABLE (16:5)

POPULATION CONTRACTION UNDER DIFFERENT CONDITIONS

1	2	3	4	5	6	7	8	9
1	b	I	E	Index B	X	X^2	X^4	P(4 gen)
2	1.5	50,000	50,000	0	0.75	0.56	0.32	20 M.
3	1.5	50,000	0	0.13	0.833	.78	0.32	37 M.
4	1.3	0	0	0	0.69	0.42	0.18	10 M.
5	1.3	50,000	0	0.133	0.78	0.61	0.37	20 M.
6	1.3	300,000	50,000	0.67	0.98	0.97	0.93	56 M.
7	1.3	0	50,000	-0.13	0.37	0.13	0.02	1 M.
8	1.3	25,000	0	.067	0.68	0.46	0.21	14 M
9	1.0	0	0	0	0.5	0.25	0.06	3 M.
10*	2.0	300,000	0	0.75	1.37	1.88	3.5	236 M

*See Note 5

Don't be daunted by the table; it's worth careful study because it is both informative and, I think, inspiring. Col (6) is simply the generational multiplier X derived from the previous 4 cols; Col (7) shows the fractional population left after two generations (66 years), Col.(8) after 4 (130 years). The last column is the consequent estimated population of Britain 4 generations from now

The highly encouraging outcome is that we could drastically reduce our island population within two generations without resorting to anything draconian – such as a 'One Child Policy', *provided* we simultaneously curb immigration. Some existing European populations already have natural breeding rates as low as 1.3[6]. But if we don't curb immigration at the same time then the drop with take well over four generations , by which time the population that remains will be almost entirely of immigrant descent.[Compare Rows 6 & 7]

6 CAPITAL & IMMIGRATION

is a subject rarely mentioned in polite company – but it ought to be, if only because of the numbers. The canary in the mine here is the current housing shortage, particularly in immigrant-rich communities such as London (below).

Britain's capital wealth has been accumulated over many generations and resides in several forms including housing, roads, sewers, power stations, factories, ports, railways, water systems, wires, pipes, schools, hospitals, pubs, libraries, shops, agricultural land, mines, parks, forests, wells, police, local governments, waste disposal, fisheries, surgeries, dentists, defences… to say nothing of education, training and know-how…. – all factors which contribute massively to citizens', health, wealth and happiness [Note 2]. Few immigrants bring much of these factors with them, so when they arrive to stay we are, in effect, handing each one a cheque, a share of our capital wealth. How large it is is contestable but according to one recent UN report (Written by economists, so beware), the average Brit's accumulated wealth is about $ 200,000 (which I believe is a gross underestimate – see Note 2, I think it's more nearly £1M. each) . So when a migrant family of 4 arrives here the UK is handing them a massive cheque . I don't suppose many Brits realise that, because it is not talked about. But let's do a little calculation:

If the average Brits' per capita wealth is W, and they give one portion of it away to each incoming migrant, which is unavoidable, then:

Total capital handed to new migrants each year = $I \times W$

Whereas fraction accumulated (at g% pa.) = $W \times P \times g \div 100$

And if Brits were agreeable to giving away only a fraction f of their annual wealth accumulating, then the immigration rate I should be such that:

$$I \times W < f \times W \times P \times g \div 100 \qquad (16:4)$$

'where $<$ ' *simply means 'less than'* (NB the W's cancel)

giving rise to the following numbers:

TABLE (16.:6)

LOSS OF NATIONAL CAPITAL PER CAPITA DUE TO IMMIGRATION

g (%)	Fraction agreeable f	Max. immigration rate
1%*	0.5	< 300,000
1%*	0.1	< 60,000
1%*	0.01	< 6,000

*The UN estimate, for what it is worth, was 0.9%.

Perhaps the easiest way to read this table is to say that at present Brits are probably giving away to new immigrants something like half of all the wealth they are accumulating. Whether or not they are agreeable to that is not for me to say here. This chapter is only about numbers. In any case they haven't been asked.

HOUSING : The canary in the mine here I would suggest is housing. There are ~ 24M. dwellings in the UK and 67M. people, implying ~ 3 per dwelling. If a typical dwelling has a lifetime ~ 100 years we need to build homes at a rate 24M./100 or 240,000 a year just to replace obsolete stock. Since

1920 we've managed to achieve that rate in only a few years (fullfact.org). Adding ~ 300,000 new immigrants a year calls for *another* ~ 100,000 new dwellings a year . Therefore many of our children cannot expect to have homes of their own. It's happening (According to Shelter there are at present 280,000 homeless people in Britain, whilst large numbers of adult children are still living with their parents*). But nobody talks about the immigrant dimension.(e.g. The *Economist*'s Briefing on the Housing Shortage of Jan 2020 *never mentioned Immigration once*. If you ask me that's totally dishonest; totally.) See the bishop's wife.

The proportion of 15-34 y.o. s living with their parents has risen from 34%(1990) to 44% (2018) in the UK ['statistica'* on web]

7 SUMMARY

Any discussion of population and immigration which doesn't take numbers into account is worthless. Who sensible would argue that all or any immigration is either wholly good or wholly bad – surely it is a question of how much; and that takes some *calculating:*

We have found that:

a) Indigenous Brits have largely descended from a few hundred hunter-gatherers who were stranded here when Doggerland was inundated around 6500 BC. There is thus no way Brits can argue that they are especially talented people who got here because of, for instance, their seafaring enterprise. The silly buggers were simply cut off. Lucky devils!

b) Subsequent invasions must have been more of ideas than people. Ideas can obviously fly.

c) The indigenous British population is approximately 400 generations old.

d) So as to make up for occasional setbacks such as plagues and droughts all animal populations must be able to grow exponentially. Such is the nature of exponential growth however that minute rates of growth or decline can lead eventually to apocalyptic changes in population. We all need an intuitive grasp of this vital process. [See Box above]

e) Many debates about immigration policy are confused, and have led to shouting matches, because educated but innumerate people have confounded immigration rates with population numbers and so have *dramatically underestimated* the long term effects of immigration. To compare a rate with a number one must first multiply the rate by *twice the life expectancy of the existing population* – 160 years in Britain. Thus the current rate of roughly 300,000 immigrants a year corresponds to a total number of 48 million migrants! This dramatic multiplier, which was by no means obvious, needs most careful thought – and acknowledgement.

NB The intergenerational Population Multiplier is

$$X = \frac{b+B}{2} \quad where\ \ B = 2IT/P \qquad (16:5)$$

$where\ B\ is\ asuumed\ to\ be\ roughly\ constant\ throughout$

(The 2 arises because only the female half of the indigenous population breeds so the fair ratio of immigration to breeding has to be I/(P/2) = 2I/P while the T converts a rate into a number.)

f) Britons are comparatively wealthy; immigrants are comparatively poor – which is mostly why they come. Thus, immigration must necessarily drain the *per capita* accumulated *wealth* of a host country. People don't talk about this. Thus the present immigration rate is halving the UK's annual accumulation of wealth – which is a very slow process.[Note 3].

This is already showing up in the present housing crisis – the canary in the mine.

g) The great news is that we can, if we want to, reduce our present population to a sustainable level (less than 20 million?) in only two generations without any need for draconian restrictions such as a One Child policy, *provided* we now halt immigration almost entirely. Because of the aforesaid 160, *small numbers of immigrants arriving per year are , in this context, equivalent to large numbers of extra babies*. Every citizen should understand that. It is not obvious, but it is absolutely spinal! [Note 4]

h) Allowing innumerate people to continue running the UK could be catastrophic, not only for Britain but for the entire ecosystem. If the Brits cannot set an example by reducing their population……..

i) It becomes obvious how Baducation alone could ruin any society [Ch.20]

NOTES

1 My mathematical model of population growth and immigration has to rely on some second year Calculus, thus I haven't put it in the text. But all numerate readers can and probably should check it out at

2 https://tinyurl.com/s2phqok

3

After all if it is wrong , so will be much else in this chapter. *I believe it makes the perfect case for why most of us must become numerate, and certainly why we shouldn't elect innumerate people to govern us* [Ch.15]. I suspect we've got into this mess because our leaders were and are incapable of understanding what is going on around them. That terrifies me. [Ch.15]. Have you ever been driven by a drunk?

2 The Capital Wealth of a nation must be distinguished from its GDP, which is merely an annual *rate*. Britain's GDP is approximately 2 Trillion £/pa. Its

housing stock is presently valued at £7T., the Stock exchange at £4T, its education, training and know-how as *at least* £6T. But that total of £17T. is a gross underestimate of the whole because most of the infrastructure is missing while a stock-market valuation is no fair measure of how much it took to actually build a power station say, reflecting only the present-day annual profit to be wrung from it. To reconstruct Britain as is, might cost 2 to 5 times as much, so my own very rough estimate of Britain's total wealth is between 30 and 80 £T. The UN estimate (by economists!) was only £10T. If I am right then our *per-capita* wealth is not $200,000 but more nearly £1M. No wonder immigrants are queuing up to come. I would.

3 The UN is suggesting we are accumulating national wealth at a rate of about 1% per annum. If true that suggest that it would take something like a century to accumulate, allowing for depreciation. Sounds roughly right to me.

REFERENCES

1 Cunliffe, B. 2012, *Britain Begins*, OUP.
2 Emigration of 15M. Brits between 1700 & 1875.
3 14% in UK and 36% in London are foreign born; *Migration Watch* website
4 Carroll, Sean, 2016, *The Serengetti Rules*, Ch.6; Princeton Univ. Press. The film based on it (BBC iPlayer) is a wonderful, sweeping account of Ecology and mankind's effects on his environment. Don't miss it.
5 Collier, Paul, 2013, *Exodus*, Ch. 2, Penguin. A lot of useful stuff in here about immigration and emigration, even though its written by an economist.
6 Spain & Italy already have breeding rates of 1.3 (World Bank, on line). Singapore's is 1.1; S. Korea's is 0.88; they are like Sulphur Crested Cockatoos. Good for them I say.

HISTORY OF THE BRITS

CHAPTER 17: INNOVATION

"But by far the greatest obstacle to the progress of science and the undertaking of new tasks and provinces therein is found in this – that men despair, and think things are impossible"

Francis Bacon, *Novum Organon*, 1604.

1 INTRODUCTION

Between 1875 and 1945 two thirds of all the transformative innovations (TIs) on Earth were pioneered by the Brits. Then the pattern abruptly changed, and America seized the Promethean fire. Why and how? These are questions that should concern thinkers everywhere. If we fail to understand, then a new Dark Age could steal through the cave entrance – it has before.

Many have sought for the secret, and some, often economist simpletons, have claimed to find it – though none convincingly. I propose to search using a method that has proved successful in pinning down the equally elusive Scientific Method. There I compiled a list of transformative discoveries, looking for patterns and discrepancies. Fashionable ideas didn't work – but something else certainly did.[Note 1]

Compiling a list of transformative innovations (TI's) , not just in science and engineering ('scieneering' for brevity henceforth), is not trivial. Some may be obvious (antibiotics) while others may seem at first obscure (VLSI). Then National or Racial Glory often trumpets unreliable claims: Popov didn't invent radio nor did the Wright Brothers pioneer powered flight. Then searching for the factors that led to a TI in a particular place and time may call for technical understanding (which many history- scholars lack), a good deal of digging, and a readiness to change one's mind. Calls for "Genius" most often reveal a lack of all three. Thus, Einstein didn't pluck Relativity out of thin air – he was merely one of two or three who couldn't resist its claims any longer [Note 2]. And, where vast sums are to be made out of patent ownership (e.g. Silicon Valley) beware of Big Law. Digging most often reveals that an idea has been floating about in several minds well before it was finally pinned down and put to reliable use. Yes, Fleming did discover the antibacterial properties of penicillin (1928), but it took several other minds and laboratories, on both sides of the Atlantic, to turn a mould into a wonder-drug (1944). Which individuals, and countries, deserve the honour?

Humans are naturally inventive creatures and I love coming upon new examples of ingenuity, especially among so-called 'primitives'. For instance:

- Innuits thrived almost within sight of the Pole because their womenfolk devised fur clothing insulated by controlled amounts of warm air, allowing them to hunt and fish out on the sea ice at 50°C below zero.
- Those same Innuits dealt with hungry and dangerous polar bears by feeding them spring-loaded bait. The bears digestive juices dissolved away the spring, exposing sharp bone spikes which pierced the creature's intestines – with fatal results.
- The aboriginal boomerang was designed to bring down flocking birds in flight, surely one of man's most ingenious inventions.
- Harmony among the Aborigines was preserved by law: mothers-in-law and sons-in-law were never allowed to speak to one another.
- To find honey an aborigine would catch a bee in his hand, then attach a long hair to its tail with spit. Thus handicapped the bee can be followed back to its nest. Then the hunter sends his wife up the tree to do the dangerous job of stealing the honey. Australians!

As a Space astronomer working at the cutting-edge, I have been peripherally involved in several innovations myself. A couple of anecdotes will illustrate the unpredictable and sometimes wry nature of the process:

In 1977, having complained too loudly, I was appointed to chair a committee to look into the future computing needs of British observational astronomers. Three of us astronomers, and three computer scientists, toured the community asking what our colleagues would need to do their research competitively. We devised a novel system of linked super-mini computers equipped with colour terminals able to display and manipulate complex images arriving from observatories both in Space and on the ground . No such system existed anywhere in the world at the time, so we had to devise much of it ourselves – including the smart coloured terminals. Called STARLINK (See refs) it quickly attracted a great deal of interest and funds [Note 4]. DEC, then the world's second largest computer corporation (now defunct, like so many) supplied the computers at well below list price. Their boss explained to me: "If your system works every goddamn multinational and bank in the world will want a copy – and we'll make billions." They did.

And so it came to pass. Now for the unexpected. A few weeks after it opened (1980) the STARLINK manager rang me:

"What are we going to do? Astronomers are using it to send messages all over the world to one another. We never envisaged that. Soon their traffic will overload all our connections. What should I do?"

It turned out that with a little money (which I had held back) we could speed up the whole network of connections. And so, as far as we knew at the time, the civilian Internet was born. No one invented it – certainly not me – but it came to transform the working lives of not just British astronomers, but of everyone. Furthermore, the computer-integrated colour terminals, which we specified but didn't design in detail, were designed and very successfully built by a small firm in Horsham in Sussex (Sigma Systems). Everybody who saw them in operation, including some influential Silicon-Valley types, were absolutely wowed. It wasn't long before nearly every Joe and Joan on the planet would have one on their desks.

At the time I also held a key position on the European side of the Hubble Space Telescope project . How was European astronomy to digest and exploit the expected avalanche of priceless cosmic data? It wasn't hard to persuade Europeans to copy STARLINK, nor to build The European Space Telescope Coordinating Facility (ESTCF) in Munich. It was largely out of the need and the expertise there that the Hubble Archive evolved. So now 30 years' worth of explorations of the Universe (still continuing) live on electronic files where they can be conveniently examined and exploited by anyone on the planet.

The point is that nobody foresaw, indeed could have foreseen, what eventuated. As much as anybody was, I was right in the vortex of all this, yet I was carried along with all the rest, like a beetle in a storm drain. Behind it all lay VLSI, (often spelt out as Moore's Law[22]).

As far as I can see, ours was the common experience. It is summed up by a quote in Buderi's wonderful book[23] : *"We invented all kinds of things (at the US Rad Lab – for wartime radar), not because we were so smart, but because we were the first people who had the problem."*

2 THEORIES OF INNOVATION

Many factors have been suggested. They include the following:

- Necessity (N) – The "Mother of invention".
- Capitalism (£) – private money to support and exploit innovation.
- Genius([G]) – of course, whatever that is supposed to be. Magic?
- Serendipity (S) – accidentally stumbling upon.
- Curiosity (C) – Pure and simple.

- War (W) : defeat, or its prospect, can lead to rapid change.
- Amelioration (A) – the unselfish desire to improve mankind's lot
- Evolution (E): one thing leading to another. Development may often be far more important than the initial idea; for example, in powered flight , electronic computers and mobile phones.
- Government (G): initiative, support and initial purchase.
- 'Good' Universities (U): i.e. ones well-funded in scieneering.
- Patent Law (P) : to preserve inventors' intellectual property rights.
- Rivalry (R): between individuals, groups or countries.
- Democracy (D).
- Infrastructure (I): permitting an innovation to thrive e.g. no motorcars without roads.
- Clusters (Cl) : of innovators working in close proximity and feeding off one another – e.g. Silicon Valley and the City of London.

3. MY TABLE OF TRANSFORMATIVE INNOVATIONS (1875 – 1975)

I have identified [Table (17:1)] 57 TIs for the chosen period , each assigned a number for purposes of identification, and a nationality [B = British, A = US, G = Germany, F = France, C = Canada, Sw = Switzerland, and Intl = International]. The last column contains various factors (by symbol) I identify as significant to each one's birth and success. They are not exclusive; several may play a role in each TI. Specifying nationalities is not always straightforward: Jim Watson was American– but did all his pioneering work on DNA in Britain, with British colleagues, so it goes down as B. Bakelund (Plastics) was Belgian but did all his work on plastics in America – so A. If I have a prejudice it probably lies (through ignorance) in undervaluing medical, agricultural and chemical innovations. There is certainly room to quibble. But as I am only interested in broad and decisive trends, mistakes at the margin shouldn't matter too much. In any case the many superscripted notes [Note 3] in the Table may help to clarify some issues as well as tell unexpected or hardly known stories about certain innovations. Readers may prefer to compose their own tables. Good luck with that: mine has involved several years of research – identifying reliable factors takes backbreaking digging in a field sown with mines laid by interested, or unqualified parties.

The list is confined to the century between 1875 and 1975 – the last because it leaves sufficient time to judge whether an innovation is transformative or not. And while it is hard enough to find out what really happened in 1950 it is harder still to separate fact from myth before 1850. I've had to change my mind several times, particularly when investigations led me down tangled byways to come upon discoveries which rather shocked me – the Wright Brothers (21) and Einstein (17) for instance.

TABLE(17:1) TRANSFORMATIVE INNOVATIONS (1875 – 1975)

DATE	NO.	INNOVATION	NAT.	FACTORS
1875	1	Completion London Sewer[1]	B	A G N
1876	2	Telephone	A	E £ P Bell R *
1877	3	Reinforced Concrete	F	N
1878	4	Electric Light Bulb	B	E P R I *
1884	5	Steam Turbine	B	(G)
1884	6	Machine Gun[2]	B	E W
1885	7	Safety Bicycle[3]	B	E I
1885	10	Motor Car	G	E I
1887	8	Radio Waves[4]	G	C U T *
1888	9	Pneumatic Tyre	B	E
1895	11	Cinema	F	E
1895	12	X-Rays	G	S
1895	13	Electron	B	C U
1899	14	Radioactivity	F	S
1900	15	Malarial Mosquito[5]	I	C U A R *
1901	18	Transatlantic Radio[7]	B	C E R £ P O *
1905	16	Electronics (Valves)	B/A	P R
1904/5	17	Special Relativity[6]	F/Sw.	C E R T *
1905	19	Plastics	A	C

1908	20	Deep Time[8]	B	C
1909	21	Powered Flight (Bleriot)[9]	F	R E *
1913	22	Atomic Nucleus	B	C U (G)
1915	23	The Tank	B	W G N
1922	24	Broadcasting	Intl.	T G I P *
1925	25	Quantum Mechanics[10]	Intl.	C T U *
1930	26	Jet Engine	B	T N £ S *
1931	27	Neutron	B	C U (G)
1930's	28	Television	B/A	E R £ G I BB *
1935	29	Autobahns	G	G
1937	30	Radar (Defence)[11]	B	W N G *
1936	31	Helicopter (Focke)	G	E
1938	32	Nuclear Fission	G	C
1940	33	Cavity Magnetron[12]	B	W N U *
1941	34	Asymmetric Gears[13]	B	S W N *
1942	35	Atomic Pile	A	W U G *
1942	36	Aqualung	F	E *
1943	37	Operational Research[14]	B	W N *
1944	38	Colossus (Elect. Computer)	B	W N G I *
1944	39	V 2 Rocket	G	W G N *
1944	41	Antibiotics[15]	B/A	C G P A I U S *
1945	40	Atom Bomb	B/A	W G R T *
1947	42	Radio Astronomy	Intl.	C W S
1948	43	Information Theory[16]	A	Bell
1952	44	Transistor	A	E W R Bell *
1953	45	DNA Structure[17]	B	C R U S *
1955	46	Solar Cell	A	E Bell
1957	47	Space Satellite	R	W G R *
1958	48	MOSFET/VLSI[18]	A	E Bell
1960	49	Plate Tectonics[19]	B/A/C	C W G U E S R *
1962	50	Open University	B	A G
1962	51	'Silent Spring'[20]	A	C
1965	52	Green Revolution	A	A £ *
1969	53	Packet Switching[21]	B/A	N G
1969	54	Moon Landing	A	W C E R £ G *
1969	55	CCD (Electronic Camera)	A	S E Bell
1970	56	Container Ship	A	£ I *
1960s	57	Birth Pill	A	A R *

KEY TO FACTORS:
A Amelioration
BB Big Business
Bell. Bell Telephone Lab.
C Curiosity, pure and simple
E. Evolution, development, one thing leading to another
G Government much involved
(G) Genius
I Infrastructure
N Necessity
R. Rivalry: Individual or group or national
S Serendipity: fortunately stumbling upon
U University significantly involved
W War
£. Money
* Challenge

Superscripts have explanatory notes[Note 3] for some individual Innovations.

4 OBVIOUS TRENDS IN THE TABLE

A) *BY NATIONALITY*

Britain (B) has made 23/57 TIs (40%)

America (A) has made 16/57 (28%)

Germany (G) Has made 7/57

France (F) has made 5.5/57

In addition only Italy (I), Canada (C), Russia (R) and Switzerland (Sw) have contributed. 3 are International.

Before 1946 Britain made 28/41 i.e. two thirds.

After 1945 American made 10.5/16 i.e. two thirds

Between them they have made 2/3 of the whole.

Such concentrations in space and time are both intriguing and puzzling, as is the abrupt switch from Britain to America post World War II.

B) *BY FACTOR*

TABLE (!7:2) DIFFERENT FACTORS IN INNOVATION

FACTOR	All/57	Britain/23	America/16
Challenge (*)	30	12.5	9
Curiosity (C)	17	7	2.5
Evolution (E)	17	6.5	7.5
War (W)	12	7.5	4
Government (G)	12	6.5	2
Rivalry (R)	11	4.5	4.5
University (U)	11	7	2.5
Necessity (N)	10	8.5	0.5
Finance (£)	8	3.5	3.5
Bell Labs (Bell)	6	N/A	6
Serendipity(S)	5		
Patents (P)	4		
Theory (T)	3		
Genius [(G)]	1		
Big Business (BB)	1		

In descending order of certainty, the main trends appear to be :

- Big business (1), with one startling exception (see below), played a miniscule role – though they often profited enormously from other people's innovations (e.g. Rolls Royce , which did everything it could to throttle Whittle, gorged on his jet engine, as did GE, once they got their hands on it); IBM computing mushroomed out of exploiting SAGE, designed by radar scieneers at MIT; US Big Pharma bloated upon orders for antibiotics pioneered in Britain.) It should be obvious really: big successful businesses abhor innovation, which frequently upsets their apple-carts.

- Only 21/57 TIs would have been eligible for Nobel prizes. Since about 900 *Science* Nobels are awarded per century only 21/900 are transformative. So counting Nobels, as some observers have done, is irrelevant.
- Genius made little contribution. The only two who stand out are Rutherford who discovered the atomic nucleus at Manchester University (22) before transferring to Cambridge, which thereafter lead nuclear physics (27) until Rutherford died in 1937, and Charles Parsons, our most complete engineer, who developed the steam turbine almost *sui generis*. Though Einstein was, if anyone was, a genius, Special Relativity (17) was shared between three or four which explains why he never got a Nobel for it. [Note 2]
- Serendipity (S), though it does occasionally occur (5/57), seems rather the romantic exception, a striking recent example being the CCD or electronic camera (55).
- America's Bell Telephone Lab, now defunct, was a matchless source of innovation. It introduced more TIs (6) than the whole of France (5.5) and a third of Americas total. It obviously deserves special study [Note 5].
- Sheer curiosity(17/57) was one of the two principal drivers, particularly in Britain (7/23). Curiosity, you will recall, is one of the Seven Pillars of Wisdom.(Ch.5)
- The other prime driver was Evolution (17/57) by which I mean the purposeful and tenacious cultivation of a seed idea into a mighty oak. Ideas it appears are cheap; on the contrary successful adaptation and improvement are not. There is another sense to Evolution here –'One thing leads to another'. Pioneering a field can often lead to unexpected problems and opportunities. Thus, the transformative transistor (44) grew out of the Bell Lab's efforts to improve crystal rectifiers (as refined at

Bristol University for radar) . Then the modern safety-bicycle (7) had a long period of adolescence, ditto the motor-car (10) and electronic television (28). (Baird's version relied on a spinning disc). It appears that TIs often come to birth after long and painful confinements, proceeded by several miscarriages. Doggedness matters.

- Government G (12/57) has been significant, especially for the Brits (6.5/23) – as a stimulant, as a facilitator, and as first purchaser. The British didn't invent radar, the Germans did, but, largely thanks to its scientific Civil- service (A definite jewel in the crown) Britain turned radar into a war- winning weapon; ditto Colossus and computers; ditto the Atom Bomb.
- . War (W) appears to be another strong but secondary factor (12/57) whose influence goes well beyond weaponry. Without the V-2 rocket (39) we wouldn't have got to the Moon (von Braun's team developed all those amazing Saturn rockets), or without the U.S. Navy's interest in the ocean bed (Soviet submarines) discovered Plate Tectonics (49) – to my mind the greatest *scientific* discovery of the last century. It relied on sensitive magnetometers developed (in Britain) to counter magnetic mines.
- Universities have also been seedbeds of innovation (11/57) if only because they employ vast numbers of folk who are supposed to do research. Whether they would be more productive in an industrial or government lab is an interesting question. The government Laboratory for Molecular Biology [Note 6] just outside Cambridge has a dozen or more Nobels in that field but is not part of the University. And what about the Bell Labs?
- Necessity (N) indeed appears significant (10/57), much more so in the case of Britain (8.5/23) than America (0.5/16), probably because Britain

has had to fight for its life. Notice how often Necessity and War go together (6 times)

- . While there have been some nasty fights over priority, and intellectual property rights (4/57) patents don't appear to be anywhere near as significant as some imagine, perhaps because private industries (save Bell) haven't been great innovators.
- On the other hand, rivalries between individuals, groups and nations have been a modestly sharp (8/57) spur.

5 THE GREAT PUZZLE.

What we learned in the last section was chiefly of a negative nature: that certain conventional explanations for Innovation, particularly those of an economic kind, are not supported by the evidence. The greatest puzzle is the overwhelming dominance of Britain and America, and the rapid transition from one to the other around 1945. We can at least rule out native (genetic) genius: whereas the Brits were Welsh, stranded on the island by chance, America is the archetypical melting pot.

What do the two dominant nations share that distinguishes them from the others?

- A common language – which may not be irrelevant. Certainly in Mathematics,(a very very different subject) better notation (language) has been absolutely spinal. However language can't be fundamental here because English has been the common working language amongst all scieneers since 1920, if only because of the then British dominance. Also, it may help to think and communicate in one's native tongue – Einstein thought so, and continued to think in German even after spending half his life in New Jersey. Britain has certainly benefited from adopting English-speaking giants such as Rutherford (N Z), Oliphant & Florey (Australia). So, language is a possible factor – though not convincing.

- Both Britain and America have both been Energy Empires, but so is Putin's Russia – a real innovation backwater.
- Both Britain and America raucously proclaim their democracy. As one of my heroes Carl Sagan wrote: "*The values of science and the values of democracy are concordant and, in many cases, indistinguishable…*". While I can't disagree, why haven't equally democratic nations such as Holland or Denmark made more of a contribution (in olden times they did)? Perhaps democracy is a necessary, but not sufficient factor.
- Compared to her continental rivals Britain has enjoyed centuries of comparative peace and security – and it may be true that contemplating the universe requires a fair share of both. While she has been in several existential wars no soldiers have ruled her streets since 1658 (death of Cromwell). America though was ravaged by civil war and deeply scarred by its Depression – which was far deeper than Britain's. Even in 1968 the academics in my (then US) university were so insecure that many came to work on Christmas Day. But that's nothing compared to the serial defeats experienced by most European nations. But peace alone hardly explains innovation. Graham Greene wrote wittily, if superficially, "*Switzerland had 500 years of democracy and peace – and what did that produce? The cuckoo clock.*". Switzerland, as I found living there, is more democratic than either Britain or America; far more. It is a different world: a referendum almost every month.

So the two great puzzles remain: why Britain and America? And why such an abrupt transfer around 1945? We'll have to fall back on speculation. Here are mine:

(A) Challenge and Response

In my experience what most good scieneers want is a challenge worthy of their steel. In that sense they are somewhere between puzzle-solvers and explorers, more akin to mountaineers that either do-gooders or businessmen. They are looking for an inspiring challenge which might give meaning to otherwise eccentrically obsessive lives. President Kennedy got it so right when he said. "*We choose to go to the Moon, and to go by the end of this decade, not because it is easy, but because it is hard.*" NASA was founded on that very principle – which inspired us all. Hubble Space Telescope teams were deliberately handed almost impossible challenges – which we somehow overcame one by one. Goethe said: "*Attempt no small thing– for it has not the capacity to stir the blood.*" The asterisks beside no less than 30 of our 57 TIs mark instances where stirring challenges of one kind or another were involved – if only it was to beat rivals to some spectacular summit. One has to be a scientist to realise just how ruthlessly competitive scientists can be. And why not? Glory and success are worth fighting for. Johannes Kepler (1609) could finally say, after spending 20 years trying to solve the mystery of Mars's motion: "*I have attested it as true in my deepest soul and I contemplate its beauty with incredible and ravishing delight.*" while Freeman Judson, a knowledgeable commentator on science, wrote: "*Science has several rewards, but the greatest is that it is the most interesting, difficult, pitiless and beautiful pursuit that we have yet found. Science is our century's art.*" Scientists can even earn immortality; Rutherford will be remembered long after Churchill is forgotten.

The Brits are a traditionally adventurous and competitive lot viz : exploration, mountaineering and organised sport (both of which last they invented). Einstein said "*Science is more a matter of character than intellect*". And anyone who has attended an American high-school football match on a Friday night, surrounded by 5,000 screaming parents, will know that Americans are damned competitive too.

(B) Traditional Culture

On the philosophical front Brits have usually been distinguished from other European cultures as being more 'empirical', more 'experimental', less 'logical' and less 'theoretical'. That goes back even beyond Francis Bacon (1605) who opined "*It cannot be that axioms established by argumentation can suffice for the discovery of new works, since the subtlety of nature is greater, many times over than the subtlety of argument.*"(Novum Organon) to the British (and American) legal system which derives from ' precedent' and not principle , from juries of common men making up their minds, case-by-case, based on the evidence and custom of the time. This is very different from the more principled approach in France say where the ancient codes of Napoleon and even of Rome, interpreted by 'experts', holds sway.

But what might such cultural differences have to do with science and innovation? Einstein (again) opined. "*Science is no more than a refinement of everyday thinking... The physicist cannot proceed without considering critically the much more difficult problem (than physics) ... of analysing the nature of everyday thinking.*" Unfortunately, he didn't go on to explain how everyday thinking works. I have therefore been struggling for 20 years to find out precisely how it does. And I've cracked it [Note 1] – or so I believe– by posing a question nobody else bothered to ask: "How do animals think" , because of course they do – otherwise they wouldn't survive.

There is no room left here to describe the links between the Scientific Method, Common Sense, Empiricism and Innovation– but they are very strong and so deserve a chapter of their own [Ch 18]. The point for now is that a deeply hidden cultural difference might be responsible for the exceptionalism of Brits and Yanks. If this is so, we must be very careful to identify and preserve it. Bad education alone [Ch 19], or bad child-rearing, could snuff it out .

The transformation in America's performance post 1945 isn't easy to explain either, if only because it was so abrupt. Four factors possibly contributed:

- The huge boost… from cooperating with Britain in the war effort – see Taffy Bowen's suitcase [Ch. 13].
- The emigration to the States of so many great European scieneers – including Einstein; Werner von Braun; Frank Whittle, Hans Bethe (head of the Theory group at Los Alamos); Kurt Goedel (Logic), Enrico Fermi (first atomic pile); John Von Neumann (Theoretical Physics) ; Freeman Dyson (Particle theory), Richard Courant (Applied Mathematics), James Chadwick (discoverer of the Neutron – for the duration of the Manhattan Project) and Riccardo Giacconi (The foremost astronomer of my generation)… to say nothing of a large fraction of all British graduate engineers – who post-war Britain could not or would not pay competitively.
- Another explanation is Dr Vannevar Bush – head of the US science effort during World War 2 , and in my opinion the foremost American of his day. In 1945 he wrote a visionary report ('*The Endless Frontier*') spelling out just how America could transform itself into a scientific superpower. Ignored for 12 years the shock of Sputnik(1957) saw Bush's plan[25] hastily effected. Anyone interested in scieneering or innovation should read Bush (on the web) and take note. He emphasised the virtues of: Pure

science (Curiosity); supporting university researchers with sufficient funds; rapidly declassifying all wartime research; appointment by performance, not seniority; proper scientific libraries; mobility, and supporting the young learning their trade. While my earlier bullets might be ephemeral, Bush's 'American Enlightenment' could stick. Let's hope.

- Finally, there is self-confidence. Britain once had insufferable amounts of it. America didn't because in truth it hadn't much to be proud about, what with its dishonourable birth, its brutality towards the indigenes, Slavery, the Civil War, ducking WW1 and the League of Nations, the Crash and Depression, turning away Jewish refugees from Hitler……. but in WW2 the US began to play a more honourable, if unintended, role [Ch 13]. It became filthy rich while Britain became bankrupt and exhausted, and lost its pre-eminent place in the world to the two Superpowers who, if they hadn't won the war, had certainly won the subsequent peace [Ch 10]. Then there was Hollywood which won the war all over again and again until even the popular military historian Max Hastings fell for it [Ch.10]. So Britain felt itself diminished, a shrinking encouraged by its new left-wing intelligentsia who wanted to deflate the old certainties, the old Establishment, in order to take over themselves. Terence Rattigan's '*The Winslow Boy'* gave way to John Osborne's '*Look back in Anger'* and many Brits did. Perhaps, after the unfairness of 19th.century society, with the Ascendency of the Parasites, they were entitled to feel disaffected, but the new elite went so far as to denigrate almost all Britain's past, including its many unique achievements, without having anything visionary to put in their place. Joan Littlewood's '*Oh What a Lovely War'* was probably the nadir. Francis Bacon, who was a very wise old bird wrote: "*But by far the greatest obstacle to the progress of science and the undertaking of new tasks and provinces therein is found in this – that men despair, and think things are impossible*" [Francis Bacon *Novum*

Organon ,1604]. If he was right, that alone might explain the abrupt changeover of 1946.

7 IMPLICATIONS

Human civilisation certainly, and most of Nature probably, now face an existential crisis brought about by the ingenuity, fecundity, short-sightedness innumeracy and greed of mankind. Given exponential growth, such a culmination , unintended though it might have been, was bound to come. Now it is here. Now is the time, perhaps the very last time we can try to put things right. Making mistakes is natural – adapting to survive is also natural (think blue-tits and milk-bottles). Sometimes humans can be pretty good at adapting too (viz. the firewood crisis led to coal-mining); it is a necessity for Darwinian survival. But we shouldn't forget. Most species don't. Survive for long .

If the ideas in Section 6 are sound we can, *with certain strong provisos*, be optimistic:

Provided politicians listen neither to half-baked economists [Ch 14] nor to Big Business (Why should it favour innovation which very likely will disrupt its existing supremacy, possible monopoly?) we could set scieneers world-wide, *very hard* challenges, with a reasonable expectation that they would be met. Just think of some inspiring recent examples:

- A doubling of life expectancy in little more than a century.
- The Green Revolution.
- Elimination of Smallpox
- Blockade of Germany (World War I) led to artificial rubber, artificial fertiliser, artificial coffee and artificial petroleum…
- Battle of the Atlantic led to Colossus then to Computing.

- D-Day landings made possible by imaginative 'funnies' including amphibious tanks (!) and floating (Mulberry) harbours.
- A safe landing on the Moon– and first time too!
- Recognition of DDTs harmful effects, and banishment.
- The discovery of the Ozone Hole, with remedy adopted.
- AIDS turned, within 3 decades, from a species threat into a manageable misfortune.

We cannot hope to see, from here, the transformative innovations that will be needed to squeeze us all through the eye of the Needle; but they will come – IF our politicians are brave enough to insist on them, and not to shirk the very responsibilities they have been elected to discharge. Issued with a challenge scieneers will, one way or another, succeed. What we simply cannot do is delay or cheat.

As an encouragement, here is one 'mad' challenge that just might work: '*Invent, by 2035, Recyclable Oil that produces no Carbon Dioxide*'. Why not? It existed once upon a time in the form of 'Pterodactyls Blood' – a liquid that could pick up solar energy, stored it until required, transported it to wherever it was needed, then yielded its energy back again while burning no Carbon whatsoever. Ridiculous? No. Unless it once existed one can prove, almost beyond a doubt, that 13-metre wingspan pterosaurs could never have flown. But they certainly did; go see their titanic skeletons hanging from the ceiling of the Museum of Natural History in New York. [Note 7]

So there is one challenge worthy of our scieneers: "*Re-invent Recyclable Oil by 2035.*"

AFTERTHOUGHT

One cannot be entirely satisfied that we have got to the bottom of TIs here. I wouldn't be altogether surprised to find that the exceptionality of Britain and America in this context is owed to something more subtle – such as better public libraries, school sports, or bedrooms of their own (BOTO) for children. We shouldn't stop looking. Meanwhile I hope we've got a reasonable working hypothesis.

NOTES.

[1] See my book *Thinking for Ourselves* (Amazon 2020); 'TFO' henceforth

[2] Einstein and Relativity: link on my TFO website **thinkingforourselves.org;** the roles he did and didn't play in its origin.

[3] **Superscripted Notes on Table (17:1)** on my 57 TIs is also on TFO website for now under the History section.

(1) John Snow's discovery that cholera was spread by contaminated groundwater (1854), the 'great stink' in the Thames (1858) and the death of Prince Albert from typhoid in Windsor Castle (1861′) led to the construction of a vast combined sewerage and water systes under London. Transformative because it dramatically increased life-expectancy, population-growth and the emergence of other megacities like London throughout the world. But it was John Newlands who pioneered this absolutely key TI in Liverpool a few years earlier.

(2) Though invented by Hiram Maxim, an American, it was the British who took the machine gun up and used it to win the Zulu wars. Ironically, cheap machine -guns (Kalashnikovs) eventually made machine-gun empires unsustainable.

(3) The Rover Safety Bicycle (Coventry) with its chain-driven rear wheel and pneumatic tyres (later) was the culmination of a long evolutionary process which commenced in France and Germany. A 2-wheel bike is a very ingenious and unlikely machine, much more so than a car. Why doesn't it fall over?

(4) Radio waves were discovered serendipitously in 1870 by David Hughes at his lab in Great Portland Street London. He was so excited by the phenomenon, with its 500-yard range, that he asked the august Royal Society to come and witness the miracle. They sent a botanist, a zoologist and an arrogant mathematician from Cambridge (Stokes). Stokes disastrously and quite erroneously pooh-poohed the whole ideas, dismissing it as "Just induction". Fortunately Heinrich Hertz working more systematically in Karlsruhe (1887) rediscovered and pinned down the phenomenon – though he could see no practical use for it. A great story, never properly told.

(5) Ross got a Nobel for discovering that bird -malaria (based on a quite different parasite) was transmitted by mosquitoes. But it was Giovanni Grassi traipsing round Italy who pinned *anophelese claviger* down as reponsible for human malaria. Malaria may have killed half the humans who have ever lived.

(6) Although Einstein always gets the publicity for discovering Relativity (after all he looks like a genius) it was actually the unavoidable development of several men, led by Henri Poincare′ – who looked like a butcher. Another great story waiting to be honestly told.

(7) Guiglielmo Marconi had an aristocratic Italian father and a very rich British mother (Jameson's whisky). Dad wasn't impressed by Guigielmo's successful efforts to emulate Hertz ,so Mum brought him to London and introduced him to Sir William Preece, head of the GPO. Preece, simmering with rage from an imagined put-down by Oliver Lodge , another radio pioneer, saw young Guiglielmo as his means of exacting revenge. With all the resources of the giant GPO behind him, including giant masts on the cliffs near Cardiff , Marconi, to great publicity, sent radio waves 10 miles across the Bristol Channel in 1897, and later, in 1901, across the Atlantic using giant kites as aerials. But radio wasn't practical until Marconi bought out Lodge's patent on the tuned circuit in 1912. It's a complex story, and one could argue that my

assigning the invention to Britain is arbitrary.[I have a radio play about this discovery on the website.]

(8) Henri Becquerel's (1899) serendipitous discovery of radioactivity led Strutt and Boltwood to use it as a way to of estimating the ages of rocks. The revelation that they were billions of years old, not millions, was to revolutionise Geology, Evolution , Astronomy, Cosmology and Nuclear Physics.

(9) Alas the claims of the Wright Brothers to have pioneered powered flight in 1903 don't stand up to close scrutiny. It was probably sensationalist puffery in the popular press. Their engine was far too feeble (12 HP). Yes they did fly later with the aid of a powerful catapult – but that is not powered flight. On the other hand Bleriot crossed the Channel in 1909 with a more powerful engine (25 HP) in a far superior design (see my website or *Thinking for Ourselves*).

(10) Quantum Mechanics is the ugly mathematical theory cobbled together to "explain" the atomic and subatomic world. It proved successful at *calculating* the bizarre phenomena that occur down there such as tunnelling and entanglement, if not really 'understanding' them. Many contributed including Einstein (Sw.), Bohr (Den.), de Broglie (F), Heisenberg (G), Schrodinger (Austria), Pauli (Sw.) and Dirac (B).

(11) German scientists employed radar as early as 1920 to detect ships in the fog. But it was the British (civil service) who turned it into a weapon capable of defending a country against aerial attack.

(12) The Cavity Magnetron developed by Randall and Boot at Birmingham University in 1940, and now powering your micro-wave, could generate the short radio-waves ideal for all kinds of radar, with 1000 times the power of its predecessors. Made Hitler's defeat inevitable.

(13) The greatest secret of WW2 was discovered by a humble Midlands mechanic; it boosted the power of British aircraft engines by 30 percent above

their German equivalents. The Luftwaffe was never in it after that {See my novel '*Against the Fall of Night*', Amazon 2020, for the story}.

(14) Operational research (OR) , developed by British 'boffins' such as Blackett in WW2, used mathematical modelling to analyse and improve complex operations such as bombing, and hunting for U-boats (Ch.4) . Quickly adopted in peace to increase reliability and productivity. For instance Critical Path Analysis can improve anybody's life. I use it to do our cooking.

(15) Although the preliminary work on penicillin was all done in Britain the Brits couldn't manufacture enough of it to cure anyone. So Flory took the idea to the States where, fortunately, it was found that the penicillin mould flourished in a Corn Syrup medium. Thus Americans were crucial to the mass production of the drug in time for use in WW2 (1944).

(16) Claude Shannon at the Bell Labs devised the vital theory underlying transmission and storage of information in a noisy world. Indispensable to the digital revolution: could and should be taught at school.

(17) Watson (US) and Crick (B) discovered the double helix at Cambridge but they utterly relied on the earlier work of Maurice Wilkins (the real pioneer) and Rosalind Franklin (the X-ray experimentalist) at King's College London. So British.

(18) Your digital tools are so powerful only because zillions of transistors can be packed on a single tiny chip. Such Very Large Scale integration (VLSI) stemmed from the development of the MOSFET transistor at Bell Labs.

(19) The new theory of Continental Drift was put together by British, Canadian and American geophysicists on the basis of geomagnetic data from the ocean depths. Sensitive magnetometers developed in Britain during WW2 to defeat magnetic mines revealed 'striping' on the sea bed – evidence of ocean-floor spreading. Our vision of the Earth would never be the same.

(20) Rachel Carson alerted mankind to the dangers of DDT in her iconic book "*Silent Spring*". It was our awakening to the damage we are doing to

Nature. The only woman 'transformer', but in the long run perhaps the most significant.

(21) Packet Switching packs digital information into discrete individually addressed packets. Thus e-mails can be sprayed out into the internet, to find their own separate ways to the addressee. Very robust, and therefore essential to reliability. Invented quite separately and independently in Britain (The National Physical Lab.) and the USA.

[4] STARLINK: see TFO website or Disney M.J. & Wallace P.T., *Quart. Journ. Roy. Astron Soc*, 1982, 23, 563

[5] Bell Labs

[6] LMB, Lab of Molecular Biology

[7] Since I couldn't get scientists to take a serious interest in the idea of Pterodactyls flying with the aid of solar power (i.e. 'Recyclable Oil'), in desperation I have written a novel about the idea called *Pterodactyl's Blood* which has now (2020) appeared on Amazon. There is an Excel presentation on the Science by my son and I, on the TFO website, see [2] above. The problem a long-shot idea like this faces is that it requires of a scientist several vastly different skill-sets, i.e. low slow-speed aerodynamics (highly mathematical), palaeontology, animal-thermodynamics, zoology…….. and so it is virtually impossible to get such papers refereed, and thus published. So far no one has been able to find anything wrong with it but. …it is intriguing. Academics like to live in comfortable little burrows where they know everybody else there. They don't like outsiders crawling in with them. But academic-burrowing stifles innovation, and has frequently done so (e.g. Continental Drift, which the experts laughed at from 1912 until 1967)

HISTORY OF THE BRITS

CHAPTER 18

THE STRANGE HISTORY OF THINKING.

As steals the morn upon the night
And melts the shades away:
So Truth does Fancy's charm dissolve
And rising Reason puts to flight
The fumes that did the mind involve
Restoring intellectual day".

From Handel's immortal duet "As steals the morn…" words by Jennens.[You Tube]

"It ain't what a man don't know as makes him a fool; it's what he do know as just ain't so." Josh `Billings

(18:1) INTRODUCTION

Thinking and Deciding are our main survival mechanisms. As such they must have been inherited from our immediate animal ancestors. But Evolution by Natural Selection is an inherently slow process which advances by minute, almost imperceptible increments. So how come that humans have advanced in a mere few generations to the point that they can hurl telescopes into Space when their closest cousins are still struggling to crack nuts in the jungle? That is by far the biggest historical question of all. The answer to it can only have profound implications for our future, as well as for our past.

I here want to give a brief outline of Common `Sense Thinking (CST) as I conceive it to be, with something of its extraordinary history, and its implications – in the sense above.

(18:2) SOME HISTORY

Because Thinking is our crucial survival mechanism Nature could not afford to leave the passing on of it to parents. It had to be embedded as deep in our organs as liver-function. And if it is to succeed CST has to work quickly, and without conscious direction. That being so it might be difficult, if not impossible, for scholars to unearth it; in fact it proved beyond them . But that did not prevent them from digging up some pretty unhealthy simulacra, and then declaring victory.

For instance the Ancient Greeks (500BC) thought they had found the secret in Deduction – which they had unravelled in the course of studying Euclidean Geometry – of which they were immensely proud. Indeed, above the entrance to his Academia in Athens Plato had inscribed *"Let no man ignorant of Geometry enter here*" . Unfortunately Deduction only works in CLOSED systems where the basic principles (axioms) are defined in advance – *almost never the case in the real world.* So Deduction is fine for playing games like Sudoku, hopeless for real subjects like Science where one is hoping to *discover* the axioms, not to obey them.

Five hundred years later the Abrahamic religions came up with the weird notion that humans were the special pets of their 'God' who had imbued Man with magic intellectual powers denied to all other creatures. Indeed the Bible gave warrant to the following creepy idea: *"Then God said 'let us make man in our image, after our likeness. And let them have dominion over the fish of the sea and the birds of the heaven and over the livestock and over all the earth and over every creeping thing that creeps on the Earth."* Since black/red/yellow… men (and certainly women) were obviously not sculpted 'in the image of God', they were included among the creatures who creeped, licencing 'us' to displace or even enslave them. Which was *very* convenient indeed. However such a dodgy philosophy clearly wouldn't bear close examination. So Saint Augustine, official theologian to the early Christian Church (~ 400 AD) pronounced *"There is another form of temptation, even more fraught with danger. This is the disease of curiosity.....It is this which drives us to try and discover the secrets of nature, those secrets which are beyond our understanding, which can avail us nothing and which man should not wish to learn."* So powerful was this prohibition that Christians stopped thinking altogether until the Reformation (1520) when, thanks initially to Martin Luther in Germany, the overwhelming reach of the Roman Church and its Inquisition was curbed. The Scientific Revolution immediately began with figures such as Copernicus (1543), Digges (1570), Brahé (1575), Galileo (1609), Kepler (1610), Hooke (1657) and Newton (1686) . They harked back to the Ancient Greeks , believing that Physics was a branch of Mathematics. But some came to doubt that Deduction would be enough, notably Francis Bacon (1604) and Christiaan Huyghens (1690) who thought that scientific truths could only be reached by translating particular instances into universal generalizations[2], a practice called 'Induction'. But clearly that involves a gamble, which David Hume (1739) argued could never be entirely justified by logic. And anyway people recoiled from gambling when it was Certainty they were after. Indeed a childish craving for Certainty, where it is not available, has been the single greatest curse which has dogged rational thinking throughout history, even today. There have always been, and there will always be, 'priests' willing to offer such false certainties to naifs – in return for power and influence.

There were two important developments in the 19th century. First, with the invention of 'Non-Euclidean Geometry' the whole analogy between Science and Mathematics was broken. Science was about the real universe, while Mathematics was just a game with arbitrary man-made rules. From time to time there might be useful parallels, but Mathematics henceforth could only be a tool, not a role-model. A second awakening was the recognition that maybe Induction (gambling) *could* work– provided it was guided by the notion of *Probability,*

[2] E.g. asserting that all swans are white having seen only 900 such creatures, which all happened to be white.

which could calculate which gambles made sense, and which did not. And so Statistics was born with ambitions to rule both Science and Philosophy, and with its birth there grew a vague expectation that there now must be a true "Scientific Method".[Note 1]

While everybody acknowledged that this Method was a good idea, nobody seemed to know what it was. As the witty zoologist Peter Medawar put it (1972): *"Ask a scientist what he considers the scientific method to be, and he will adopt an expression that is at once solemn and shifty-eyed: solemn because he feels he ought to declare an opinion; shifty eyed because he is wondering how he is going to conceal that he has no opinion to declare."*

Alas, Statistics soon broke down into warring sects which stridently denounced one another so that bewildered folks like me, who had to teach the subject at university, began to question the lot of it. As far as I could see there were two, mainly historical, problems involved: a craving for the old Certainties of Classical Greece (Deduction) and a refusal to acknowledge that Darwin's discovery of Evolution (1859) had made the whole idea of Abrahamic religion redundant. But many scholars found it impossible to discard cultures they had imbibed at school and afterwards. Instead of arguing over how humans think they should now have asked "How could animals think?" because that is what we all are.

I entered this bloody fray back in 1997 when my own research area (Hidden galaxies) was descending into chaos. There was plenty of strong evidence bearing on my pet theory – but it conflicted! Conferences on the subject broke up in controversy, even acrimony. It was clearly time to consult that legendary Oracle "The Scientific Method" which everybody assumed existed, but where?

It took 20 years of stubborn digging, and some luck, to unearth a treasure that had never seen the light of day before. The Scientific Method turned out to be very largely Common Sense Thinking (CST) – which is like a boy scout's penknife for the thinking mind. It has six key implements:

Bayes' Rule for gamblers (known since 1763)

Ockham's Razor (Classical '*lex parsimonae'*)

The Detective's Equation (New; the 'E= mc^{2}' of thinking)

The Principle of Limited Variety (J M Keynes, 1920)

The Principle of Animal Wisdom (PAW) (New)

The Inference Table (New)

This is no place to go into all the details but, in case you think I have gone mad in claiming so much, I must explain one thing: *You do not have to be a great mind to make a great discovery*. The perfect illustration of that is Charles Darwin who stumbled upon the greatest scientific discovery of all: Evolution by Natural Selection. Darwin was basically a lout. He spent his entire boyhood and much of his younger manhood mindlessly slaughtering wild animals and birds. He failed at two universities in two different subjects (medicine and the priesthood) and the only constructive pastime he appears to have had was collecting beetles. His exasperated father thundered "You wouldn't even make a decent rat-catcher" and packed him off to sea for 5 years in the humble situation of "gentleman's companion" aboard *HMS Beagle*, a RN survey vessel commissioned to chart the Southern coasts of South America.[Note 2]

It was the custom of the day for RN Captains to remain in splendid isolation from their crews, a practice which not infrequently drove them mad . So Captain Robert Fitzroy hired Darwin to keep him company and keep him sane in the aft cabin for 5 interminable years at sea.

How lucky Darwin was; Fitzroy was a cultured, humane man with a good library. That induced Darwin, on the long sea passages, to read seriously for the first time. And Fitzroy allowed him to go ashore and indulge his passion for slaughtering, and sometimes collecting, the local fauna. And , as we all know, it was on one such foray on the Galapagos Islands that Darwin noticed that the finches on separate islands had very different beaks. Twenty years later, spurred into action by the realization that Wallace had independently come to identical conclusions, Darwin published *"The Origin of Species"(1859)*

So I don't feel entirely foolish to claim that I have discovered how Common Sense Thinking works. My obsession with galaxies simply drove me to ask questions which no one had bothered with before, such as 'How do animals think?' Which of course they do. If you don't believe that then for goodness sake read *"Are we smart enough to know how smart animals are?"* by Franz de Waal, a world expert on primate behaviour. There you will learn that primates (and others) can plan ahead, work in teams, show empathy, imagine solutions to problems in their heads, demonstrate inference, live not just in the present, use many tools in an intentional way, act generously and behave unselfishly.[Note 3]

In any case all the evidence is against genius in science . If there was such a thing then where are our genii today when more than half of all the scientists who have ever lived are active now? I've never met one, and neither have the hundreds of colleagues I have asked about it.[Note 4]. Claims for scientific genius usually come from those unqualified to judge.

For any who want to delve further into these matters there is my recent book '*Thinking for Ourselves*'[Notes 5&9]. Suffice it here to say that CST can be fruitfully applied to very tricky questions like Immigration, where the arguments, the evidence and the opinions sharply conflict. There [next chapter] I shall utilize an Inference Table of the kind we have already encountered in Table (5:2) – Detective's Thinking; in Table(8:2) – Scottish Independence; and in Table (11:1) – the British Empire.

(18:3) SOME IMPLICATIONS OF COMMON-SENSE THINKING.

(A) The spectacular ascent of mankind is entirely owed to the invention of writing (5 to 7 millennia ago). The Detective's Equation reveals that the decisiveness of evidence rises virally with the number of clues involved. Writing enabled us to collect, store, assess and combine many more clues than we could hitherto. Thus the doubling of evidence can easily increase one's power to decide a complex issue wisely by 5000 % or more! Literate humans suddenly became a million times more capable than their illiterate forbears. Our spectacular ascent is NOT due to greatly superior brains, but to writing. As Einstein put it : "My pencil and I are smarter than I am." [Note 6]

(B) Since we all need to think to survive Nature couldn't afford to hand out significantly unequal capacities to do so to different individuals. Brilliance, IQ, the capacity to pass exams, call it what you will – is of little use when it comes to serious thinking. That requires other qualities including curiosity, breadth, relevant knowledge, judgement, imagination, flexibility, integrity – and above all doggedness. Don't be impressed by, or defer to, superficially clever people.

(C) Serious thinking is almost always based on Induction , which is to some extent guesswork – and indeed a gamble. We cannot live without constantly gambling, and so we all need to become familiar with betting Odds, and the means to compound them. They are essential to sound Thinking.

(D) Beware of very strong arguments or immovable evidence, they could well be dependent on Systematic Errors, the Elephants in everybody's room. Far better to rely on a network of weaker clues which generally cohere with one another. This is the Principle of Animal Wisdom (PAW).

(E) Successful Induction often requires the implicit assumption of certain *Principles of Uniformity* such as 'Tomorrow will be much like today' or 'Atoms over there will be the same as atoms over here'. While such principles seem to apply across the natural sciences there is little reason to assume that like principles will apply more generally. So beware of "scientific thinking" misapplied – especially in the humanities.

(F) Because we desperately need to understand a subject does not mean we can – *or ever will*! God, The Mind, Consciousness…..if the tools of CST cannot get a grip on a subject, then we are helpless to progress. For instance the Principle of Limited Variety reveals that neither Economics nor Psychology are sciences – and are mostly irreproducible hocus-pocus.[Note 7]

(G) Much of conventional Education is a waste of time and money – because it doesn't comprehend Common Sense. While Education is a good idea in principle, in practice much of it has been, and remains, designed more to benefit the teachers than their students – let's be honest about it. Many young lives, with their future savings, are being wasted in class-rooms. People should never let their scholastic experiences, however bruising, deter them from aiming high or becoming wise. Conversly the UK is full of Baducated people whose confidence in their own abilities is misplaced because what they been taught is largely without foundation. Qualifications are no guarantee of Common Sense. Selling degrees and selling Indulgences can be equally fraudulent. [Ch. 20 on 'Baducation']

(H) THE fundamental truth we all need to understand is that *almost all serious arguments about the real world can only reach provisional conclusions.* The best any of us can hope for are good betting odds deriving from a wide variety of evidence. Once we recognize that single truth we might be less hostile to folk who don't believe the same things as we do. Provisionality is the only soil in which any progressive civilization can germinate or flourish. A craving for Certainty is childish, futile and sometimes destructive. Had we rejected that we might have had the jet engine before the birth of Christ. [We have already argued that most of the Seven pillars of Progress are justified by Provisionality [Ch. 14] while many of the worst evils in this world such as dictatorship, racialism, religious hatred and terrorism derive from its denial.] [Ref 8]

NB Note that cleaving to a provisional philosophy does *not* imply weak thought or governance. On the contrary. More weak clues, more democratic committees and more avoidance of dogmatic arguments can, in the end, lead to more, not less decisive, policymaking. [Chap. 6]

(18:4) THE BRITS AND THINKING

Thinking is not a exclusively national pastime but in a history of the Brits it is worth recalling British successes, failures and disasters in this connection. Britain *should* score highly because of its early escape from the clutches of the Roman Church – and its Inquisition. Thomas Ockham (14th century) is renowned for his eponymous Razor ('choose the simplest hypothesis first') but its roots lie back in Classical times ('*lex parsimoniae*'). Francis Bacon was an early(1604) and eloquent advocate for Induction and Experiment (indeed he died in the course of one, catching pneumonia in the snow). Thomas Bayes (and his executor William Price) spotted that eponymous Rule we all need to update our confidence in any hypothesis (1763) when a new clue turns up. They were Non-Conformist ministers from North London now reburied in leafy Bunhill Fields near Liverpool Street railway station. With no half-decent universities in England, Ireland or Wales, for further progress we have to look North to the Scottish Enlightenment where vigorous debate flourished in the taverns, particularly at night. Had you attended a supper at the Oyster Club in Edinburgh during the late 1700s you might have seen David Hume (Philosophy), Joseph Black (inventor of both Chemistry and Thermodynamics), James Hutton (the 'father of Geology') and Adam Smith (begetter of Economics) supping together and discussing each other's work – arguably the greatest concentration of intellectual gunpowder ever gathered in history. Edinburgh was then referred to as 'The Athens of the North', which seriously under-rated Edinburgh; Athens was never in the same league. Oxford and Cambridge didn't teach science until about a century later; they were primarily seminaries. So thank goodness for the Scots, the Quakers and the Non-Conformists who built the Industrial Revolution, and hence the modern world, in unfashionable locations such as Glasgow, Ironbridge (Shropshire), Manchester, Newcastle, the Potteries and Birmingham. Unfettered by a classical education they could experiment to find out what worked (called 'Empiricism', an especially British trademark).

After Darwin and Wallace (1858) one might have hoped for an acceleration of good thinking. But never underestimate the British capacity for snobbery. Oxford and Cambridge, now deprived of their monopoly of Holiness, quickly substituted Cleverness instead. Thus J M Keynes and Bertrand Russel for instance gave spectacular peacock displays which impressed all too many, while R A Fisher and Harold Jefferies almost succeeded in burying CST in a fog of irrelevant mathematics.

Yes the Brits have produced some spectacularly bad thinking, and damaged themselves frightfully in the process. In that connection I would highlight the invention of Economics (Adam Smith 1776); 'The Essay on Population' (Thomas Malthus 1798); the canonization of Free Trade (David

Riccardo & successors 1817), the uncritical acceptance of Statistics (Galton and Pearson at University College London, UCL 1900); Popperism (London School of Economics 1950) and the foolish, not to say criminal adulation of IQ (Burt, also UCL, 1950s).

Yes CST matters to history. Experience demonstrates that it cannot safely be left in the hands of academics, at least not the British variety.

(18:5) SUMMARY

Nothing is more important to humans than sound thinking. Evolution has thus endowed us with an exquisite mechanism for doing so – Common Sense. Unfortunately it is buried so deep within us as to defy easy analysis. Amongst others, Greek philosophers, Abrahamic priests, and latterly modern philosophers, statisticians, psychologists and economists have all got it wildly wrong. Thus for the past two millennia humankind has been thinking much less well than we might have done . But that misfortune was overbalanced by the invention of writing, a transformative tool which enables us to store, recall, and combine far more evidence together, and so accomplish complex tasks utterly beyond the capabilities of our cousin apes, or indeed of illiterate humans. This is our secret, not superior IQ. [See Ch. 16 *Thinking for Ourselves,* Note 4 for a clear demonstration.]

Because they didn't understand Common Sense Thinking, especially as it should apply to a modern world of culture and technology, the British people have suffered some appalling and unnecessary misfortunes, most often inflicted upon their poorer classes. One thinks in particular of: Free Trade, Malthusian demography, half Baked Economics in general, Friedmanism in particular; Victorian mal-investment and malnutrition; Psychology; their mis-grading as hereditary fools on the basis of forged IQ tests (Burt); an innumerate ruling elite; appalling management; a thieving financial sector; mass immigration never condoned by the democratic process (next chapter); and wholly unjustified snobbery based on Baducation. As a result we have had a last century very much less happy than it might have been. But those who can not or will not think straight must pay.

The clumsy obfuscation of Thinking by scholars and priests has all too often led to the handing over of that vital task to self-appointed, self-seeking and self-deluded 'experts'. We need to take back control of Thinking for ourselves, especially now that the Internet can supply the information needed to do so. When we do, truly spectacular dividends, both for individuals, and for enlightened societies, can be expected.

NOTES

NOTE 1: Hugh Gauch Jr. : *Scientific Method in Practice*, 2003, Cambridge University Press, gives a scholarly survey of the history of this subject. I have read it cover to cover six times, picking up more insights every time.

NOTE 2: Charles Darwin, *The Voyage of the Beagle*, 1839, Google Books.

NOTE 3 : Frans de Waal: '*Are We Smart Enough to Know how Smart Animals Are?*' , Granta books, 2016. Despite the clumsy title this is the authoritative account. Indispensable and very readable.

Note 4: In my book '*Thinking For Ourselves*' *[Amazon Kindle 2020]* I analyse (Chapt.3) about 20 important scientific discoveries to find out how they were made. In most cases they were made by someone who narrowly won a race for the line. Some even came in second but somehow won more popular acclaim (Einstein for instance over Poincaré). That's not genius.

Note 5 The table of contents for my book *Thinking for Ourselves* can be found by looking for it on Amazon. 610 pages, £14:50.

Note 6 The meteoric ascent of Mankind is justified in Sect (16:8) of the above where writing is shown to increase our decisiveness by a factor of millions.

NOTE 7: Sects. (13:3,4&5) of *Thinking for Ourselves* show how the Principle of Limited Variety completely undermines Economics, Psychology and Psychiatry as sciences. Statistics is undermined in Ch. 11

NOTE 8:You can find an account of why all Serious Thinking must be provisional in Appendix 8 of *Thinking for Ourselves* entitled: '*Certainty, Falsifiability and Common Sense'*.

NOTE 9: If animals can neither write nor calculate then how on earth could they use CST as I have described it, with its Detective's Equation and its numerical Weights? Yes that was puzzling, extremely so. Then the penny dropped with the most melodious clang. It's the other way round! They use what I call "*Categorical Inference"*. All our literary and numerical tools are simply clumsy imitations. When I discovered this I knew I'd got CST right. I was so excited I had a stroke two days afterwards. For *Categorical Inference* see Appendix 9 of *Thinking for Ourselves.* If you don't like betting odds you can use that instead of my scheme for CST; it ought to be good, its been working out there in the wild for hundreds of millions of years!

HISTORY OF THE BRITS
CHAPTER 19
MASS IMMIGRATION –THE BIG CREEP

"So, uncomfortable as it may be, there are large cultural differences (between countries) that map into important aspects of social behaviour, and migrants bring their culture with them." (P68*)........*

. *"What migrants are escaping from, though they may not realize it, is the dysfunctional institutions that as settlers they appear to want to bring with them.*" (p103)

Paul Collier, '*Exodus*' Alan Lane Press, 2013,

(19:1) INTRODUCTION

In Chapter 16 we deliberately avoided any discussion of values, to concentrate on the numbers —which was hard enough in itself. Here we plunge head-first into controversy. We are going to employ Common Sense Thinking (CST), otherwise we will get in to one of those irreconcilable deadlocks which so often characterise this subject. A will choose argument or evidence X, and give it high Weight, while B will choose a quite different argument and give *that* high Weight instead, making any constructive discussion hopeless thereafter. If not actually said, words like 'racist' and 'feebral' then hang in the air. There may be good arguments on both sides; but what is needed is some impartial weighing mechanism to choose between them.

You will recall that The Principle of Animal Wisdom (PAW) disallows the setting of high Weights on *any* single piece of evidence (or argument) – no matter how passionately a protagonist believes in it . Why not? Because all too often Time has shown up such Elephants of the Mind-Room as false. The wise, the only thing to do, is to look for concordance amongst a wide variety of weaker clues and arguments – using an Inference Table. [Chap. 18]

(19:2) IS LARGE SCALE IMMIGRATION BAD FOR BRITAIN?

The Inference Table bearing on the hypothesis *"Large scale Immigration is bad for Britain"* is followed by notes on individual clues/ arguments:

INFERENCE TABLE (19:1)

HYPOTHESIS 'MASS IMMIGRATION IS HARMFUL TO BRITAIN

	Clue/Argument	Weight	Balance	See Note
	Prior	1	1	
1	Makes nation more colourful	1/4	2^{-2}	
2	Is owed to ex-colonials of the Empire	1		1
3	Immigrants will do dirty jobs Brits won't	1/4	2^{-4}	
4	Will make Brit exports more competitive	1/4	2^{-6}	2
5	Will provide us with key skilled workers	1		3
6	Being younger they will pay our pensions	1		4
7	Is drastically increasing Population growth	4	2^{-4}	5
8	MI has never been democratically approved	4	2^{-2}	6
9	Has kept British workers' wages down	4	1	7
10	Helps the rich but harms the poor	4	2^{2}	8
11	Has led to the drastic shortage of housing	4	2^{4}	9
12	Has led to serious strains on NHS, schools, etc	4	2^{6}	10
13	Has ruined many indigenous businesses	4	2^{8}	11
14	Is undermining investment in fut. infrastructure	4	2^{10}	12
15	Reduces programs of training and investment	4	2^{12}	13
16	Has largely displaced help for genuine refugees	4	2^{14}	14
17	Imports some very backward cults/behaviours	4	2^{16}	15
18	Imports foreign enmities & terrorism	4	2^{18}	16
19	Little integration; ghettos	2	2^{19}	17
20	Severely weakens Social Cohesion	4	2^{21}	18
21	Have to export more to pay migrant remittances	2	2^{22}	19
22	Encourages weak businesses to 'sell citizenship'	2	2^{23}	20
23	Encourages massive dishonesty and corruption	4	2^{25}	21
24	Imports much appalling treatment of women	4	2^{27}	22
25	This isn't Britain any more	4	2^{29}	23

NOTES on Table(19:1):

1 I gave my reasons in Chapter 11 for why this is false. The vast majority of ex-colonials greatly benefitted from British colonialism. (That may not be true of the Spanish, Belgian, French, US, German, Russian….varieties. But that is not *our* problem).

2 Yes, but only because they represent sweated labour . It has sometimes been forced upon us' by practices elsewhere (e.g. Germany imported Turks to undercut other European car manufacturers). But never excusable. Another disastrous consequence of bloody Free Trade.

3. We could easily train more doctors, nurses, programmers etc, but we don't. Restrictive Practices (e.g. the BMA see Chapt. 7), dodgy CEO's who won't spend money training their own, cheapie or short-sighted governments, appalling universities who issue worthless degrees, missing apprenticeship schemes, snobbery toward some vital crafts, over-respect for others. If given the chance I believe most Brits would want to learn a valuable trade / craft/ skill/ profession. But don't underrate the opposition to this from incumbents.

3 Clearly nonsense. Do we deport them when they grow old in turn ; or do we import others? This shows how false/threadbare half-baked economic (HBEs see Chap14) arguments for MI most often are. (See also Collier)

4

5 See Ch. 16

6.Disgraceful arrogance on the part of our ruling elite.

7. This is contentious .The effect *may* be small and selective. [see 'Migration Watch' website]. I am persuaded that workers in care-homes and hospitals for instance would be much better paid if migrants couldn't be exploited instead. Anyway the effects can propagate internationally, as in the car industry (see 2 above). And if not true why have so many industries clamoured and conspired to bring MI about?

8 Cheaper restaurants, cleaners, child-minders, hotels, hire-cars, gardeners, loft-conversions, parent-carers…Lower wages and lesser opportunities for our poor. Disgraceful I say.

9 See Ch. 16; the Housing Crisis is the canary in the mine.

10 Go to a GP's surgery, an A&E, a city school, an MP's surgery… in an area favoured by refugees.

11 Corner shops, taxi-driving, café's, car-cleaning, chip-shops, hair-dressing, plumbing, house renovation, handymen, petrol stations, ….going, going, gone!

12.See Ch. 16 and the "Million pound Immigrant Cheque"

13 Why train your own people, or invest in labour-saving equipment when you can import cheap labour instead? A deliberate and disastrous brake on Progress. Back to the 19th century or earlier. In the end it will make us *less* competitive. Obviously.

14 An emotive subject [See Sect. (19:3)] Many immigrants are quite wealthy and have to lie or bribe to get here – they are not refugees at all.

15 e.g. Violent Jamaican gangs (the murder rate in Jamaica is 50 times higher than it is in the UK); drug-trafficking (& associated knife crime), People- smuggling; Asian paedophile rings targeting vulnerable British girls; bride-selling, female circumcision, fanatical religious sects, Ayatollahs preaching hatred…

16 Bombings, KGB-murderers….

17 Too rapid (Mass) Immigration leads not to Integration but Segregation, even Dis-Integration. Obvious really, but see Collier (ref) and Sect (19:5)

18.See Section 5 below.

19 Nobody seems certain how large remittances add up to, but probably of order £10 Billion a year [see scholarly articles Migration Observatory website]. We have to export that much more to compensate.

20 Hotels, care-homes, small shops and businesses of many kinds. Even weak universities lure foreign students with vague promises of employment here afterwards with the prospect of 'eventual citizenship'.(You can understand them trying that on, what with foreigner's tuition fees of £27,000 a year for often naff degrees; everybody can become a Professor then, just everybody.)

21 Apparently many, perhaps most immigrants are comparatively wealthy, are not political refugees, and only get here by lying about their backgrounds. This undermines our national moral fibre. Sects(3&5) and Collier [Note 1].

22 Look around you. To some, burquas are an affront to progressive civilization, while others will object to paying for the upkeep of the offspring of immigrant males with a poor tradition of supporting their own.[the highest proportion of single parent families with dependent children in the UK (18.9%) are black (GOV.UK). In the US it is far worse; two-thirds of Afro-American households are single-parent; the large difference reveals that this is a cultural not a racial characteristic.

23 Many parts of Britain, usually in urban areas, have become foreign ghettos where you can go for a walk and scarcely see a British face. [Note 3 below]

What is the bottom Line of Table (19:1) ? The final balance reads Odds of 2^{29} to 1 on the proposition that "Large Scale Immigration is bad for Britain." But what is 2^{29} in more familiar terms? Well 2^5 is 32 so 2^{10} (32 times 32) is about a thousand, and so 2^{30} is a thousand, thousand thousands or a Billion. Thus 2^{29} is just a factor 2 short of a Billion, i.e. about half a billion. And surely Odds that high should convince anyone. There is no point in quibbling about the details, even with several entire arguments in the Table. They cannot make any difference to the final outcome. Mass Immigration is, and has been, bad for Britain. You might even argue, with Odds like those, 'Very bad indeed'.

Here we can see the value of learning to think in a Common-Sense Way. One can, *by assembling enough evidence*, arrive at unassailable conclusions.

The only way that I can think of to challenge the overwhelming conclusion is to undermine my prescription for CST itself [Chap. 18]. Have a go! If you succeed you might even be able to insist that MI is actually OK for Britain. And if you fail you will at least have learned how CST works; 'win-win' as the PR men say.

(19:3) MASS IMMIGRATION & SOCIAL COHESION

Social Cohesion (SC) is a clumsy phrase for a clutch of invaluable characteristics: cooperation; group loyalty; shared identity; willingness to self-sacrifice for the common good; empathy for fellow citizens; teamwork; national morale; *esprit de corps*; sharing both pain and pleasure; patriotism; neighbourliness ... If we are going to adapt as drastically as we must to the approaching environmental catastrophe will MI enhance or hinder that process? Since I am not a sociologist I can only appeal to the conclusions of those who are[3] .An accessible source of information on these matters is '*Exodus*' by Paul Collier [Note 1] who has summarised much of the scholastic literature on both Immigration and Integration. The message that comes across is clear: MI seriously undermines Social Cohesion, not just here and now, but everywhere

[3] Though I am not convinced that Sociology, fascinating though it unquestionably is, is any more a Science than Psychology, or Economics. Too many possible hypotheses perhaps, with some disastrous exponents such as Margaret Meade.

where it is too rapid, not only amongst the newcomers, but amongst the indigenous population too (e.g. Jamaican gun- and knife- crime has spread amongst local gangs here as well.) Any doubters should read in particular the first half of Collier's Section 2 which deals with the social consequences of MI on host countries. Here are some quotes:

"Trust and cooperation beyond the family do not arise naturally.....The evidence suggests that (they) accumulate in a modern progressive society. One reason that poor societies are poor are that they lack these attitudes." (For instance it is impossible to purchase Life Insurance in Nigeria) (p 64).

"The vital ingredient of successful cooperation is that enough people should be willing to punish those who do not cooperate. But if those who adopt opportunistic rather than cooperative strategies are disproportionately immigrants, punishment is misconstrued as discrimination.....(p74) (e.g. the Tottenham Riots)

"The sustained migration rate will be greater the more culturally distant is the country of origin from the host country." (p 91) (because it is the local diaspora which drives the immigration rate: more relatives, dependants, servants etc., etc... }. Collier calls this 'The Diaspora Effect'.

".... children of immigrants (in Europe) are more resistant to adopting the national culture than are their parents." (p 69)

It seems then that MI undermines Social Cohesion and will so make it harder for Britain to adapt to the environmental crisis. America is an excellent example of a second-rate society paralysed by racial diversity.

What we are to do about all this is another matter. Personally I believe we have to try and bring about the rapid integration of migrants already here, and do away with the hypocrisy of a benevolent Rainbow culture. The world simply isn't like that, however much Feebrals (below) might wish it so. Immiscibility (failure to mix) is a widespread human characteristic (Note 3)

(19:4) INFERENCES

- The case against Mass Immigration (MI henceforth) seems unassailable. MI is not only bad for Britain but, it might be argued with Odds so High, is very bad indeed. That being so everyone should be able to openly discuss MI without being branded "a racist" . Just as bad, if not worse, are "Feebrals", my name for feeble-minded liberals who refuse to discuss tough issues – or let anyone else do so either. My profession (university academic) is packed with 'Feebrals', timid souls too frightened to express any opinion their fellow Feebrals won't endorse. They substitute "virtue signalling" for honest debate. Personally I believe such Feebrals are a far greater menace to society than racists – and that's *really* saying something.
- It should not surprise us that different citizens can hold widely different opinions on MI, because their experience of it, and its personal consequences for them, can be so wildly different. Some, particularly rentiers and the metropolitan elite, benefit enormously from MI; others, particularly poor indigenes, lose out disastrously. Then there is geography; overhasty MI leads not to Integration but to its very opposite—drastic and rapid ghetto growth (see above). For instance Bangladeshis huddle together in Tower Hamlets , distancing themselves from British culture to such a ridiculous extent that their women now wear veils –which are *not* worn back in Bangladesh itself (Collier). If you are a Brit stranded in such a neighbourhood you might feel cheated,

even hostile. What has happened to the society you grew up in and expected to live out your days within? In effect you have been forcibly exiled and impoverished – through no fault or volition of your own. On the other hand if you live in Bath, or Barchester you may not see an immigrant face from one month to the next, and can afford to hold a lofty opinion of MI. The subject is bound to be highly divisive. All the greater reason for open discussion.

- Personally I feel that MI is but one symptom of the general vandalization of this planet by thoughtless or weak human beings. The real question is how are we going to save it, and ourselves, in time to survive. There is only one answer: by a drastic reduction in the human population before it is too late. In my opinion that will only come about if comparatively rich, civilized societies like Britain set the example, and set it *now*! If the Brits cannot preserve their own island paradise, setting an example to the rest – then I believe we are all doomed, man and beast. In Ch.16 we showed how rapid depopulation could be achieved here, without draconian measures, but only if MI is halted immediately. From that point of view the present rate of MI is an absolute disaster – but so many of us do not realise that because we are innumerate. It is worth repeating the mantra: "**The present rate of Mass Immigration corresponds to 3 British mothers out of 4 raising an extra child**."
- Whatever way you look at it Slavery is a very bad idea (that's why we British abolished it in 1834, and forced abolition on nearly everybody else in the world too). Happily it destroyed both Classical Greece and Imperial Rome. It enfeebled and has since depopulated the Southern states of America. It left the West Indies in such a mess that large numbers want to emigrate even today; especially today, now that places like Jamaica have descended into drug-led gang violence. Yet

importing cheap labour, which is what MI is largely about, is a half-way house to Slavery, with many of the same dire consequences. For instance:

- It undercuts and cheats the indigenous poor ('po' white trash').
- It puts off investment in labour-saving devices and practices. Thus it is *by design*, anti-progressive.
- It enriches those who can exploit cheap labour, and impoverishes those too principled to do so.
- It encourages all manner of lazy habits: for instance not training enough local doctors, nurses, vets, dentists, programmers, plumbers, electricians, mechanics, craftsmen. ….('import 'em from abroad'). And thus denying some of our own children the 'prizes' in life.
- It saves feeble politicians from having to confront crux issues; for instance care of the aged and dying: 'Shove them into care homes, out of sight, where either immigrants, or the local poor, can look after them at artificially low costs.' In 2015 the House of Commons was thus able to duck the whole question of Assisted-Dying, and dignity at the end of Life. Personally I found that utterly contemptible! As one who was looking forward to going out on my own terms, and with my flags still flying, I'm dismayed too; now it will have to be Switzerland . But why should I , or anyone else, have to sneak out of my own country to die in dignity? Bloody Feebrals! Without MI the wages of poor carers would have to rise significantly and politicians would have to face hard decisions, *which is all they are bloody paid and elected to do*! We cannot afford weaklings in government, whatever party they espouse.
- We cannot go on as we are, raping the planet, and Britain itself. But to change drastically will force us to take many extremely difficult

decisions, and to take them soon. Only stable, coherent societies will manage that, and even they may falter. For instance:

1. Do we encourage or discourage globalization?
2. Do we do away with the nonsense of Free Trade [Ch. 14]
3. Do we confront the issue of Assisted Dying?
4. Do we continue to poison our environment with chemical farming?
5. To what extent should our island become self-sufficient?
6. By how much, and how quickly, should we reduce our population?
7. How quickly, and how best, should we divest ourselves of Carbon fuels?
8. Should we look to find if there is a safe nuclear alternative : e.g. the Liquid Thorium Reactor?
9. How are we going to solve the disastrous housing shortage so that our children can have homes?
10. Should we, can we, and could we bring MI to an end?
11. How much of our island must be rewilded to preserve its ecosystem for the long term.?
12. Do we discourage mass air-travel, cruise ships, tourism to fragile areas, monster cars, trade in wild animals.....
13. How are we to preserve our local seas and their inhabitants?
14. How much meat, fish and other environmentally degrading foods do we continue to consume?
15. Do we continue to support a culturally fragmented, even disintegrating society, as against far more Integration?
16. How are we going to solve the plastics (packaging) problem? Its urgent.

All these issues, and others, will test our Social Cohesion to the limit.

(19:5) THE HISTORY OF BRITISH MI.

If MI to Britain is as disastrous as the evidence suggests, how did it come about in a nation which wasn't helpless to decide otherwise (as Japan has done; less than 2%)? The main reasons, I suspect, are as follows:

(i) Our ruling elite are so innumerate they had/have no idea what was going on. And of course they don't live in racial ghettos.

(ii) Britain is riddled by Feebrals who are either too ignorant or too craven to acknowledge MI and preach that all diversity is good. Anyway, they say, MI is our fault for having the Empire.

(iii) Temptation – those million-pound immigrant cheques I mentioned in Ch 16. This is a matter that needs to be brought out into the open.

(iv) Half-baked Economists who can justify anything, including MI. Some have even suggested it is necessary to pay for our pensions.[Ch.14]

(v) In particular, the disastrous Free Trade policy meant many key British industries (e.g. cotton, wool, cars, metallurgy, ….) became uncompetitive and were tempted to import semi-slave labour to survive. In all cases it failed in the end, leaving large unemployed diasporas in former industrial areas such as Manchester, Leeds, Leicester, Bradford, the Midlands……..[To be fair some were forced into this by European competitors who were importing sweated foreign labour themselves] It's that Free Bloody Trade again!

(vi) 'Disaster Creep' describes a phenomenon which steals upon a society too slowly to be easily recognized in time. Before the Red Indians (2 children/ female) realized, they were sharing their territory with European immigrants (10 children / female), and the game was up for them. Innumerate, Feebral societies like Britain are especially prone to Disaster Creep.

(vii) MI accelerates dramatically when immigrants do not integrate. This 'Diaspora Effect' (Collier) leads the growing diaspora to press for even more immigration of their kind (family, dependants, servants, friends, unpaid labour) in a vicious and often corrupt circle. The surgeries of MP's in immigrant favoured areas are already taken up 95% of their time by immigrants wanting to bring in more relatives and others of their own kind.(Collier). The British can't be all that racist: take my own city, Cardiff. Once it was a small city, but with the world's largest port. In consequence all manner of seamen settled down here a century ago and intermarried with local Welsh girls; we even have a suburb called Canton; and you've heard of Tiger Bay. But that happened because there was time for gradual mixing, and incomers didn't bring their families. Mass Immigration with whole families arriving and settling in ghettos, which is what we have had recently, is a recipe not for integration but dis-integration. It's obvious really.

(viii) Feeble unions have not looked after their members' considerable interests in this connection. Low wages, long hours, flimsy employment rights were all causes which should have been fought more stoutly. Alas the Labour Party became infiltrated by too many Feebrals, Marxists and Blair-alikes to effectively look after poor Brits. I bet not many of the Labour Party elite live in ghettos.

(ix) American mass culture which floods British screens, makes a Rainbow society appear normal. It is not! Just look at America now; Trump has been voted in to build barriers against further immigration.(His Mexican 'self-financing' Wall). Outward appearing Rainbow societies so often are not so in reality: look at Hawaii for instance. I used to go there in the course of my work. The Polynesians, the Japanese and the Whites appeared to loathe one another. Racialism is not merely white against black, its much wider than that. Look at the way post-colonial nations have broken down along tribal lines: the awful Biafran war in West Africa which killed a million; Kenya is totally split between Kikuyu, who have managed to breed the fastest, the old Masai elite who have been wracked by venereal disease, and the smaller number of Luo in the East. South Africa politics is increasingly about tensions between Zulus and Xhosa. By the way, the colours in a rainbow are distinct, not mixed.

(x) Finally, and most disastrously, the British ruling elite have never been educated to think in Common Sense terms. (Chapter 18). Had they been properly educated they might have figured all this out 50 years ago, when there was far more room to do something about it. Instead, when Enoch Powell raised the subject in 1968 they blenched, and threw him out of main-stream politics. [See Note 2 for his infamous speech]

(19:6) IN CONCLUSION

Mass Immigration into Britain started as a trickle but has now become an overwhelming flood. And it is breaking up the United Kingdom as migrant diasporas huddle together in ghettos which may then incubate those very dysfunctional cultures which drove them here in the first place.

Personally I don't trust either of our main political parties to clean up this mess. The Conservative Party contains too many rentiers, who profit immensely from over-population, while many of its supporters and funders think of cheap migrant labour as a blunt knife for castrating the unions. And it was the Conservatives who recently threw out the introduction of Identity Cards, very necessary, some thought, to identify and discourage massive illegal Immigration.

The Labour party on the other hand has been taken over by Feebrals, by Marxists, and by Metropolitan Blair-alikes (Ugh!) ,none of whom care much for Britons in the large. Anyway they know that 4 out of 5 immigrants will continue to vote Labour.

That leaves only an urgent Referendum (or series of referenda) to clear the air once and for all. Is this to be a United Kingdom, or some kind of loose rainbow confederation? This time there needs to be an unambiguous undertaking by Parliament to rapidly implement the outcome(s) – unlike the recent Brexit farce.

NOTES

NOTE 1: *Exodus*, by Paul Collier, 'Immigration and multiculturism in the 21st century', 2013, Allen Lane UK. Although, as an academic economist, he is suspect, I feel this is an honest attempt to spell things out, without regard to preconceived opinions. Since I didn't know much about immigration at large beforehand, I found it highly informative. *The Children of Sanchez* by Oscar Lewis is by a sociologist who embeds himself among an extended Mexican family living in a city favela. It illustrates just how a selfish culture actually generates its own poverty by bringing the enterprising down. Depressed me for days, as we were living in Arizona alongside a lot of Mexicans at the time.

NOTE 2: I had never read the infamous (1968) speech before because at the time I was on my way to America. I was therefore surprised to read it 51 years later[24] Apart from some language that is unacceptable today [e.g. 'negro' and 'pickaninny'] it mostly seems pretty rational to me. Basically he was urging Parliament, on behalf of his constituents in the Midlands – who were being submerged in an inundating ghetto – to at least debate MI seriously, before it was too late . And many ordinary Brits apparently marched in his support. So why didn't Parliament heed, or put MI to

[4] I came across it in *The Penguin book of Modern Speeches* ,ed .MacArthur, 2017, p348. No doubt it can be downloaded.

a referendum, instead of bursting into hysterical indignation? I suspect partly because a weakling PM (Heath) feared that Powell would displace him, and partly because Feebrals, on both sides of the House, ducked an issue of the very kind they are elected to decide. Isn't that decadence? Whatever we may think of him Powell was arguably the finest scholar to grace the Commons this past century: starred double First in Classics, published poet; youngest professor in the Commonwealth (at 25 in Sydney), later youngest Brigadier-general in the British Army (32), Powell doesn't sound like a fool to me. But read the speech itself, not second-hand hysteria.

NOTE 3: Immiscibility. It is very natural, and sensible, for humans to seek out others like themselves with whom to mix and live. It's far easier, it feels more secure, it leads more naturally to trust on both sides, so that is what we all tend to do. We all need to 'identify' and feel part of a community, not aliens amidst a crowd of strangers. So much is obvious. But think of its implications for immigration: an unwillingness to integrate, and ghettos .They don't have to be forced on the incomers by the indigenes, as Feebrals like to pretend, they may be the natural incomers' choice. The feeling of 'them against us' develops quite naturally and may have nothing to do with race. Look how newly independent India immediately broke up into two and then into three, on the basis of religion. Politicians love segregation into artificially homogenous groups who will faithfully vote for them (Think Hitler & Modi). Immiscibility is such a widespread human characteristic that it probably has considerable survival value. To deplore it is as foolish as branding anyone opposed to MI "a racist". The real problem for all of us in this debate is sheer ignorance of the other side. We need to swap stories of our own experiences in this context before making up our minds. So here are four of mine , mainly for those many readers who live in 'exclusive' areas where MI is unknown. They don't prove anything but I hope they illustrate that there is another side:

A) In 1994 we spent 3 months at the Raman Institute in Bangalore. Every day the local paper would contain pages of advertisements from Indians living in

Britain along the following lines; "Daughter, BA, MD, aged 29, Birmingham area. Government doctor with salary of £...... Bride price £....in pounds sterling, cash only. Box...." No wonder so many Asians in Britain are doing well financially : by selling British citizenship.

B) In 2012 I go to my local Post Office to post a parcel. In front of me are half a dozen pregnant ladies in full hijab gear, all with several young children. One by one they go up to the counter and collect several hundred pounds each in notes from the post-mistress. Then they make their way out. Parked right across the pavement and almost blocking the entrance is a moustachioed Asian gentleman at the wheel of a very high-end BMW. As each woman passes she hands him *all* the cash she has just collected. All of it. How many wives has he got I wonder, watching in astonishment. Nice if you can do it: procreation for profit ,at other people's expense.

C) The Welsh Refugee agency installs an Indian lady, with her two young daughters and her servant, in the other half of our semidetached in Cardiff. She had applied, and been granted asylum, on the grounds that their Muslim father (back in Asia) was forcing his daughters to become Muslims, whereas she herself was Christian. Later, she confides in my wife, that it was a cock-and-bull story concocted so that she can come over here to live with her boyfriend, who had come to settle in London. Then drama. Her servant runs away and claims separate asylum. The lady is furious, never having done a hand's turn before. The Welsh Refugee Agency races to the rescue and provides another very desirable residence for the servant just 5 doors away. But the servant prefers to become a nightclub singer in London. So she sublets her WRA-provided house to half a dozen other Indians and only comes back once a fortnight to collect her benefits, and their rents of course. Indian lady in fits, but eventually departs for London, and one hopes, amorous bliss.

D) My wife is a linguist who sometimes acts as translator in immigration courts. There she translates all manner of dramatic tales. When these succeed the delighted ‘clients’ often tell her the truth. Example: parents with two young kids from the FSU arrive in a container, fleeing to Britain because the husband has been ‘tortured’ by the local police. Court sympathises and they are granted refugee status, generous financial support for several years and a new and handsome flat in Devon. Soon arrange council-house swap so they can live with others of their nationality in central London. Neither parent learns English but mother does occasional casual jobs like child-minding. Husband work-shy and anyway stoned most of the time. Truth: they own 6 houses ‘back there’, he was never ‘tortured’, they are quite wealthy and had had themselves smuggled in across the Irish border (a favourite route apparently) and have since managed to import enough of their gold into Britain to buy yet another house in London. If nothing else these stories demonstrate the virtual impossibility of British courts checking on immigrant tales. Our tradition of giving people the benefit of the doubt cannot help but lead to ever accelerating Mass Immigration.

E) Forcible banishment from your own society was once a punishment hardly better than execution. Now it’s happening to innocent Britons every day as their neighbourhoods become swamped by foreign immigration. It’s happened to us. In 1977 I deliberately returned after 8 years abroad, to live in what I felt was my home, Wales. We bought a house in a leafy cul-de-sac and designated Conservation Area near the centre of the civilized city of Cardiff. Gradually we came to know many neighbours and shopped in the two local shopping areas. Eventually I became chairman of the local Residents Association set up to promote social interaction and to preserve the area’s trees and general tranquillity. It was a lovely neighbourhood; we would never have considered leaving. Then things began to change. Population pressure built up, very largely from immigrants. Money was to be made by subdividing and subdividing properties again and again. Gardens were overbuilt to erect multi story flats. The local school was converted into a sort of Muslim madrassa; we never quite knew for sure because they never communicated with us before they vandalized the property and scrammed. Where there had been one car now there were ten. The local library was fitted out with terminals so that mainly immigrants could use the internet; now it has closed for ever. If I go to my doctor's surgery I might as well be in Dakar. If as many as one local shop in twenty is British owned and run I'd be surprised. We know nobody in our cul-de-sac where once we knew everyone. We have tried but it seems the incomers are not interested in us; we're alien. In what was once our little bit of paradise we have become exiles. If you tell me I have no right to be sad I will feel only sadder. Perhaps you will only know how the many people like us feel – when it happens to you.

HISTORY OF THE BRITS.
CHAPTER 20
BADUCATION

"I never allowed my schooling to interfere with my education."
Mark Twain

(20:1) INTRODUCTION

If, as I argued in Ch. 1, Britain is the uniquely best location for humans to thrive, then why aren't we far out ahead of our contemporaries as judged by those progressive measures which really count? We certainly were, back in 1820, but ever since we've been gradually sliding back. It's a great conundrum which any decent historian must confront. If the answer were obvious one political faction or other would probably have fixed it.

When an organism is sickly without apparent cause one's instinct is to suspect parasites, particularly parasites in the brain. Imperial Rome was brought down by such parasites, and so was Almighty Spain – priests in both cases. Could they be responsible here? I believe so, but in a subtle way.

The youthful human brain is a highly malleable organ, thus the temptation to mould it is almost irresistible. Thus priests, fanatics, tyrants, missionaries, militarists, quacks, psychologists, tycoons and psychopaths are all very keen on educating other people's children. Bertrand Russel didn't say many sensible things but one certainly was: *"Men are born ignorant, not stupid. They are made stupid by Education."*. Don't forget, Stalin was a great educator, so are Chi, Erdogan and Tony Blair.

I am going to argue that England and Wales have been crippled by a bad education system driven at its heart by arrogant and ignorant university dons, descendants of priests. That Britain progressed at all was largely thanks to the efforts of Non-Conformists, Quakers and Scots who escaped those priestly clutches. Surprisingly those dons have only increased their baleful influence of late. The most wounding effects of this odd Education System (ES henceforth) include:

- A population that has been and is being bamboozled out of Common Sense Thinking (CST). Priests don't understand it, and would hate it if they did.
- A narrow-minded, cliquey and innumerate ruling elite.
- A huge waste of human resources through forcing children to choose careers much too early in life to do it well.
- Far too much pointless testing and grading, which can only blunt youthful curiosity and self-confidence, while forcing 'teaching to the test'.
- An unhealthy tolerance of powerful/reactionary incumbents.

Any effective national policy on education could only spring from widespread agreement about what education is for. Without such a philosophical grounding, failure is pretty well guaranteed. Irreconcilable prejudices then lead to confusion and frustration all round. In particular schools are then expected to perform far too many incommensurate tasks to really succeed at any. And, as always, honesty is essential, but is all too often missing here. Many parents simply want their kids out of their hair so that they can hold down two full-time jobs. Others demand that schools give their offspring an unfair start in life. University teachers believe they are entitled to well paid, demanding occupations *guaranteed for life*. Private schools can only ensure their continuance by brainwashing their pupils into sending their own kids in turn. And so on. We need to brush all this hypocrisy aside — before drawing swords.

After 40 years in the teaching profession I am distrustful of anyone with dogmatic views on education. After all it is bound to be a *personal* and unpredictable affair whose long-term consequences can only be judged late in life, and then with difficulty. From the individual's point of view a single inspiring teacher, or a single unfortunate occurrence, can make all the difference. For instance my father wet the bed when he was first sent to Christ's Hospital boarding school as a child; a priest flogged him with a thick ebony ruler until he was unconscious; only the school doctor showed any sympathy. Dad became a children's physician and life-long atheist.

What is unquestionable is that human childhood is uniquely long, and even longer from the perspective of Human (i.e. logarithmic) Time. An education lasting from calendar ages 5 to 24, which is becoming the norm nowadays, actually takes up 50% of our entire (Human) lives [Note 1:Human Time]. Fifty per cent! I believe that is an absolute tragedy. Surely we've got to get out there and live, instead of sitting in classrooms and taking exams for half our sojourn on Earth! That's my view anyway. I suspect a classroom education that long will hardly turn out mature men and women, just big babies.

A particular problem here is that we all have only one childhood, and one education. None of us is therefore well placed to pontificate about education in *general*, yet many of us do, not least government ministers, and my colleagues in the teaching profession. If we are to employ CST here, as of course we must , recall that it can only reach *provisional* conclusions – which enjoins tolerance all round. If I have anything novel to say here it springs solely from a 20-year study of CST. When measured against CST our ES shows up badly. We *could* put it right, though the problem is first to get people who have been immersed in it themselves, to recognize just how bad it is.

(20:2) THE UNIQUENESS OF THE BRITISH EDUCATION SYSTEM

I will here concentrate on the system at university level in England and Wales because that is where the rot apparently starts (Scotland's has been quite different and much better). And it is the exceptionality of our universities which imposes most of the stress upon the secondary and primary schools lower down.

I won't put in many facts and figures, but they can be found in David Willetts magisterial *"A University Education"* [Note 2]

The oddity of our ES lies in these factors:

- It is uniquely *specialised.* No one else expects their children to make decisions at age 15/16 that will limit their career choices thereafter.
- The university experience is largely *residential* – boarding schools for big boys and girls.
- Because of this residential feature, every university/department (U/D) finds itself in direct competition with every other in the land for the 'best' prospective students, while every prospective student is in a nationwide competition with every other to get into the 'best' U/D. The joke is that nobody really knows which are the best prospective students, nor which are the best U/Ds. So both debilitating competitions are utterly futile, but blight young lives.

Note:

(a) Examinations are made to seem the coinage of success, but no paper exam has ever been devised capable of measuring one's capacity to think well in a CS (inductive) way – the only way that matters in real life.

(b) CST demands a broad range of disparate knowledge, not a narrow range of strong arguments. It is breadth which generally counts far more than depth – the very antithesis of what we now provide.

(c) Swotting for exams (cramming) cannot but destroy Curiosity, the very quality most valuable to any progressive society, or to any individual interested in life-long learning, as all must now become.

(d) Students are fooled into the belief that the hardest U/Ds to get into must be the best for them. But U/D's are rated (by journalists) considerably by how hard they are to get into. A dog chasing its tail.

(e) It is extremely hard to rate teaching quality, the very thing students should care about. It probably has little to do with 'research excellence', frequently used as a proxy. Most 'research stars' find undergraduate teaching a drag. Anyway departmental health can change almost overnight as key staff come and go.

(f) Let's face it, asking students about "the quality of their educational experience" can be no reliable guide as to how well they are being taught. For instance weak teachers can ingratiate themselves with students by avoiding the hard parts of a subject, telling the students what their exam questions are going to be, even hinting at the answers. That happens all the time; all the bloody time. The most popular lecturers are often the worst and most dishonest.

(g) British universities insist on setting their own exams and then grading their own students, *without any supervision from without*. An irresistible invitation to corruption. Irresistable. Massive grade inflation of degree classifications is the sure stink of corruption .

(h) Short of 'moral turpitude' no university teacher can be sacked, certainly not for incompetence. They insist on, and amazingly get, 'tenure for life'. The philosophical reason they give for this is laughable. [Note 3: tenure]. Imagine that in any other trade.

(20:3) SOME OF THE DIRE CONSEQUENCES

- British students acquire the narrowest education on the planet
- Many students make bad choices at a tender age, often maiming them for life.
- Because they are 'captured' by their residential education, students leave with a stunted critical faculty, and a false sense of their own learning. Difficult to quantify but potentially serious.

• School is blighted for many by quite unnecessary cramming, and 'teaching to the test'. What a shame. Frequent quite pointless exams can only dent self-confidence, an invaluable quality in life.

• Of OECD countries Britain has the lowest proportion of students who get any part of their education abroad (Willetts). Suicidal I believe .It's those residential universities clinging on again.

• Employers tend to select employees on the basis of those almost valueless university exams .They get the wrong staff, while students get the wrong jobs, impoverishing the nation.

• Because of their narrow education our ruling elite are largely innumerate.[Ch.15]

Blighted childhoods, disappointed ambitions, an inefficient economy and an inferior government. Considering how hard so many have worked to bring all this about – what a disaster.

(20:4) HOW MODERN DEVELOPMENTS ARE MAKING THINGS WORSE

• Student loans mean that half the population is now participating in this folly – at their own expense.

• Universities have persuaded recent governments to put an ever growing share of their support for Research and Development, particularly in Science and Engineering, into universities. But that is entirely against the grain of our history and of much foreign experience. Much research has to be 'close to market', while dogged development is often far more important and far more expensive, than simple ideas. Universities are ill-equipped to manage that. This could be a suicidal tragedy, a final step off the cliff. [Ch 19 on Innovation]

- Governments are encouraging students to stay on longer and longer in full time education, half already of their *Human* lives. But dons generally make bad mentors (next sect) so that could be highly unwise.

(20:5) HOW DID THIS FOLLY COME ABOUT?

Since I am not a member of the British Establishment I am tempted to suggest that that it was planned by Captain Mainwaring of 'Dad's Army' and executed by Basil Fawlty of the eponymous 'Towers.' But if that was not so perhaps the following speculations are worth considering:

- The Establishment decided that that the best possible education should be modelled upon the very one they got themselves, mostly at Oxbridge. But Oxford and Cambridge were never intended to be proper universities. They were seminaries funded by papal bulls in the 13th century, to turn acolytes into priests. Until the late 19th century only ordained priests could teach in them, only Anglican (males) could attend, and they didn't teach Sciences. And they certainly didn't do research. After all the influential Saint Augustine had laid down the precept for Christians "*There is another form of temptation even more fraught with danger. This is the disease of curiosity……..It is this which drives us to try and discover the secrets of nature, those secrets which are beyond our understanding, which can avail us nothing and which men should not wish to learn.*" They put their own students under oath never to teach in any rivals and they succeeded, *for no less than 600 years*, in preventing the setting up of any other such institution across England or Wales [until UCL in 1829]. It is a quite appalling tale of greed, corruption, restricted-practice, and overweening pride.(Read Willetts if you don't believe me; better still go and examine the buildings at Oxbridge; don't they resemble a seminary?).It was so bad that some wealthy Non-Conformists had to send their children *across the Atlantic* to be educated!

•. The whole purpose of a seminary is not education but *indoctrination*, for which purpose residence, i.e. total immersion, makes eminent sense. You don't want the novitiate harbouring doubts. Having been thoroughly brain-washed myself I know just how irresistible total immersion can be [Note 4].

•The longer they survived in their fiercely defended exclusive state, the more influence these pseudo-seminaries came to assert upon our upper class, almost the only class that could afford to go to them. Eventually that class could hardly imagine any other kind of model for a proper university. It is touching, but tragic: even David Willetts couldn't see through his alma mater. Total immersion at a young age is almost impossible to escape – as of course is intended

In such rarified environments you would hardly expect the dons to grow up properly, and by and large they did not. And in my experience at least, that immature sensibility is widely spread through British academe. It could hardly be otherwise. After all your average don is the swot who never really ventured out of school, and is in no danger of facing such perils of life as earning a living, or losing it to redundancy. How *could* one grow up in those circumstances? Timidity is the common, almost invariable result. How could such timids be good mentors for a maturing life? Perhaps that wouldn't matter so much if our young weren't exposed to them so immersively, and for so bloody long. [NOTE 4 on dons under stress]

(20:6) WHAT IS AN EDUCATION FOR?

Until we can answer this fundamental question no point is served in proposing reform. For what it is worth here is my answer:

"A good education ought to help the individual towards becoming a successful and happy citizen of a successful and happy society".

That may sound bland, but wait:

(a) The "help" implies that we cannot expect too much of education – which is only one component of growing up. Parents, family, friends, play, sport, music, dancing, arguing, competition, bullying, gangs, misfortune, tears, risk, setbacks….. they are surely all components of really growing up. For instance I doubt that bad parenting can be remedied by good education .. though it may help.. just a little.

(b) As a minimum "successful" implies that the recipient can eventually expect a sufficiently well paid occupation to raise a family of their own.

(c) "Happy" is even harder to define, but as a minimum it implies that a recipient will be able to earn sufficient leisure-time to pursue their own inclinations, irrespective of their eventual employers' demands.

(d) And "Society" presupposes that a distinct and well defined society actually exists, if not entirely in fact, at least in intention. If anything goes, if all cultures are regarded as equivalent, if there are no tacit underlying rules, ambitions or expectations, then education can become little more than job-training.

Thus a nation that demands a good education for its offspring cannot shirk the responsibility of first defining, and then declaring, what kind of society that education is aimed towards. 'Feebrals' who try to wriggle out of this responsibility disqualify themselves from taking part in the 'education debate'.

(20:7) SO WHAT SHOULD BRITISH SOCIETY BE LIKE?

This is bound to be contentious, but contention and progress are opposite sides of the same coin. Since I cannot bear to think of Nature dying, since I cannot leave my grand-children to wilt in a concrete nightmare resembling the outskirts of Chicago, and since I cannot imagine that anyone has a better chance than the Brits of setting the example we all so urgently need, I have to be bold, very bold here. So here is my stab at an answer:

"British Society should aim to become as Progressive as possible, as fast as possible so that it can attempt to lead the human race away from the environmental brink towards which it is now sliding headlong."

'Progressive' here has no vague meaning. We defined it in Chapts. 5, 7 & 8 , where it was derived from what we there considered the fundamental lessons of CST. You might recall the salient features : Curious, Honest, Adaptable, Numerate, Tolerant, Literate and Democratic [CHANTLiD remember?] That is a firm foundation from which to start, but in the circumstance we have to add "Sustainable". For myself I would also like to add "Fair" but as I cannot justify that on CS grounds I refrain. It is taken for granted that Common Sense (Inference) is the only sound way to think about serious problems (not games).

One can see one immediate consequence of a Progressive ES. Since, Curiosity, Tolerance and the drawing of *provisional* conclusions must all be a part of it, Religion is ruled out. Not out of society, but certainly out of the national education system itself. Faith-based schools would have to go. [Note 6;Blair]

(20:8) IMMEDIATE MEASURES THAT COULD BE TAKEN.

• Beyond specialized facts everyone hopes that education would impart some extra 'wisdom for life'. But that wisdom turns out to be effective Common Sense Thinking or CST. But that is not taught in any UK university or school at present, because they simply do not know, or appear to care very much, what it is (it's the influence of those old priests once again) And anyway there's no money in it. So an extremely cheap but effective measure would be to teach CST to *all children* before they reach age 15. It would put us far ahead of any other nation in the world. Zoom!

• Legislate in favour of a broad liberal education until as late in it as possible, with fateful decisions on specialization generally delayed. {According to Willetts (p349) " the English education system can be seen as offering a one-way street out of the sciences with no traffic the other way"}

• Reward citizens (of any age) for passing just a few nationally set tests in *key* subjects (e.g. Numeracy, Literacy, CST, Team-working……). Only pass/ fail; no grading please. More like driving tests for the progressive citizen.

• Discourage residential education and hence the current ridiculous nation-wide competition which has its roots in olden days when we could afford to educate only a tiny few. For goodness sake, universities are now screaming out for students. Instead boost *local* education opportunities, if only because Life Long Learning has to be a top national priority.

• Encourage *professional* grading mechanisms to help employers choose employees much better than they presently do, relying on unreliable university grades. Anything would be better, anything… and less corrupt.

• Reduce substantially the share of R & D funds spent in universities, and set up a broad range of alternatives elsewhere. [Note 7: university R&D]

• Insist that students be allowed to accumulate transferable credits, so that they can pause, move, change, at *any* age. *Life-long learning is surely the future,* but in fits and starts. That may mean national supervision of university exams. And it pretty much rules out much residential education because working parents obviously won't be able to leave home all the time to pick up vital new skills.

• Teach and reward teamworking as an essential skill, starting age 14

• Why should residential universities and their academics be the sole models for tertiary education? That's another uniquely British, and actually recent, folly. Restore all those other Institutes of Technology, Colleges of Further Education, Technical Colleges and the like, competitors which universities and snobs don't like. Even The Open University, which I would argue is by far Britain's greatest modern achievement, is languishing. It was, and should remain, the exemplar for future advanced education.

• Reduce the influence of university academics over *all* aspects of Education. And encourage those same academics to broaden themselves (perhaps by paying only 9-month salaries, as they often do in the US).

• Only 30,000 British undergraduates spend part of their study abroad, far less a share than any other OECD country (Willetts). But a year studying abroad could easily be the most valuable part of their academic lives, particularly in broadening experience, which is so invaluable in life. It's those bloody residential universities clinging on again. A gap year on the beach is no substitute. Put this right!

- No more taxpayers money for faith-based schools, including Christian varieties.
- Allow failing universities/schools/ to go bust

There will of course be howls of protest. But such are the inevitable accompaniments to *any* progress. Look back to reactions to the Factory Acts, to all extensions of suffrage, to female emancipation, to blood transfusions, to the abolition of the death penalty and corporal punishment, to immunisation (even today), to abortion on demand, to in vitro fertilization, to Transportation for minor offences, to Brexit, even to the abolition of slavery …… If Reactionaries, Feebrals and Incumbents don't howl it's not progressive. It's simply not.

(20:9) PARTICULAR MODERN CHALLENGES

- Globalization fuelled by the massive container ship and the jet cargo-plane, together with a disastrous and unnecessary addiction to "Free Trade"[Ch 14] means that nobody's working life is now secure. Redundancy, change, moving, commuting .. all pose huge challenges to family life and traditional education. Megacities like London and Kolkotta grow, not because they are healthy but because they offer more alternatives for struggling groups and families.
- Rapid change brought about by modern communications, particularly mobile phones and the internet, means that nobody's training in youth can be adequate for life. Whether we like it or not the whole emphasis must now turn towards life-long learning. A once-and-for-all residential education will only suit one for extinction.
- Massive Immigration imposes huge additional and unanticipated strains upon schools in certain areas, particularly for early-years. Language difficulties, illiteracy, poverty, ignorance, poor diets, anti-feminism, resistance to integration, ghetto-isation, exotic religions with

fanatic priests, imported gang-culture, racialism…. How can normal education cope with all that? In short it can't, and it isn't.

(20:10) SOME MORE RADICAL IDEAS WORTH CONSIDERING

The news isn't all bad; of course it isn't. There are huge untapped resources in the community which could revolutionise affairs – if only we had the imagination to employ them. I'm talking about *Volunteers*. The longer we live, the fitter we are, the wealthier we get, the earlier we retire, the more valuable time and leisure we could devote to others, not least to our (i.e. the community's) children, if only we got some encouragement. So:

(A) Childhood should be fun – not all grind. If working parents (following the very rich) can't or won't look after their children much of the time, kids need a secure club to go to every day where they can meet their friends, play games, relax, make music, keep fit, build tree-houses, learn guitar….whatever or whatever. So they need to go to two *quite different* schools every day; a grinding school worked entirely by professionals, devoted exclusively to 'getting on'; and a **Club-school** for the fun side of life – largely worked by Volunteers, for instance off-duty parents, retirees, grandparents, neighbours, enthusiasts for this activity or that – be it football, tango-dancing , art or gaming…. With regular minibuses between the two campuses (volunteers again) kids could commute between the two while remaining secure. And Club-schools wouldn't have to close at 15:30 sharp or whenever, to allow full-time paid staff to leave work. Such a Club school would be largely manned and womanned by the community, ruled by the community and what is so important, *owned* by their community. It would no longer be an arm, or the full-time responsibility, of central government. And nearly all the good features of a residential education, and there *are* many, would be at hand for all.[Note 9: Club schools]

(B) We all need good **Mentors** in life. According to Willetts so many of us fail because we are either ignorant of the opportunities, or make wrong choices early in life. This calls for a new profession: mentoring of the young. Young people might meet their mentor-team only once a quarter, or at critical moments of choice, but such meetings could make all the difference, especially to the presently disadvantaged. Who would elect to be a NEET ('Not in Employment, Education or Training') if there were better alternatives out there? And there certainly are.

(20:11) REFLECTIONS

We have only to look back on the history of British education to see how awful/ridiculous it can be – for instance birching Ancient Latin and Greek into boys for five hundred years. God only knows what that was about. Or not allowing females to have the same education as males (Priests were responsible there too.). Or dividing children on the basis of an 11-plus exam into those who were worth educating, from the majority who were not.(Incidentally the rationale for this came from a crooked fantasist, Sir Cyril Burt [Note 9])

I suspect a good part of the truth is that while people want children they want someone else to do most of the child minding (I don't think that's unnatural; it is the consequence of the unnatural nuclear family; for instance in an Indian village the children are part of a community looked over by everybody). The result is a class of child-minders referred to as 'teachers' or 'educationalists' . You can't blame some of them for teaching what they happen to know, rather than what the children actually need. Nor is it surprising that some self-important 'educators' rise to the top and try to run the show, mainly for their own selfish ends. They're the 'Academics' (I was one for 35 years)

And then there are the priests, an even sadder lot; they see youth as the ideal opportunity to indoctrinate young minds with all manner of daft poisons, against which the young *must* be protected. When an unholy alliance develops between priests and academics the consequences can only be dire. And that is what appears to have happened on this blessed isle, at least to its South. Our Northern citizens would have none of it and so Edinburgh became 'The Athens of the North', giving birth to 'The Scottish Enlightenment' which was to revolutionise Britain, then Europe, finally the entire world. So our weird English/Welsh ES was not inevitable, nor is it irreversible if, and it's a big if, we can at last see its egregious faults. [NOTE 10: Scotland]

One must never forget that Education today is a vast business, with many vested interests, practiced upon largely helpless children. No wonder it is often so disastrous. I suspect that our successors will look back upon us as barbarians, as we look back upon those generations who sent young boys up chimneys.

Nothing is this field is going to be either easy or uncontentious. We all feel we 'own' Education – which is both good and bad. As I see it the huge challenge will be to get both a better and a more renewable education while spending *far* less valuable Human time a'getting of it— viz Mark Twain. Anyone who swallows my argument for Logarithmic Time will realise that something radical has to be done about Baducation, and done very soon. But perhaps because it is so ridiculous it may be easy to improve, if not entirely fix.

But do we really have the time, seeing how rapidly the whole world is sliding towards the environmental brink? That's what haunts me. If you believe, as I do, that the Brits have to take the lead, once again, in finding a quite different way to thrive, then we have to act fast. In my opinion there really is no other hope. Maybe that very urgency will rouse us to shrug off timidity and act. We could you know; we could.

NOTES

NOTE 1: Clock-Time (t) a 17th century invention, and Human-Time (T) are entirely different concepts, utterly confused by giving them the same name. Here they are compared, year below corresponding year:

t	4	5	11	18	22	23	30	50	60	70	80
T	4	9	27	38	43	44	50	62	66	70	73

Note that an education lasting from t = 5 until t = 23 (now typical) occupies (44-9)/73 or 48% of a human life. Tragic I think. Follow up Logarithmic Time at
https://tinyurl.com/thvvvob

NOTE 2: "*A University Education*" by David Willetts, OUP 2017 is a magisterial account of the subject full of facts and wisdom by an ex-minister in the field. Even so he cannot escape the clutches of his alma mater: a truly touching example of how even the most intelligent of us are indelibly marked by an immersive education.

NOTE 3: Academic Tenure is usually justified on the grounds that academics can then speak out against any kind of government intimidation. But they are the timidest creatures on the planet. The only English academic I can think of who did so speak out was Bertrand Russel (against conscription) – who was then *sacked by his own university.* They didn't wait for the government. The only Welsh one, Bill Bevan, principal of University College Cardiff, who openly joined the Labour Party on television in 1987 as a protest against Thatcher's curmudgeonly support for universities. She sent two bully boys down from London who declared (falsely as it turned out) that the college was 'bankrupt'. Bevan was fired but his academics, whose jobs he was trying to protect, were too terrified to support him.(Note 5)

NOTE 4: I've been deliberately brainwashed twice, both times most effectively – I'm ashamed to say. It was all about total immersion, which is almost irresistible in youth. As an 8-year old boarder I became a real "toughie"; as a demon fast-bowler I found I could intimidate anyone, even big bullies. And at the end of 26 weeks of sheer hell in the British Army I would have leapt out of a trench and led my 36 infantrymen into a hail of gunfire – in defence of the Queen. I was actually disappointed when no such opportunity presented itself. Such experiences teach one to be suspicious of immersion. It's all too effective to be part of a liberal education.

NOTE 5 ; I had the rare experience of seeing dons under real stress when my university, University College Cardiff, was declared bankrupt by Mrs Thatcher in an act of spite (1987). During the following Senate debate I never heard a single don speak out for anything beyond the preservation of his or her own job – dressed up in learned hypocrisy of course. Timidity, burrowing (down a safe, highly specialized hole), and virtue-signalling make most of the many dons I have encountered quite unsuitable as mentors for the young. And layman should be wary of academic titles; nowadays they are as meaningful as the ecclesiastical variety; no one fails a doctorate while a modern professorship can be obtained by filling in a form to be endorsed by one's colleagues; since they are all eager to become professors themsekves, perhaps you can guess the outcome? {Our 'bankruptcy' is briefly covered in my novel "*Crouching Giant" (*Amazon Publishing 2020). It deserves the attention of a far better comic novelist than I.}

NOTE 6: Tony Blair it was who re-introduced "faith-based-schools". In retrospect one can see how suspicious his behaviour was. Before the election which brought him to power (1997), he flew to Australia to get the support of Rupert Murdoch's British right-wing newspapers which, to general amazement at the time, he got (Murdoch is a militant Catholic). Then, weeks after Blair resigned, in somewhat murky circumstances, he joined the Catholic Faith. Uh-hum. I suspect he was and is primarily an undercover papist, intent on reasserting that mediaeval authority over Britain; why else his current outrage at us for daring to leave the EU?

NOTE 7:Less than 5 out of Britain's 23 Transformative Innovations were made in universities [Ch. 19]. That's not surprising because, while universities may be good at fundamental research ,"…they do not have the firepower or skills to bridge the valley of death from research to proper commercialization (Willetts p 266)". We are a miserable 18th in the world when it comes to filing international patents while, because of 'The Haldane Principle', the government is barred from telling universities what research they might do in the national interest. For very much the same reasons Germany has set up 60 Frauenhoffer Institutes employing 22,000 scientists to master such problems. We are still mesmerized by "university independence" which sounds very fine, especially to dons, but which could, in the long run, prove disastrous. If we retain Haldane then far more government-funded research *must go on outside universities*. It's no good blaming big industries; they're not much good at research either [Ch.19].

NOTE 8: Club Schools are not my original idea. My wife went to a so called 'Pioneer School' in the FSU and absolutely loved it, while at the same time attending a normal school for ordinary lessons. Why should secondary schools be expected to do so much beyond classroom education? There *are* other ways; for instance the UK's three most successful sportsmen all went to Whitchurch Comprehensive School, Cardiff, *which doesn't do sport*: Sam Warburton (Rugby), Gareth Bale (Soccer), and Geraint Thomas (Cycling) were all nurtured by enthusiasts in local clubs, enthusiasts who've got far more time for it, and better facilities than harassed school-teachers in between lessons. Come on councils and government: get things started.

NOTE 9: Professor Sir Cyril Burt, University College London, was the first knighted Psychologist. He was entrusted to analyse the IQ tests of identical twins separated at birth throughout Europe in consequence of the turbulence of WW2. He showed that IQ was 75% inherited. To the government that implied that there was not much point in educating dimmer kids. Only after his death in 1971 was it found, by an American researcher, that the man was a complete fraud and fantasist. He'd not only forged the data but he'd forged the imaginary research assistants whose authoritative reports had earlier affected government education policy for almost a generation afterwards. Anyway IQ is no measure of capacity for CST. It was a catastrophe which people, particularly psychologists, would rather not talk about. In Chapter 13 of *Thinking for Ourselves* I demonstrate that Psychology can *never* be a Science, and is largely unrepeatable hocus pocus. It's like Half Baked Economics[Ch.14], and for the same reason, only worse. It was a 'Not-the-Nobel-Prize-Winning' economist who persuaded governments to splurge on early-year education'; unfortunately he'd got his 'sums' badly wrong (Willetts p153). But how many Economists and Psychologists we are treated to in the media every day! They have become a bloody menace to society. One needs CST to see through them.

NOTE 10: I want to say much more about the huge contribution made to British progress by Scottish education, and will later. The Scots founded proper universities at which academics were actually paid to teach students useful knowledge, not just to preach at them. And at a time when the only two English universities weren't even teaching science 19-year-old Glasgow University undergraduate Joseph Black invented the Chemical Balance (1750) and so founded Chemistry. He went on to discover Carbon Dioxide and Magnesium and then came up with Latent Heat, the foundation of another core science – Thermodynamics. He became James Watt's boss and set Watt to massively improve the then primitive Newcomen steam-engine, which he eventually did with Mathew Boulton in Birmingham. Not bad for one man? It was the lowland Scots who first took up coal-mining seriously, while another Scot, John Crichton-Stuart (Marquess of Bute), turned South Wales into the industrial powerhouse of the world, which it became in the 1870's; at one stage 75% of the world's steel was coming out of the Merthyr Valley. Thank goodness English Baducation didn't reign everywhere. Loxonbridge had very little to do with all this wealth creation; but you can bet they gorged on it later.

HISTORY OF THE BRITS
RETROSPECT AND PROSPECT

I have attempted a portrait of the Brits , seen from the point of view of a scientist. It is therefore sceptical, quantitative where possible, and very much based on Common Sense Thinking – as I have come to understand it. We have had an exceptional history, in no small part due to our almost uniquely favourable location, an island from which, by fair means and foul, we were able to dominate Europe and much of the Atlantic for three centuries. During that time we have faced two truly existential crises: the Firewood Crisis of the 18th-century when we had to turn to coal and invent industry, and the Environmental crisis of the 21st to which we are now sliding relentlessly. We escaped the first through a mixture of ingenuity and geological good fortune : escape from the second looks more doubtful because it is squeezing the entire planet. It is the second crisis which has come to dominate this book, in a way I never anticipated. Any satisfactory story has to have progress and direction, it is no mere catalogue events – 'one damn thing after another'. And if there is no future for our grandchildren – beyond gradual degradation, what point is served by bringing up the past – which can only remind them of their shrivelling prospects – which will be almost entirely the consequence of our gutlessness – our unwillingness to try and fight for them – when there was still time to do so.

Guts demands self-confidence, and if the British can't find that who can? In 1945 we had almost insufferable amounts of it, but drip by drip it has fatally bled away. Although we had won the war we were to be comprehensively robbed of the peace by America. Newly independent countries wanted to rewrite history to make themselves appear far more heroic than in truth they were, and so it was necessary to blackguard Britain & its Empire (Especially true of Ireland and India). Then the British intellectual Left wanted to denigrate the past in order to steal the future. And not least was the overwhelming presence of the American media on British cinema and television screens. We can't blame Hollywood for casting America in all the heroic roles: that is how it built its vast 'empire of the mind'. I was taken in myself – until we went to live in Arizona (1968–70) and found out the true and shameful story of how the Americans had defrauded the native Indians of their land. America is not a model, it is a warning. Indeed the Americans are even greater victims of Hollywood History than the Brits. Its bloated and fraudulent braggadocio almost brought the world to an end in 1962 – over Cuba.

So if we are going to try to save our grandchildren's future we have to rescue our history first, for without it we won't have the guts to even try. And that history is remarkable – if only we dare to look it straight in the eye. We have made, and are making, many foolish mistakes, nevertheless we have transformed the world to an extent no other civilisation can remotely claim. What are Pyramids, Parthenons and Terracotta Armies besides Antisepsis, Representative Democracy and Industrialization? The point is not to crow about it, but to gird our loins again, and try to get all of humankind, and most of our fellow creatures, through the gathering tempest ahead. Of course it would be nice if all the world's statesmen were to gather round a table to act in enlightened concert. But can you see Trump, Chi, Putin, Modi, Ursula van der Leyden (7 children), Ayatollah Al Khamanei… and the rest of them doing so? I can't. That leaves very little choice. It's the Brits or nobody! We probably won't succeed – but we just might. We will have to make extremely painful decisions, embrace controversy, risk unpopularity and blame, tolerate mistakes, ignore Feebrals, try experiments, frequently alter our minds and, above all, show endless moral courage. Endless. It's all a very very big ask. But what is the alternative? If you have one please tell us. Our grandchildren need to know. Now.

IF I HAD MY WAY

I would, in *something* like this order:

(1) Prevent the break-up of the United Kingdom for at least a generation. This island makes no sense divided up in any other way. At the same time I would radically decentralise. But that is about better administration, not identity.

(2) Found a Progressive Party to push for Progressive (CHANTLiDS) reforms, whoever is the government of the day.

(3) Halt Immigration now (with no exceptions; they will just lead to an endless running sore) . We have to de-populate; otherwise what is the point?

(4) Replace mindless Free Trade with a Fairplay Tax**; before we have to sign all those post-Brexit trade deals**. This will make us rich again , and far more secure.

(5) Teach Common Sense Thinking to all 13-15 year olds.

(6) Pass a bill on Assisted Dying.

(7) Enumerate Britain .

(8) Double support for Research and Development, but mostly *outside* universities. They're not that good at it.

(9) Reduce school examining by 75%.

(10) Ban oil-tankers weighing more than 30,000 tons from British waters and force them all to carry proper insurance policies to clear up any spills they cause.

(11) Bring Public Libraries back from the dead by employing volunteers and removing computer terminals from them.

(12) Introduce Volunteer-based Club Schools and Libraries.

(13) Appoint a Royal Commission to look into the use of chemicals in Farming and its effects on ecology.

(14) Close *all* Faith -Based Schools. We shouldn't let priests, *of whatever denomination*, anywhere near our children.

(15) Raise Inheritance Tax to a high level and invest the proceeds in Rewilding.

(16) Introduce a progressive Carbon Tax.

(17) Introduce a progressively rising Packaging Tax; some of the proceeds to go into a Rubbish Lottery. Each package would carry a number and whoever salvaged it would be eligible for a huge weekly .prize. We'd quickly become the tidiest country on the planet.

(18) Invest heavily in Life-long-learning.

(19) Introduce "Money II" which could *only* be earned by Good Works on behalf of the community. Sole means to purchase especially desirable properties, holidays in spectacular areas, residence in the best suburbs and towns , etc etc,…. *Absolutely* un-exchangeable for the grubby variety. Let's put the noses of the rich out of joint and have a new and *worthy* elite. Not inheritable.

(20) Introduce a Ministry of Depopulation and examine all issues in that light, Annual targets.

(21) Ban all foreign ownership of our media. All.

(22) Deport all illegal immigrants. Introduce Identity Cards to find out who they are. Burden of Proof on dodgy immigrants.

(23) Shorten the working week to a normal 4 days; to help family life.

(24) Tax Multinationals e.g. by using a Delivery Tax etc

(25) Put a steep tax on Advertising. Much needless poverty, overwork, discontent and globalisation is caused by purchasing stuff we have been mis-persuaded to buy. Who needs an £60,000 car? Only a jerk.

(26) Restrict Parliament to sitting for only 4 months a year. We want *representatives* not careerists. Watching parliament intensively during the

Brexit debates convinced me most of it was pure theatre; showing-off not legislating.

(27) Do all we can to encourage 'Integration' and disperse ghettoes.

(28) Defend our sea life, open more sea parks, make sure all fishing is sustainable.

(29) Triple number of doctors under training.

(30) Reduce court hearings to limited times.

(31) Introduce National Service, not for fighting, but for community service and so that we can all learn about one another, not separate into rigid class streams as we do now – which is *so* impoverishing. We all learn quickest when kicked out of our comfort zones. If everybody spent the equivalent of one day a week 'in the trenches' this would be a far kinder, richer, happier, far better educated and wiser society. Even some parasites might come to see the error of their ways.

(32) Halt university loans for substanceless voodoo subjects such as Economics, Psychology, Management 'Science'….. They're simply modern priesthoods, as dangerous as the ecclesiastical varieties.

(33) Ban all academic title ,which academics themselves have rendered worthless anyway by shameless grade-inflation. It's pure priestliness.

AU REVOIR

Dear Rudi (my grandson, born 2005),

I started this for you and your generation. I would like to bang on about some other stuff – but there may not be time – what with this bloody virus and me being a fairly dodgy 82. So here it is, incomplete, but better for being too short than too long. [If I get the time I'll add some more on the web, which you could download, if you wanted].

I've had a good deal of excitement writing this, and several big surprises. And when a scientist surprises himself that's often a sign he's onto something big. Perhaps the biggest surprise of all is the hugely positive response I have been getting from the dozen wise old friends amongst whom I have been circulating this manuscript as I went along (hardly any of them scientists). Where I expected the kind of mild derision you usually receive, and even welcome from old mates, they've been spurring me on, calling for more copies, the next episode, and urgent publication before it is all too late. So here it is.

The other big surprises I mentioned are:

- Just how urgent the situation has become, particularly the ecological crisis. Do you know I've hardly seen a single Swift swooping over our rooftop in Cardiff for years. Not so long ago (after you were born certainly) we used to sit in the garden of a summer evening to admire dozens of them racing through the blue savannahs in search of insects. Even more terrifying, my friend Mac reports from his farm in Pembrokeshire that where he was accustomed to seeing two hundred nesting swallows every day, this whole *season* he has seen just two! Chemical agriculture, which hardly anybody mentions, is wiping out our insects, and perhaps with them the whole *unfathomable* web of life on which we depend. That absolutely terrifies me, and Mac by the way. He's a rare breed ; a lifelong industrial chemist who became a farmer late in life. He refuses to use a single chemical on his property; he knows only too well just what they can do.

- Britain's real uniqueness – something which nobody doubted in 1920, but which has almost been forgotten now. Like bumptious children America, Russia, China, Hollywood and Silicon Valley have clamoured for our attention, but they are not, by some long way, as interesting, or as progressive as us.
- While we made important contributions to inventing the modern world, and to winning the Second World War, I never realized, until I dug into the details, the degree to which we dominated both.[Chs.17 & 10)
- It is fashionable nowadays to decry empires, and most are indeed pretty awful, not least the current American and Russian empires, which are never acknowledged as such (but. ask the Navajo, the Chechyens or the Circassians – if you can find any of the latter left alive). It turns out however that the British Empire, with exceptions of course, was a gentle, enlightening influence upon nearly all those involved , who, don't forget, very largely assented to its rule. If nothing else it abolished slavery worldwide. I particularly mention this because , as you will recall, this conversation, and the idea for this book, started while we were walking the Pembrokeshire Coast Path and you remarked that we Brits had 'enslaved the Indians', a complete untruth you must have picked up from your school in London. Look out for Fake History, there's obviously a lot of it about, especially up Hackney Way. It is NOT intended to do you any good; of that at least we can be sure.

But we British have made some terrible mistakes too amongst which I would highlight:

- The invention of Economics, a sort of half-baked religion which confuses every issue , stalls every kind of progress, excuses any number of vast financial crimes, yet has no rational basis.(Ch.14)
- Championed Free Trade, a curse that has brought Western Civilization to its knees.(Ch. 14)
- Turned a blind eye to massive immigration, which is now totally out of control. The numbers are equivalent to 3 British mothers out of 4 raising an extra child. Not a lot of truth being talked about this either!
- In doing so deprived your generation of the kind of housing you had every right to expect. As Jane Goodall put it in the wider context: "We inherited the Earth from our parents, but we have stolen it from our. children."
- Forgotten that this island only makes sense as a *United* Kingdom.
- Allowed Feebrals, with their pathetic virtue-signalling, to stifle vigorous public debate. Any progressive society *must* be constantly taking hard and often divisive decisions – that's what 'Progress' means. Why are we ignoring Assisted Dying; the potential break-up of the United Kingdom; the Baumol Effect; large pension deficits; accelerating ghettoization; widespread financial theft by parasites; tax-evading multinationals; foreign ownership of key UK businesses and media; monopoly in the so called 'professions'; massive greed and corruption by the management class; Baducation… and so on and so on? Because Feebrals don't like taking decisions, and they don't like anyone else taking them either! Did you see Feebrals in Parliament trying to stop 'Brexit', not because they appeared to have any convincing arguments (I was listening hard in hope), but because they hate the thought of change? Any change.

The truth is Rudi that the human race, roped together willy nilly, is accelerating towards a cliff edge. Somebody has got to turn round, dig their axe into the ice and halt that slide before we all plunge into the abyss. Because of their amazing site, and their unexampled history, the Brits should be much the best able to do that. After all we completely changed the world once before (~ 1750). If *we* do not then I cannot alas see anyone else who can. So it's up to us; or rather it's up to you and your generation of young Brits. So *please* don't become a Feebral. You can't leave it all to Greta Thunberg; you can't. Dig that axe hard into the ice, or we've all had it. The very best of luck !

Love Mikey.

PS:
TOPICS I HAD INTENDED TO COVER AND MIGHT STILL:

Modern Priests, Time & History; United Kingdom; Blockade; The Scottish Connection; The British Constitution; Class & Snobbery; Security – the Government's Main Job; Taxes – the sinews of any civilised state; Party Politics; Britain & Europe, The Irish Question.

ACKNOWLEDGEMENTS

I would like to thank:

Adolf Hitler who bombed us out of our home when I was 3, thus inspiring a precocious interest in (military) history.

The Birmingham Public-Library System where I got much of my teenage education and entertainment.

The US Office of Naval Research which paid for my PhD studentship in Astrophysics in London. 1965-68.

The three smartest people I have known well, as it happens all women:

Mum (Linda, née Picton) who taught me to read when I was two by reading me a story and, when I was hooked, closing the book and telling me to finish it myself. Mum believed in a wide range of experience. After her kids had left home she went to work in factories and offices just to see how others lived.

Patti (Eileen Coffey) Gilkey an extraordinary Irish-American story-teller and wit from Long Beach California. At her funeral (in London) the British Foreign Secretary said : "During World War Two she was worth at least two armoured divisions". She is portrayed in my novel *"Against the Fall of Night"* .

Aunty Joan Fairbridge (née Duff): Australian poet, song-writer, code-breaker (Bletchley Medal), journalist, farmer's wife, wit and sage. She is the central character in my novel *"Strangle*", coming soon.

My old mates who egged me on to finish this book including: Russ Holloway, John Macdonald, Dave Soutter, Pete McLeod, Tony Pollard and Huw Lang. Blame them.

The USS Pension scheme which has allowed me to go on making a nuisance of myself in old age.

Rudi my grandson (b 2005), a typically opinionated but ill-informed male Disney, who got me going by explaining what a crime the British Empire had been.

Printed in Poland
by Amazon Fulfillment
Poland Sp. z o.o., Wrocław

61223298R00154